KU-549-150

The Construction Industry

The Construction Industry

Balance Wheel of the Economy

Edited by
Julian E. Lange
Harvard University
Daniel Quinn Mills
Harvard University

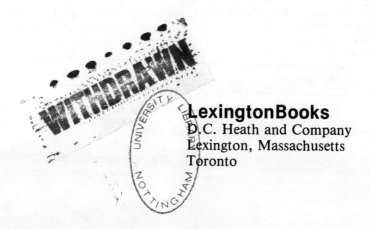

LexingtonBooks
D.C. Heath and Company
Lexington, Massachusetts
Toronto

Library of Congress Cataloging in Publication Data

Main entry under title:

The Construction industry.

Includes index.
1. Construction industry—United States—Addresses, essays, lectures.
I. Lange, Julian E. II. Mills, Daniel Quinn.
HD9715.U52C585   338.4'7'6240973   79-1562
ISBN 0-669-02913-0

Copyright © 1979 by D.C. Heath and Company.

All rights reserved. No part of this publication may be reproduced or
transmitted in any form or by any means, electronic or mechanical,
including photocopy, recording, or any information storage or retrieval
system, without permission in writing from the publisher.

Published simultaneously in Canada.

Printed in the United States of America.

International Standard Book Number: 0-669-02913-0

Library of Congress Catalog Card Number: 79-1562

To my family

J.E.L.

To Deborah Scott Mills

D.Q.M.

Contents

Acknowledgments

The editors wish to express their thanks to both the Ford Foundation and the Harvard Business School Division of Research, both of which provided financial support for this volume.

Foreword

John T. Dunlop

This volume constitutes a report on significant areas of research and the generation of ideas related to the construction sector—bidding and price formation, labor relations and technological progressiveness, residential financing, and electric power construction.

The construction sector is still a very neglected area of research, partly because it is so different from manufacturing (with continually shifting work sites and nonstandardized output), partly because it is fragmented and specialized, and partly because scholars and academics have been so remote from construction, despite its critical importance to the performance of the economy in economic growth, for shelter and for public activities throughout the country.

This volume brings together the work of seven authors who have done careful and significant work and who know the construction sector. Here they make their separate and collaborative research and ideas available to a larger audience of scholars, practitioners, and private and public policy makers who are directly affected by the performance of construction. A better understanding of construction is vital not merely to that sector but, in view of the strategic role of construction, to the performance of the whole economy.

The conventional wisdom of public policy discussion contains a great many propositions regarding the construction sector. It is high time we assess the validity and applicability of these propositions. This volume is an excellent beginning. Rapid increases in construction costs are often solely attributed to labor and material cost increases, but they may also reflect improvements in quality. How much of each? What about land values? Financing? Construction is often depicted as a technologically backward sector, but how does this preconception stand up to close scrutiny? Housing construction is often depicted as the balance wheel of the economy after World War II, with recessions in housing necessary to eliminate previous excesses. But is it possible to cool the economy without shutting down housing construction and incurring the very high costs of instability to builders, producers, and labor? It is often presumed that large scale construction operations are more efficient than small operations, but what are the special problems of managing large-scale projects such as power-generating stations? It is often said that industrial relations in construction are disastrous and antisocial. Does this judgment stand up to careful scrutiny? What is the standard for comparison?

The popularly held premise that construction is inefficient, backward, and susceptible to widespread and easy reform needs scrutiny by the sort of research papers presented in this volume. An alternative premise that emerges here is that given the instability in construction demand, the diversity and nonstandardization of construction products, the geographical diversity and isolation of sites, and the peculiarities of construction purchasers, the construction industry (with its specialized firms and labor force) is a highly efficient response to these conditions.

These chapters have the further value of perceptively portraying the institutional arrangements in which construction operations are conducted. Thus, the description of the bidding arrangements (chapters 2 and 3) constitutes a distinctive contribution that helps a great deal to give meaning to the concept of "price" in construction. The description of recent collective bargaining developments and of changes in mortgage instruments in housing are no less significant.

These studies should serve to encourage further work on other aspects of construction and to infuse new views into the more general debates over construction and general economic policies.

1

An Introduction to the Construction Sector of the Economy

Julian E. Lange and
Daniel Quinn Mills

Construction, one of the most important parts of the American economy, is often referred to as an industry but is more accurately described as a sector of the economy, such as manufacturing, transportation, or services. It is not a single activity, but a group of activities loosely related to one another by the nature of their products, technologies, and institutional settings. Were construction viewed as an industry, it would be the largest one in the economy. As a sector of the economy, it is one of the smallest, whether measured in terms of the value of output, or number of persons employed in its activities.

Construction's importance is not determined by its size, however, but by the function of its products. Construction produces those products that permit us to feed, clothe, and shelter ourselves—the structures in which our goods are produced and stored, over which goods are shipped to market, and in which goods are consumed. The products of construction are manufacturing plants, roads, houses, water systems, and similar structures. Half of the capital investment of American industry has been placed in the products of construction; the other half involves tools and equipment.

Measures of Construction Activity

Construction involves both new construction activity and maintenance and repair work. New construction is the larger part, but maintenance and repair are significant. The only direct estimates of total maintenance and repair activity were made in 1963. In that year, new construction constituted 75 percent of total construction activity, and maintenance and repair 24 percent. Although direct estimates of new construction activity are made each year, analysts customarily use the 1963 survey to account for maintenance and repair as one-third of the volume of new construction activity. This is surely a mistake. Maintenance and repair work fluctuates in volume and perhaps expands most rapidly when new construction is low. Building owners probably stretch out the life of structures by means of maintenance and repair when new construction seems inadvisable.

A considerable amount of information about new construction is available each year. New construction activity has accounted for about 11 percent of the nation's gross national product (GNP) on average since World War II. This figure fluctuates, however, because construction follows a business cycle of its own. In

1

some years, new construction has been as high as 14 percent of GNP; in other years as low as 9 percent.

Construction employs about 5 percent of the nation's labor force. Work in the industry is seasonal, so that the percentage of persons employed in construction rises to more than 6 percent in summer and falls to less than 4 percent in winter. The proportion of total employment in construction is less than the proportion of GNP because the GNP measurement is based upon the final use of products, not their intermediary stages. Construction involves the installation of materials and components produced in manufacturing industry. When expenditures on new construction are counted, they include the value of materials and components installed. However, a calculation can be made in which the total expenditure on construction is reduced by the value of inputs to its production process. This estimate is called income-originating in construction and is about 6 percent of the GNP, about the same proportion of the GNP as construction employment is of total employment.

Among the major types of construction are:

1. Residential buildings
    a. Single-family houses
    b. Multifamily houses
    c. Apartments
2. Nonresidential buildings
    a. Industrial plants
    b. Commercial buildings
    c. Schools
    d. Churches
    e. Hospitals
3. Highways and streets
4. Military facilities
5. Conservation and development construction
6. Sewers and water treatment systems
7. Utility construction
    a. Telephone and telegraph
    b. Railroad
    c. Electric light and power
    d. Pipelines

Table 1-1 shows the percentage distribution in 1977 of the value of total new construction and additions and alterations by type of structure and by ownership. Several interesting points are observable:

1. The relative role of public versus private ownership varies greatly among the types of construction. Government agencies are major purchasers of such items as highways, streets, military facilities, and the like, but very minor buyers of residential construction.

Table 1-1
**Percent Distribution of Value of Total New Construction and
Additions and Alterations by Ownership, 1977**

| Type | Public | | | Private | Total |
	Federal	State/Local	Total Public	Total Private	Public and Private
Residential	0.1%	0.4%	0.5%	47.5%[a]	48.0%
Nonresidential building	1.1	5.7	6.8[b]	18.2[d]	25.0
Public works and utilities	3.1	11.5	14.6[c]	12.1[e]	26.7
Other	–	–	–	0.7	0.7
Total	4.3	17.6	21.9	78.1	100.0

Source: U.S., Department of Commerce, Bureau of Census, "Value of New Construction Put in Place," C-30 Series (Washington, D.C.: Government Printing Office, 1978).
[a]Includes nonhousekeeping buildings.
[b]Industrial, educational, hospital, and other buildings.
[c]Highways, streets, military facilities, conservation and development, sewer systems, water supply facilities, and miscellaneous public construction.
[d]Includes nonresidential farm buildings.
[e]Telephone and telegraph, railroad, electric light and power, petroleum pipeline.

2. The government role as an owner is a large one, consisting in 1977 of 21.9 percent of all construction expenditures. Most of these expenditures came from state and local government, but much of the money spent by the states and localities was provided by the federal government (not shown on the table).

3. There are thousands of government agencies in the United States, and hundreds of thousands of private organizations. None individually constitutes a large factor in the purchase of construction. The federal government is the largest single buyer of construction and in 1977 accounted for only 4 percent of all purchases. The producers of construction sell to a very large and diverse group of buyers.

The distribution of construction activity among types of structures does not remain constant over time. Instead, substantial shifts in the type of construction take place from year to year. Residential construction, for example, was at an annual rate of 2.4 million new starts in 1972, but only 1.2 million in 1975, one-half the total of three years earlier. By 1978, housing starts were again above 2 million. These are very large changes—the greatest in both absolute and relative magnitude since World War II. Expenditures on residential construction did not decline by as much, however, because of inflation during the years 1972 through 1975. By contrast, industrial construction reached a low point in 1972 and expanded thereafter. In 1977, residential construction was 48 percent of all new construction, and nonresidential building was 25 percent.

Characteristics of the Construction Product

The construction sector has many unique features. There is physical product, as in manufacturing, but instead of being produced at a plant and shipped to a customer, it is produced at a site selected by the purchaser. Nor is the product standardized. Instead, in general each facility is designed to order, on a custom basis. The product is not priced and advertised for sale, but instead a unique price is determined for each project. Rather than the customer buying a completed product, the customer contracts with a construction firm to build the project for a fixed price on a cost-incurred basis.

Product Characteristics in Construction:

Assembly at a particular site.

High degree of product specificity including detailed plans and specifications drawn for each unit to be produced.

High diversity of technological requirements of varying degrees of complexity.

An individual price for each structure.

Construction Firms

There are a vast number of construction firms, and they range greatly in size. General contractors take responsibility for an entire project but subcontract most of the actual construction. Most firms operate in a particular locality or region, but some are national in scope. Those that are national are generally specialized to a branch of the sector or a type of work. The major branches of construction by type of product include residential buildings, nonresidential buildings, highways, dams and other civil engineering projects, pipelines, electric transmission lines, and industrial and power plants. If the specialization of contractors is used to categorize them, the resulting major classifications are general contractors, heavy and highway contractors, and specialty trades contractors (for example, electrical, plumbing, and masonry contractors).[1]

A large number of relatively small enterprises make up the construction sector. In 1972, according to the most recent federal census of construction firms, the average contractor with a payroll had only 9.5 employees.[2] (Even this figure understates the industry's dispersion, since it does not include the more than 467,000 proprietorships and partnerships without payrolls.) Of the more than 430,000 establishments with payrolls, nearly 62 percent had fewer than 5 employees, while fewer than 10 percent of them had 20 or more employees. Put another way, about 60 percent of all contract construction employees worked for establishments employing fewer than 50 persons. The average establishment had total receipts of about $345,000.

Many contractors specialize in a particular kind of construction work. General contractors tend to specialize more than special trades contractors, and their most frequent specialization is residential building. The Bureau of the Census defines specialization as having over half of the firm's receipts from a given type of construction. By this definition, about 90 percent of all general contractors had an area of specialization, and about 50 percent of them concentrated their efforts on one type of project to the exclusion of all others. Firms that specialize in residential building, especially the construction of single-family homes, are most likely to do that type of work exclusively, while firms specializing in other kinds of construction tend more often to have some receipts from outside their area of specialty.

A large majority of construction contractors perform their work in the region of their headquarters. In 1972, for example, over 90 percent of all contractors operated exclusively in their home states. Moreover, even those contractors working in more than one state obtained the preponderance of their receipts from work within their home states. Not surprisingly, it is the largest contractors who tend to operate over multistate areas. While representing only 7.2 percent of all contractor establishments, such firms nevertheless accounted for 29.1 percent of all construction receipts.

Despite the atomistic structure of the industry, a number of large engineering and contracting firms have annual receipts in the billions of dollars. These establishments typically operate on a nationwide or even worldwide basis and are called upon to undertake such massive construction projects as dams, power plants and skyscrapers. In 1972, 3,863 contractors (less than 1 percent of the total), who had receipts of $5 million or more, accounted for over 33 percent of the industry's gross income and about 23 percent of its employment.

The construction industry also experiences an inordinate amount of business turnover. Establishing a firm is relatively simple and often requires little capitalization. As a consequence, the rate of business failure is high, especially among the smaller subcontractors. Although the total number of establishments has remained fairly stable over the years, the ratio of new and discontinued businesses to operating businesses is considerably greater in construction than in most other industries.

Characteristics of Employment in Construction

The peculiar characteristics of the product, of its pricing, and of firms have major effects on the characteristics of employment in construction. Below are listed several aspects of construction employment that, taken as a whole, cause the sector to have a unique place in the American economy. Especially important is the assembling of contractors and subcontractors with various specializations for the building of a particular project, with the resulting specialization of the work force and the intermixing of the employees of different employers.

Summary of Employment in Construction:

Considerable shifting of employees among work sites.

Considerable shifting of employees among employers.

Identification by the employee with his craft or occupation, not with his employer.

A relatively large proportion of skilled workers.

Much self-supervision.

Very unstable employment opportunity.

Dangerous and often difficult work conditions.

Intermixture of employees of different employers at a single project site.

Construction of nonstandard (that is, custom-designed) products.

Characteristics of Management in Construction

The management of construction firms and construction projects is surprisingly complex. Construction involves aspects of management that characterize such other branches of the economy as manufacturing, defense contracting, and research and development. What is peculiarly characteristic of construction, however, is the complex interaction of managers of firms on a project site.

Construction management is similar to manufacturing management in many ways. Construction firms fabricate or assemble products as well as install them. Some firms, particularly in the mechanical specialties, maintain centrally located shops that, in fact, are small manufacturing plants. Sheet metal, piping, and iron and steel contractors are examples. Many other construction firms operate out of offices, however, with a storehouse or yard attached for holding equipment and materials. All fabrication is done at the job site itself. Other firms do not even maintain storehouses but operate out of a one-room office and use a truck to transport materials purchased for each job to the site. In effect, the contractor doing this has shifted all inventory costs to his materials suppliers. Management in construction may entail, therefore, the full range of manufacturing managerial tasks (including purchasing, fabrication, inventory control, and shipping), or virtually none of them.

Management in construction is like that in defense contracting (which incidentally involves some construction) in that a firm's work ordinarily involves only a limited number of projects at a given time and a close relationship to the purchaser of the product. Disputes about costs are as common in construction as they are in defense work. Whether the job is done on a cost-incurred basis or on a fixed-price basis, the ordinary avenue for disputes over costs lies in the additional charges made to an owner (construction's term for customer) as a result of changes made in the design of the structure after its price has been determined. Such changes are common.

Management in construction is like that in research and development activities in two important ways. First, it involves professionals, in particular engineers, in the management process. Second, construction draws operating managers from technical specialities, especially engineering. These two factors have a very significant impact on the performance of the managerial function in construction and upon the view that managers from other sectors of the economy have about construction management generally.

Architects and design engineers are largely responsible for the performance of structures. In many instances, design firms are expected by their clients not only to design a structure but also to oversee its actual construction and ultimately to certify its satisfactory completion. In the past, the architect was perceived as the owner's representative at the construction site with virtually full authority to inspect work, to require changes, or even to require that work be taken out and redone. Architects have become uncomfortable in this role. In recent years, the position of the national professional association of architects has been that the architect is not the owner's representative on the site but is instead merely an interested observer. Such an arrangement is intended to limit the legal liability of a design firm or designer if something goes wrong. But in whatever capacity, the designers still play an intimate role in the management of construction at a job site.

Construction has traditionally drawn its managers from two groups. The first, and probably the larger source, are workmen who have been employed in a blue-collar capacity in the industry. The second group comes from the engineering disciplines. Managers in construction as a group are not graduates of business schools or law schools, but of engineering schools. Graduates of civil engineering curriculums are particularly important as a source of managers in construction. Unfortunately, the result is a managerial cadre that although highly competent technically, lacks certain supervisory and managerial skills. The management of purchasing and inventories, the organization of the flow of work, and the supervision of the work force are poorly developed in construction, when compared, for example, to manufacturing.

In construction firms of more than a minimal size, management is specialized to a certain extent. It is common for the head of the firm to concentrate on financial matters and relationships with customers. These managerial functions are often performed with great practical sophistication. This is especially true of certain aspects of financial management. Construction firms ordinarily involve little invested capital; they operate on short-term business loans and on money advanced by the customers (generally unwillingly and often unknowingly). The daily management of construction projects is usually under the direction of another officer of the company who is, in effect, a general superintendent. The managers of site operations and of fabrication shops, if any, report to him.

The managerial revolution in the United States, which has involved the professional training of many thousands of graduate students and extensive research and experimentation into various functions and aspects of management, has largely bypassed construction. Only a very small proportion of graduates of business schools enter the construction sector. Few academic courses are offered in construction management, and little research is conducted into the problems of construction management. In recent years, however, some interest has developed, particularly in engineering schools, in providing managerial instruction to students.

This is not to gainsay the several dramatic developments in managerial techniques and structures in construction in recent years. Among the most important are the development of sophisticated work scheduling techniques, such as those labeled PERT (Program Evaluation and Review Technique) and CPM (Critical Path Method). These are planning devices that attempt to coordinate the many separate aspects of construction projects for the purpose of minimizing time of construction, costs, and confusion at the site among the work forces of various firms, and of permitting better control over the sequence of operations. Another important development has been better utilization of materials on site, especially the sequencing of deliveries and storage. The orderly construction of high-rise, large-volume buildings on very narrow urban lots has motivated and, in turn, been made possible by these developments. Both scheduling techniques and materials utilization have been much facilitated by the application of computers to these tasks.

The Problem of the Large-scale Project

The size of construction projects has continued to outgrow the industry's capacity to manage. Very large projects, such as new towns, nuclear power stations, or the Trans-Alaska Pipeline, have dwarfed the capabilities of construction firms to manage both their financial and operational elements in the traditional manner of a general contractor. In consequence, experimentation with a new kind of organization, purely managerial in its motivation, has developed. A number of construction firms now advertise themselves as "construction managers." For a fee, they propose to manage a project for an owner, that is, to design it (in some instances, but not all), to plan its schedule of construction, to obtain contractors and subcontractors for the owner, to supervise construction and to deliver a completed project to the owner. These firms are selling not one product, but a group of managerial (and sometimes design) services.

Large projects, with their substantial dangers of financial loss, have forced architects and engineers to reduce the managerial responsibility they will undertake, and contractors have done the same (although they offer management services much like an architect offers design services). As a practical matter, it is not too much to say that very large projects are frequently not managed at all! The ultimate responsibility returns to the owner, who alone has the financial exposure that requires undivided attention. Owners are, therefore, attempting to enter the managerial gap in construction by closely overseeing the construction process. But most owners do this as a last resort, recognizing that their own staffs also lack the competence to manage very large projects well.

Recent developments in the scale of projects are dramatic. A nuclear power station now necessarily consumes about ten years from the start of design through construction to operation, about six years of which involve on-site construction. Few nuclear projects take less time, and many take considerably longer. Such a project will involve the expenditure of $2 or $3 billion. Similarly, the Trans-Alaska Pipeline consumed some eight years of planning, design, and construction. Cost savings or overruns on these jobs can be enormous. Shortening construction time on a large nuclear power station by two years can save as much as $710 million in interest charges alone to a public utility.[3] The Alaska pipeline, projected in 1970 to cost less than $1 billion, appears in 1979 to carry an ultimate price of some $8 billion.

Completion schedules, cost control, and quality of performance of the structure are managerial responsibilities. When these factors get out of hand, it is common to identify their proximate causes (increased interest charges, increased prices of materials, increased wage rates). But what is common to all major construction jobs today is a crisis of management and the need to regain managerial control of the construction process. At this point, growth in the scale and technological complexity of certain construction projects has outstripped managerial capacity.

Notes

1. Government statisticians use the classification by contractor specialization in reporting employment and earnings data, and by branch in reporting expenditures and output.

2. U.S., Department of Commerce, Bureau of the Census, *1972 Census of Construction Industries,* Industry Series CC 72-1- (Washington, D.C.: Government Printing Office, 1975), pp. 1-2, 1-12.

3. Authors' estimate.

2 Pricing Private Construction

Julian E. Lange

Prices in the construction industry are usually set by competitive bidding or negotiated contract. In the public sector, prices for the majority of construction projects are reached by competitive bidding because of government procurement statutes. These regulations are designed to prevent political favoritism and corruption in the awarding of contracts that often involve very substantial sums. (See chapter 3 for a discussion of the particular requirements for bidding in the public sector.) Although reliable statistics are not available for the private sector, it is generally acknowledged that most construction is priced by means of a form of competitive bidding. In recent years, however, a growing proportion of private nonresidential construction has been awarded by negotiation between owners and contractors, utilizing several forms of "cost-plus-fee" arrangements. Most private residential construction is performed by speculative builders, who fabricate housing units on their own account for resale. Finally, certain types of repair and maintenance work and simple construction tasks are accomplished by force account, that is, with the owner acting as contractor and directly employing the labor.

The unique nature of the construction product has determined these diverse and distinctive pricing arrangements. The insistence of buyers on a custom-designed product requires job-order production and the calculation of a separate price for each unit. The construction project contains thousands of individual components, even if the structure is a simple one, and the exact requirements must be enumerated in a set of detailed plans and specifications.

In addition to the complexity of the product, several other features of the construction process contribute to the uniqueness of individual projects. Construction activities must be performed largely on site, with the result that physical conditions peculiar to a site must be considered in the design of the structure. Since construction takes place over time, some changes in detail undoubtedly occur as the structure begins to take shape, initiated at the suggestion either of the owner or of the contractor. Further, since the projected use of most structures is measured in decades, owners contemplate building new structures infrequently. This creates an incentive to include unique features in the design of the building, to meet present needs and probable future requirements. Finally, the owner's and architect's style preferences must also be included as major contributors to product uniqueness.

The concept of submarkets is extremely important in understanding pricing arrangements in construction. Few general statements can be made about pricing

11

for the construction "industry" as a whole because there is no single construction industry, but rather a group of industries that are loosely related to one another by the nature of their products, technologies, labor relations arrangements, and institutional settings. The most useful hypotheses about pricing practices in construction are those made with reference to a particular submarket or group of submarkets.

Construction can be described with reference to four major dimensions: industry branch, technology, geographical breadth, and project size. The submarket of a given project determines the universe of contractors from which the eventual bidders will be drawn. For example, some general contractors concentrate on building construction while others devote their energies to highways, bridges, and tunnels. Further, there is a wide range of structures within the category of buildings, from the simplest warehouse or garage to huge office buildings, industrial plants, or power plants. Because a contractor must acquire expertise in a given branch of the industry to become efficient, contractors tend to specialize in related industry branches (for example, power plants and large industrial plant facilities). Hence, the number of general contractors able to coordinate the construction of a $20 million industrial plant will be substantially smaller than the number of general contractors who can build a simple $500,000 warehouse.

In the technological dimension, contractors acquire skills that apply directly to some construction projects but not to others. For example, some painters specialize in building interiors, while others concentrate on bridges; mechanical contractors who specialize in installing one-way, controlled-flow air ventilation systems in research laboratories possess a different sort of expertise from contractors who install home air-conditioning units in single-family houses.

The geographical dimension of a construction submarket varies for projects of a given size and technical complexity. For example, the awarding of a contract to build a two-story, 30,000-square-foot office building may attract local contractors (both general and specialty contractors), whereas the construction of a sixty-story office building may attract contractors (general and major specialty contractors) from all over the nation.

The size of a project is often related to its technical complexity. In general, as project size increases, the number of firms with the skills to undertake it will decrease. This holds even within a given specialty. A small electrical contractor who is adept at wiring two-story office buildings will not possess the experience, manpower, or financial strength to undertake the electrical subcontract on a fifty-story office building. Consequently, project size and geographical breadth are closely related; larger projects tend to attract general and major specialty contractors from a wider geographical area than do smaller projects.

Alternative Pricing Arrangements

Many features of the pricing process are representative of particular construction submarkets in only the most general way. For example, the steps in the competitive bidding process described below most readily apply to commercial or industrial submarkets; to apply them without modification to the power plant submarket would be misleading. They are presented here to acquaint the reader with general institutional practices in construction, so that the analytic framework suggested further on can be viewed in perspective.

Competitive Bidding

Many construction projects are priced by means of competitive bidding. In the public sector, the steps are carefully delineated and strictly adhered to, while in the private sector the owner has considerable latitude in setting the rules. Nevertheless, the basic features of the bidding process remain the same in both. The structure is designed by an architect, often with the aid of an engineering firm, based upon the objectives and requirements of the owner. Detailed plans and specifications are formulated, which are then distributed to interested contractors. In the public sector, statutes usually require that all qualified contractors be allowed to compete for the work on an equal footing. (The definition of *qualified contractor* usually calls for some minimal evidence of previous experience, financial stability, and the payment of a modest license fee.) In the private sector, the owner can do as he wishes, with the options ranging from an open competition for all interested parties to the restriction of the bidders to a few favored firms.

The contractor's activities during the bidding stage are comparable for both public and private buildings of similar complexity. A quantity estimate of the type and amount of materials must be made, based on a careful examination of the plans and specifications. Different contractors carry out their estimating tasks in a variety of ways, ranging from rough estimates based on average technical coefficients to a careful delineation of the order of production tasks. The more detailed estimates are generally more accurate, while the procedures based on average factors often miss the mark by 25 percent or more of actual cost.[1] The cost of submitting a bid varies with the complexity of the project and is often substantial.

The final bids are normally submitted on either a lump-sum or unit price basis, with the former being used for most projects. A lump-sum bid is the total price for which a contractor offers to complete a structure according to the plans and specifications. Managerial judgment plays a key role in determining the single price. The cost estimate for each component—materials, labor, capital and subcontractor charges, overhead, and profit—represents a contractor's best guess about an uncertain future. Wage and price increases, technological change, strikes, and unfavorable site conditions are just a few of the pitfalls that a contractor may encounter. A contractor's assessment of the likelihood and impact of such occurrences must be reflected in his cost estimate. The bid price must also be adjusted to take competitive factors into account. Because of its central importance, the task of selecting the final bid price is usually the responsibility of top management, typically the president or another principal with a large financial interest in the firm.

Usually, unit price bidding is called for on projects where the uncertainty about the quantity of materials needed or the labor involved in certain key tasks is particularly pronounced. In such cases, the contractor selects a unit price for each task. Managerial judgment about cost-related and competitive uncertainties again plays a major role in the decision-making process. The unit price is weighted to take direct and indirect overhead and profit into account. A lump-sum final price is computed by multiplying the unit price by the owner's engineering estimates for the quantities involved in each task. The price used to determine the lowest bidder is the final computed lump-sum price. However, the payments to the winning contractor will be based on the *actual* quantities used multiplied by the quoted unit prices.

In unit pricing, a contractor will often submit an "unbalanced bid" when he discovers what he believes are large discrepancies between his estimates and the owner's engineering estimates. Depending upon his preference for risk and his confidence in his own quantity survey, a contractor will often raise the unit prices on tasks that he believes to be underestimated while lowering the unit prices on other tasks. The price of the lump-sum final bid remains unchanged. If the contractor has guessed right, this practice can result in a substantially increased profit because the final payment is based upon the *actual* quantities. This bidding practice, however, is not without its risks. The awarding authorities or owners will often disqualify a bid if it appears to be heavily unbalanced, and it is always possible that the contractor misjudged the accuracy of the engineering estimates.

Awarding the Contract. A public awarding authority must generally award the contract to the lowest responsible bidder. (*Responsible* in this context means having a reasonable probability of completing the job as specified.) In contrast, a private owner has autonomy, being bound only by the common law of contracts. The private owner may choose any bidder (including the highest bidder), reject all bids, or select a contractor and attempt to alter the bid through negotiation. If a private owner has not restricted the number of bidders to those whose work he believes to be comparable, he may reject some of the bidders because of his (or the architect's) uncertainty about their ability to meet performance standards and complete the project on time. Frequently, the bids are not opened publicly, and unsuccessful contractors may or may not be informed of the details of the winning bid.

The private owner's behavior is not completely unconstrained. It is the usual practice for an owner who has restricted a bid list to award the contract to the low bidder. If competing contractors feel that they were treated unfairly, they may refrain from bidding on any further projects for a given architect or owner. Hence, to the extent that an owner regularly engages in the construction of facilities, he is under pressure to adhere to the rules that the contractors assume to be the basis for the contract award. However, since a large number of private owners undertake construction projects infrequently, they enjoy relatively wide latitude in making contract awards.

In both the private and public sectors, once the award has been made, the contract documents may be completed quickly or may take two or three months to finish. In the interim, the owner or awarding authority will usually send the general contractor a letter of intent, giving him notice to proceed. The general contractor must then award the subcontracts as soon as possible, to ensure that the subcontractors will hold to their quoted prices. In several government jurisdictions, statutes require the general contractor to award subcontracts to those specialty contractors that were quoted in the winning bid, but in most states and in the private sector, the general contractor is under no legal obligation to do so. For a large project with several subcontract specialties, subcontracts will be awarded in the order that the tasks are to be performed; for example excavating work will be among the first subcontracts awarded while painting will be one of the last.

Postaward Price Modification. Virtually all construction projects entail owner-initiated changes and extras that occur during the construction period. Once the contracts have been signed, subsequent price changes are the subject of negotiation between the owner and the general contractor. Design changes often require the reorganization of production tasks, and thus they entail additional costs. In the postaward price negotiations, the contractor and owner find themselves in a situation with many characteristics of bilateral monopoly bargaining. Contractors often view design modifications as an opportunity to increase profits. Indeed, it is sometimes the case that contractors have intentionally submitted bids below fully loaded cost (at or below short-run marginal cost) in anticipation of recouping general overhead and profit through the price adjustments that result from design changes.

Negotiated Contracts

Given the latitude of private owners to adopt any pricing method, many of them choose to award construction contracts by means of negotiation with one or several contractors. There are three major reasons for this:

1. An owner may contemplate building a project of large size and great complexity (for example, a power plant). In such a case, he will prefer to hire an experienced contracting firm that possesses a high degree of managerial and technical expertise. Because of the project's complexity and the fact that technology may be changing during the several years of construction, it may be difficult to describe the structure precisely in the plans and specifications at the outset of the project, making the calculation of a lump-sum price very difficult.

These uncertainties make the expertise and professional integrity of the contractor extremely important. It is equally important that the owner's staff be highly knowledgeable, so that they can evaluate contractor proposals and monitor subsequent construction activities.

2. An owner may place great weight on the quality of the workmanship that will go into his proposed structure. He may therefore decide to engage the services of a contractor with an excellent reputation for technical competence. The contractor will often be one that the owner has used previously with good results or, alternatively, a firm that has been highly recommended by the architect. Presumably, the contractor's good reputation will not be limited just to quality of workmanship, but will extend to fairness in financial matters as well. If the contractor has worked for the owner in the past, or contemplates possible future opportunities to do so, he will have an incentive to keep his production standards high and costs competitive, in order to keep potential competitors for future awards at bay. Again, the owner's technical competence must be relatively high in order to monitor contractor performance.

3. An owner may be both price conscious and knowledgeable, and wish to construct a building that is well defined and simple in design. A department store chain, for example, might plan its tenth branch store, with a design essentially the same as the nine preceding ones. In such a case, the owner's staff is likely to be able to estimate the cost with great accuracy. For reasons of convenience, the owner may choose to select a contractor of good reputation and negotiate a lump-sum price directly. Of course, if the contractor insists upon a price that the owner's staff judges to be unreasonable, the owner always retains the option of negotiating with another contractor or inviting competitive bids on the project. (This alternative also exists in the first two situations described above.)

Negotiated contracts generally fall into the "cost-plus" category, although occasionally, as in the third example, a contractor will negotiate a lump-sum price. The cost-plus arrangements may take on several forms, differing mainly in the method of determining the contractor's fee, but all include the reimbursement of the contractor for the direct project costs including materials, labor, subcontractor payments, and equipment purchases or rentals for use on the project. In most cost-plus arrangements, only the general contractor is hired on a fee basis. Subcontract awards are ordinarily made through the use of a competitive bidding system, with the subcontracting firms bidding at the invitation of the general contractor, subject to the approval of the owner.

The cost-plus-fixed-fee contract is the most common form of the cost-plus arrangements. The fee is usually fixed at a percentage of the target cost estimate that is determined at the inception of the project. In some cases, the contractor receives an incentive to reduce costs by sharing in any cost savings. In addition, some contracts penalize the contractor for cost overruns and failure to complete the project on time. Open-ended cost-plus-percentage-of-total-cost contracts are rare, since the contractor is given an incentive to increase costs, and potential abuses loom very large. When a percentage fee arrangement is used, an upper limit on the fee is ordinarily set in advance.

Speculative Building

The second exception to the general rule of competitive bidding in private construction is speculative building. Speculative builders are firms "primarily engaged in the construction of single family houses and other buildings on [their] own account, for sale to others, rather than as contractors."[2] Typically, a speculative builder will build a few houses at a time and set a price on each house according to what he believes the market will bear. If buyers do not materialize within a reasonable period, he will adjust his price. Hence, speculative builders do not ordinarily build a structure for a specific owner. Instead, they build for a general buyer in a particular price range.[3]

There are two major reasons why speculative building is feasible in home construction but impractical in nonresidential construction. First, the basic needs of home buyers are very similar, and housing designs can be reduced to a few standard patterns. A speculative builder can select a price range within reach of many potential buyers and build a house acceptable to a large number of them. Second, lending institutions are willing to finance the construction of housing units because of the high probability of locating buyers within a short time. The builder-developer is thus able to "stockpile" housing units, a practice that is untenable in nonresidential construction because of the high degree of project specificity.

In contrast to the many owners who award nonresidential projects to a general contractor on a cost-plus-fee basis and then rely on competitive bidding for the subcontracts, most speculative builders negotiate prices directly with their specialty trade subcontractors. The fairly standard and repetitive nature of the tasks performed by the specialty contractors appears to be responsible for the lack of a bidding system in the letting of subcontracts by operative builders. The operative builder makes an intuitive trade-off between the amount of price saving that could be achieved by taking bids on standard specialty work and the difficulty of breaking in a new member of the construction team. For work that is less standardized, bidding may be utilized. Such work may include "new work, unusual work, work during periods of shifting prices, and tasks which vary with the design of the house."[4]

Force-Account Construction

The last important category of private construction that does not use a competitive bidding process is force-account work. A substantial amount of construction is performed by an owner with his own labor forces and not by contract with outside workers. Force-account work is ordinarily limited to repairs, maintenance, and simple construction tasks. More complex work involving several specialty trades and/or specialized manpower is usually accomplished by securing the services of specialty contractors, with either the owner or a hired firm acting as general contractor.

Basic Bidding Models

A simple bidding model can serve as a useful introduction to a detailed examination of price setting in construction. Such a model delineates the main issues faced by prospective bidders.

In a typical case, the architect and engineer have prepared detailed plans and specifications for a project. Several contractors submit bids on the work; the project will subsequently be awarded to the lowest bidder. Each contractor must go to some expense to prepare a bid, and the first decision must be whether or not to submit a bid on this particular project. After deciding to compete for the work, the contractor must then select a bid price. Obviously, a higher bid price will increase the profit that can be realized, but it will decrease the likelihood of being the low bidder. Thus, the contractor's strategy is to bid as high as he dares while attempting to be low bidder.

The selection of the bid price, therefore, has two important elements: estimation of project cost and formulation of contractor strategy, that is, choosing the bid price that represents the best trade-off between higher profits and low bid. Figure 2-1 illustrates a simple model of bid price selection. In figure 2-1, a and b represent the practical boundaries of the bid prices for a particular project. It is assumed that c is the estimated direct cost (marginal cost) of the proposed project, including materials, labor, equipment rental or depreciation, and overhead directly related to the project (such as the salary of a field superintendent), all adjusted for management's best guess about the likely impact of cost-related uncertainties. It is further assumed that the estimated direct cost c will be equal to the *actual* direct cost of the project after it is completed. Hence, if p equals the bid price submitted by Contractor X, p minus c will represent his contribution to profit (if any) and general overhead (that is, *non-project-related* overhead, such as the taxes on his home office) associated with the bid price p. Thus, a schedule can be generated of profit (or loss) plus general overhead payoffs associated with each price p in the relevant range between the outer limits a and b. (It should be pointed out that c represents Contractor X's cost estimate. But a is still a possible bid price even though it is less than c, since another bidder might be a more efficient producer, have a lower project-related overhead than Contractor X, have made different adjustments for cost-related uncertainties, have used a different estimating procedure, or simply have made an estimating error. The upper boundary b represents the bid price at which the owner will reject all bids.)

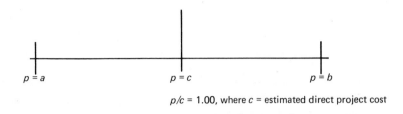

p/c = 1.00, where c = estimated direct project cost

Figure 2-1(a). Relevant Range of Possible Bid Prices

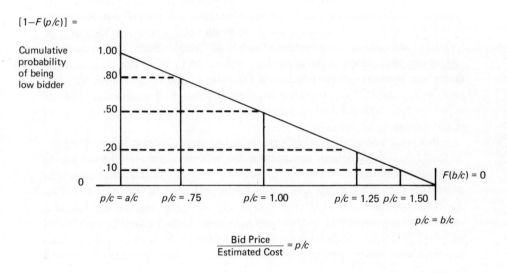

Figure 2-1(b). Cumulative Probability of Being Low Bidder

It is clear that the higher a contractor's bid, the less likely he is to emerge as the lowest bidder. Hence, for each price p there is also an associated probability of being lowest bidder, and one can further assume that this probability is a decreasing function of p. (In the example in figure 2-1, arbitrary values have been assumed for the probability of winning the contract award associated with each bid price indicated.) With this information, one can compute an expected contribution to profit and general overhead for each bid price: the profit plus overhead figure associated with a bid price multiplied by the probability of being low bidder at that price, assuming the independence of contractor bidding behavior (see table 2-1). The contractor would then submit a bid p for which the expected contribution to profit and general overhead is highest. If a contractor repeated this procedure in its essentials for all jobs he was competing for, he would maximize expected contribution to profit and general overhead in the long run.

The model illustrated by figure 2-1 and table 2-1 represents the basic features of the optimal bidding models that are found in the literature.[5] These models all have several shortcomings. Almost all of them assume the estimated project cost to be equal to the actual cost—a most unrealistic assumption.[6] They also compute the probabilities of being low bidder on the assumption of independence of the individual bidder.

To assume that the project cost is both known and equal to the *estimated* project cost removes at a stroke one of the major sources of variation in construction bid prices. Contractors adjust their cost estimates in accordance with their judgments about cost-related uncertainties, and it is unlikely that the resulting estimates will generally coincide with the actual project cost. Moreover, errors of estimation are commonplace. In smaller projects (where the entry of specialty and general contractors is relatively easy), inadequate estimating procedures and contractor inexperience often result in errors that produce wide divergence in bid prices (sometimes on the order of 200 percent or more).[7] But even with competition among experienced, sophisticated contractors, lack of sufficient time and qualified personnel can sometimes result in substantial errors of estimation.

Independence among bidders is usually assumed because it simplifies the expected profit calculations and because the pattern of interdependence among competing contractors is not easily specified. But in practice, it is clear that experienced contractors are influenced by the existence of other bidders. This influence becomes more apparent in the case of larger projects, which have a relatively small number of bidders who are known to each other. The likelihood of interdependence of contractor bidding behavior in the large majority of cases greatly diminishes the precision of the profit-maximizing bid price estimates of

Table 2-1
Expected Value of Possible Bid Prices

Bid Price	Profit (Loss) Plus General Overhead as Percent of Cost	Probability of Being Lowest Bidder Given Various Values of Bid Price	Expected Contribution to Profit and General Overhead as Percent of Cost
$p = a$	−.50	1.00	−.50
$p/c = .75$	−.25	.80	−.20
$p/c = 1.00$	.00	.50	.00
$p/c = 1.25$	.25	.20	.05
$p/c = 1.50$	.50	.01	.005

Note: Hence choose bid price = 1.25c, given these choices, since expected contribution to profit and general overhead is maximized.

the simple models, and hence their usefulness both in the explanation of contractor bidding behavior and in the formulation of optimal-bidding rules.

Simple models of bid optimization are clearly inadequate for a thorough understanding of the fundamental influences that affect the contractor's bidding decision. Assessing the relationship between the bid price and the probability of being low bidder is a highly subjective matter for most contractors. An analysis of the factors that influence the contractor's judgment is a crucial step in understanding the bidding process.

An Analytic Framework for Price Setting

A contractor's bid price depends on his estimate of the direct project cost and the amount added on over the estimated direct cost (sometimes referred to as the markup or contribution) to provide for profit plus general (indirect, non-project-related) overhead. Cost estimation is not simply a technical activity. Differences in cost estimates arise from differences in managerial judgments about uncertainty as well as from the utilization of estimating techniques that vary in precision. Contractors are well aware of the possibility of unexpected changes in prices and wages, strikes, adverse site conditions, and the like. Cost estimates are adjusted to reflect the contractor's guesses about the likelihood and impact of such events. The determination of the amount added on for profit and overhead also depends on a managerial assessment of competitive factors. It resembles a game of strategy in which the contractor selects the additional amount that he hopes will result in the low bid, while also meeting his minimum requirements for profit and overhead.[8] Since determining the final bid price involves a substantial input of managerial judgment, the weight given to the presence or absence of particular factors in a bidding competition differs among contractors (and also for the same contractor at different points in time). The analytic framework described below provides a way to identify the factors that determine the final selection of a bid price and the interaction of these factors.[9]

Estimating the Direct Project Cost

The most salient feature of the cost structure in the construction industry is the high ratio of direct costs (materials, labor, and variable cost of equipment) to total costs. A rough estimate for the average markup for all construction taken together amounts to 15 percent of total construction expenditures, with direct costs accounting for 85 percent of the total (see table 2-2). Variations in cost estimates of 25 percent or more are common, particularly for small projects under $100,000, and such differences can account for the major portion of the variation in the total bid prices submitted by contractors.[10]

Table 2-2

Breakdown of Aggregate Construction Expenditures for 1972

(entire United States)

Item	Expenditures (thousands of dollars)	Percent of Direct Cost	Percent of Total Construction Expenditures
Materials	46,426,441	36	31
Payroll	40,004,782	32	27
Value of subcontracted work	38,197,317	30	26
Equipment rentals, depreciation, etc.	1,972,054	2	1
Subtotal: Direct cost = materials, payroll, subcontracts, equipment	126,600,594	100	85
Total construction expenditures	149,429,496	118	100
Markup for general overhead and profit	22,828,902	18	15

Source: U.S., Dept. of Commerce, Bureau of the Census, *1972 Census of U.S. Construction Industries* (Washington, D.C.: Government Printing Office, 1975) I:1-8-1-9.

The Techniques of Estimating. Cost estimates vary because the techniques vary substantially in their degree of precision. The most accurate technique is the most arduous, costly, and time-consuming for the contractor: a detailed plan that takes into account not only the quantities of materials and labor inputs but also the problem of coordinating job tasks and attempting to ensure that the order in which the separate operations will be carried out is the most efficient available. This procedure requires a careful study of the plans and specifications, and must be prepared by an experienced estimator and/or a field supervisor in combination with clerical personnel.

Because of the time and expense, a contractor may decide not to assemble a very detailed project cost estimate. Methods of lesser accuracy involve less attention to coordinating production tasks and place greater reliance on "rough and ready" average measures, such as the average cost factors for square footage of commercial office space put-in-place. Since construction projects are a complex amalgam of thousands of separate parts and assembly operations, the use of average gross measures may result in estimates that differ from "true" cost by 30 percent or more.[11]

Contractors may opt for the less precise methods of estimating for several reasons: (1) simple inexperience; (2) a shortage of technical personnel to perform the estimating task; or (3) assumption of their slight chances of being low bidder. This last practice, in which the contractor is prepared to gamble without investing a great deal of time and money, is frowned upon by the larger and more experienced contractors, who point out that it may lead to winning a contract at a price that will guarantee a loss. Most contractors, however, and especially the smaller firms, admit to taking a chance once in a while. Since contractors attempt to be low bidder, and since most estimating errors tend to be errors of omission, the practice of "taking a flyer" exerts a downward influence on the bid price.

The Quality of Contractor Experience. Varying degrees of expertise are another cause of differences in contractors' estimates of costs for the same structure. Estimating retains many of the characteristics of an art, despite its more straightforward aspects, such as the quantity take-off. An estimator's previous experience with similar projects can result in greater accuracy in assessing cost-related uncertainties and in suggestions for production shortcuts. He is also aware of the hidden pitfalls caused by ambiguities in the plans and specifications. In addition, since some contracting firms concentrate on certain types of projects (such as office buildings or shopping centers), over time these firms may have developed absolute cost advantages over the contractors who lack such experience. For example, such firms are probably more knowledgeable about the availability and productivity of labor in a familiar locality than are firms new to the area. The "learning curve phenomenon" may enable some contractors to underbid competitors effectively, but only if a skilled estimator is able to apply the firm's previous experience to the project at hand.

Absolute cost advantages over competitors may also result from differences in worker productivity that reflect differences in the skill mix of the work forces of competing contractors. Some contractors are able to attract and hold better than average supervisory personnel and craftsmen through guarantees of steady employment and incentives, such as minimum amounts of guaranteed overtime. The increase in productivity of the work force in general can thus be translated into a lower bid price. Absolute cost advantages can also result from locational advantages and volume purchases of materials and equipment. For example, larger contractors who are working on several similar projects simultaneously can often secure volume discounts from materials suppliers and reduce their bid price accordingly.

Many of these relative advantages can be obviated by similarities among contractors who are competing for the work. For example, buildings that will cost more than $10 million are complex enough to be built by only a small number of contractors. In such cases, it is likely that the skill differential among large, established, and sophisticated contractors is minimal, particularly when compared to the differential that is likely to exist between a medium-size firm bidding on a $500,000 building and a smaller, inexperienced contractor bidding on the same project.[12]

Future Changes in Production Costs. Construction takes time, and both the physical characteristics of the project and its actual cost will differ somewhat from the original plans and specifications and the estimated project cost. Contractors take this into account by anticipating cost escalations in their project cost estimates. Labor, materials, and capital equipment rental or depreciation are the main categories of factor costs. The proportions differ from one branch of the industry to another, but labor and materials generally consume the lion's share of the direct project cost, with capital depreciation or equipment rentals accounting for about 1.5 percent (see table 2-2) of the total direct construction outlays.[13]

For unionized contractors who are bidding on projects likely to be completed before present local wage agreements expire, labor rates are standard for a particular area. Since average worker productivity is not likely to change significantly during short periods of time, contractors can estimate these labor costs with a good deal of accuracy. For projects that are expected to continue past the expiration of current labor agreements, however, contractors must include a percentage increase in the labor cost for those activities that are to be performed toward the end of the project, as well as provide for the impact of possible strikes. The cost of materials also involves uncertainty, and contractors must estimate increases in the price of materials that are likely to take place during the course of a contract.

Other Elements of Uncertainty. Clearly, a significant element of judgment enters into a contractor's project cost estimate. Contractors must adjust cost estimates to take account of many uncertain factors. In addition to those already mentioned, they must consider the possible impact on costs of unfavorable weather, community protests, inefficient or late subcontractor performance, political influences, and litigation stemming from disputes with the owner or subcontractors. On the other hand, owner-initiated changes necessitate postaward price bargaining between the contractor and owner and often afford contractors an opportunity to increase profits. Contracting firms differ in their ability to reduce uncertainty; no one can predict the weather one year hence with great precision, but some contractors may have more information than others concerning the efficiency of various subcontractors. Consequently, differences in contractors' ability to reduce uncertainty will produce variations in project cost estimates.

Subcontracting and Its Effects on Uncertainty. Subcontracting a portion of the work offers the general contractor the opportunity to reduce some of the uncertainty entailed in a fixed price agreement with the owner. The degree of subcontracting differs in different branches of the industry, and it is often dictated by technical considerations. In some cases, the general contractor becomes more of a broker of subcontractors than a provider of actual production services with his own work force. Subcontracting allows the general contractor to be sure that a certain portion of the direct cost is fixed, thus diminishing that portion of the project on which he is subject to cost overruns. Hence, subcontracting provides the general contractor with a larger percentage return on his actual input of direct construction services on a project than the percentage profit that is computed on the basis of the total project cost. Viewed in another way, for a given project a greater amount of subcontracting reduces the amount of uncertainty that a contractor faces compared to that entailed by the performance of the work with his own forces. This arrangement allows him greater leeway to reduce his percentage markup accordingly.[14]

Two important qualifications must be added. First, since construction is such a complex process, in which the different production tasks are highly interrelated and interdependent, in some cases subcontractors may well *add* an element of uncertainty to the general contractor's situation. If a subcontractor falls behind schedule, performs shoddy work that must be redone, or requires increased supervision by the general contractor, the costs will increase. Hence, some general contractors prefer to work only with subcontractors of demonstrated ability who can be counted upon to perform quality work on schedule. Second, the process of bid shopping enables some contractors to increase their profit by obtaining subcontractors who will perform their tasks for less money than was provided in the winning bid to the owner. In many cases this increased profit for the general contractor imposes an implicit cost on the owner—reduced quality of workmanship.[15]

Clerical Mistakes. No discussion of the causes of variation among contractors' cost estimates would be complete without mention of the ever present clerical errors. The pressures of meeting the bid submission deadline, which are intensified by the reluctance of many specialty subcontractors to submit early bids to a general contractor for fear of being undercut by a competitor, produce clerical errors. There are numerous last minute price changes and consequent recalculations of the final bid price. In cases of large and obvious clerical errors, statutes concerning public sector bidding provide for the release of the contractor from his obligation to enter into a contract with the awarding authority and also for the return of the bid deposit. Private owners will also ordinarily return the bid deposit and nullify the contractor's commitment in cases of substantial clerical errors, since common sense dictates that forcing a contractor to complete a project that he knows will result in a certain loss provides him with a substantial incentive to cut corners and perform shoddy work.

Minor clerical errors have a more subtle effect on a contractor's bid. Errors of this type generally do not show up until work is in progress, at which time the contractor must try to absorb them or offset them through increased productivity or other savings (sometimes entailing inferior workmanship). Many such errors are errors of omission and, as such, clerical errors tend to exert a downward influence on cost estimates.

Determining the Markup for Profit and
General Overhead

The estimated direct project cost provides a contractor with a minimum bidding figure; it represents his best approximation of the short-run variable cost, modified by his assessment of the cost of related uncertainty. The contractor will further adjust the final bid price to take account of competitive factors. This adjustment depends on many factors, including the contractor's willingness to take risks, his operating procedures, and his judgment about the strength of demand in the relevant submarket and characteristics specific to the particular project. The weight placed on these separate factors will be subjectively determined; no precise formula will be used. The same contractor may apply different subjective weights at different times. Since relatively small differences in the final bid price may well mean the difference between winning or losing the bidding competition (particularly in the case of larger projects), the factors taken into account in determining the markup represent an extremely important aspect of contractor bidding behavior.

To understand the bidding process, the differences between the uncertainties affecting costs and those relating to competitive factors must be analyzed separately. It is important to realize, however, that a contractor's selection of a single final bid price reflects his simultaneous assessment of both types of uncertainty, and in the final analysis represents his best judgment concerning how well the proposed project fits into his overall strategy for the survival and growth of the firm.

Contractor Characteristics. One of the most important determinants of the size of the markup is the contractor's "hunger for work"—his desire to win a particular project and its potential importance to his overall mix of work in progress. In determining how anxious he is to secure a given contract award, a contractor must consider his present backlog of work and his cash flow needs. If he has a sizable backlog of work, he may feel less anxious about adding an additional project than if he has little or no backlog.

To many contractors, the cash flow implications of winning a particular project competition are even more important. Since construction work takes place over time, progress payments are made periodically to the general contractor (who in turn pays his subcontractors). Industry custom (and prudent owner behavior) dictates that a certain percentage "retention" is deducted by the owner from each progress payment, which is eventually paid to the contractor upon the satisfactory completion of the project. Retentions may amount to 10 to 15 percent, often more than a contractor's markup for general overhead and profit. In addition, a contractor may have one or several projects whose owners are slow in making payments, creating a short-term cash flow shortage. For some contractors this sort of situation may become chronic. But even in the best of circumstances, a contractor will ordinarily have to seek short-term credit from a commercial bank to provide necessary working capital. Such loans are granted in keeping with the contractor's present in-house volume of work. For this reason, a contractor may be particularly anxious to secure additional projects in order to increase loan collateral, especially when cash flow is tight. Such a strategy may in fact succeed for some contractors in the short run. In such cases, the intense desire to secure additional work will exert a downward influence on the contractor's bids, prompting the sacrifice of future profits and even essential general overhead in order to obtain a positive short-term cash flow. Chronic inability to provide for general overhead costs however, is likely to lead eventually to bankruptcy.

Some contractors' bidding strategy can be influenced by a policy of either a minimum or standard percentage markup for profit and general overhead. This is more likely to be the case among the larger, more established contractors than for the smaller or newer firms. The larger firms are more likely to have larger home office staffs and more elaborate physical plants than the smaller firms, and hence a greater fixed overhead. In addition, in both small and new firms, most of the estimating, as well as a large part of the administrative work, is performed by the firm's few principal officers, further reducing their out-of-pocket general overhead costs. Hence, even if the smaller and newer firms have minimum markup policies, their minimum is likely to be smaller than that of the larger, well established firms for similar size projects.

An additional factor that affects the intensity of a contractor's efforts to secure a particular job is the availability of key supervisory and production personnel. Certain experienced estimators and field supervisors represent a quasi-fixed cost to the firm, since a contractor cannot realistically consider laying them off without losing the firm's investment in their specialized skills and risking substantial damage to the management team. In making the decision to bid and in formulating a bidding strategy for a particular project, a contractor must consider which of his key personnel will become available in the near future. He must then attempt to secure projects that suit their specialized talents. In most industry submarkets, the procedure is largely intuitive, but this is not always true. In power plant submarkets, for example, the contractor's proposal must include the names and résumés of key members of the design and production team, and this "personnel dimension" of the bid proposal is considered carefully by the owner.[16]

The contractor's willingness to accept risk is the final factor in his bidding strategy. It is important here to distinguish between risk and uncertainty. Uncertainty, as it was explained earlier, involves knowledge or the lack of it, and contractors differ in their command over knowledge and their capacity to reduce uncertainty. Two equally knowledgeable contractors can differ, however, in their respective willingness to accept risk.

Contracting is a risky business under ideal circumstances, and a contractor's willingness to gamble will affect how much he chooses to reduce his bid price in order to stand a better chance of winning the contract competition. Consequently, differences in risk aversion among competing contractors will account for some of the dispersion in the final bid prices. Further, the same contractor may be willing to gamble to a greater or lesser degree at different points in time, depending upon his backlog and net cash flow position and his prospects for securing other jobs in the near future.

State of Demand in the Industry Submarket. The level of demand in a submarket at a particular time can influence the number of bidders participating in a project competition and their willingness to reduce their markup in order to improve their chance of being low bidder. Demand will often vary between particular submarkets, even though overall construction demand may display a definite trend. This influence on contractors' bidding behavior can manifest itself in at least two important ways.

First, when work is relatively plentiful, the average number of bidders for projects in each submarket will be smaller than in times when work is relatively scarce.[17] As demonstrated in the literature, the greater the number of bidders in a given competition, the less the chance that any particular contractor will emerge as a low bidder.[18] Second, the state of submarket demand affects the mobility of contractors between submarkets, that is, a contractor's propensity to expand into new or unfamiliar submarkets. The lines between closely related submarkets tend to blur, and in the short run, movement between submarkets for projects of roughly the same size takes place primarily along the geographical and industry branch dimensions.[19] Contractors tend to enter related submarkets that require technical skills similar to those they already possess. Hence, in times of slack demand, contractors probably travel farther and venture into closely related industry branches in order to obtain work. The net result is likely to be an increase in the average number of bidders per project and downward pressure on the bid price. In such instances, the probability of winning a bidding competition decreases, forcing firms to bid on a greater number of projects. Alternatively, in times of high demand in a submarket, the reverse effect can occur.

Another important exogenous economic factor affecting the contractor's markup is the rate of price increases in construction and in the economy at large. The contractor's *perceptions* of the course of prices in the recent past and his *perceptions* of the rate of likely future price increases will influence his bidding decisions more than the *observed* rate of recent changes in prices as reflected by index numbers. When construction costs increase rapidly, contractors are wary of committing themselves to long-term fixed price contracts, and they tend to increase the contingency in their cost estimates for increases in labor and materials costs. The increased uncertainty that results from an inflationary trend in the economy influences contractors to hedge against the future by increasing their cost estimates and bid prices to a greater degree than they would in times of relative price stability. The degree of extra hedging varies according to each contractor's willingness to accept risk, but the net result will usually mean higher prices for construction projects.

Characteristics of a Specific Bidding Competition. The strategic aspect of bid preparation resembles the notion of a zero-sum game: there is only one winner of a bidding competition, and barring illegal collusive agreements among contractors, there is no compromise position. The object of the competition is to bid low enough to win the contract, but just barely. A contractor attempts to minimize the difference between a potentially winning bid and the second lowest bid—in industry parlance, "to leave as little as possible on the table." It is therefore desirable for a contractor to have as much prior knowledge as possible of his competitors' estimating methods, willingness to accept risk, and other factors affecting their selection of a bid price.

Since computerized optimal bidding systems have not come into general use, the majority of contractors use their information in a highly intuitive manner; they do not compute subjective probability distributions. It is likely that a contractor's assessment of his *own* business situation (for example, his backlog and the necessity of obtaining work for key personnel) will override his less accurate knowledge of competitor motivations. And, of course, it is often the case in an open bidding competition (such as most government agency procurements) that many of a contractor's competitors will be completely unknown to him, thus rendering any generalizations about a hypothetical "average bidder" highly speculative. Nevertheless, it is important to look briefly at those factors in a particular bidding competition that a contractor finds useful in subjectively reaching his final bid price.

First, a contractor must consider the number and identities of the known and potential bidders arrayed against him. For most projects, this information is readily available in the *Dodge Reports* or similar publications that provide names of general contractors and subcontractors who have taken out plans and specifications.[20] It is sometimes possible to determine who the serious bidders are by more informal means. For example, information may be gained by estimators talking with other estimators in the plans room at the architect's office or by simply observing the amount of effort certain contractors put into the analysis of plans and inspection of the job site. Knowing the potential competitors helps a contractor to assess his relative strengths and weaknesses. He may know, for example, that one of his competitors has lost several bidding competitions of late or has just finished work on a large project and is therefore anxious to secure additional work. Alternatively, he may know from experience that another of his opponents carries a fairly large overhead that must be included in his bid price. At the simplest level, every competing contractor has the intuitive notion that the greater the number of competitors, the more difficult it will be to emerge as the low bidder.

A second group of project-related factors that can influence a contractor's selection of a final bid price includes the size and complexity of the job, its geographical location, the time of the year at which the competition takes place, and the proposed duration of the project (as indicated in the plans and specifications).

The size and complexity of the project determines the number of contractors who will compete for the work and their level of technical expertise. Very few general contractors possess sufficiently experienced management and production organizations to complete successfully a multimillion dollar commercial office building, and the contractors competing for such large projects tend to be somewhat familiar with each other's estimating procedures and strategies. It is likely, then, that contractors competing for very large projects will emphasize strategy more than those vying for smaller jobs. In contrast, a small project may attract a dozen bidders possessing varying degrees of estimating skill and technical competence. Many of these firms are likely to be unknown to each other (possibly because several are new entrants to the submarket). In such cases, a competing contractor is quite likely to ignore his competitors, and he will simply compute his best cost estimate, include an average markup for overhead and profit, and hope for the best.

The time of the year during which the bidding competition takes place may be an important factor in determining how eager competing contractors are for work. Because of seasonal influences, the winter months are ordinarily a period of reduced activity for construction firms in most states, often accompanied by declining contractor backlogs. In such circumstances, a relatively large number of contractors may be anxious to obtain work, and this pressure may exert a downward influence on their bid prices.

As noted above, uncertainty about the factor cost estimates increases with the proposed duration of a project. Moreover, in periods that are perceived by contractors to be inflationary, the greater the proposed length of the project, the greater the contingency cushion a contractor will be likely to add to his bid. On the other hand, in times of relative price stability, the duration of a project will exert a less dramatic effect on contractors' bid prices.

Finally, the geographical location of a project will influence the number and identities of the competing contractors. Since contractor mobility is related to the level of economic activity in construction industry submarkets, other things being equal, smaller projects are likely to entail competition among predominantly local contractors. For such projects, geographical location may be an important factor in determining the number of contractors competing for the work. For larger, multimillion dollar projects, relatively few contracting firms possess sufficient capital and expertise to complete the work, and the bidding competition will most likely attract firms from a regional or even national geographic area.

Miscellaneous Factors Specific to a Bidding Competition. Two other important considerations exert some influence over the amount of the markup in a contractor's bid.

1. By submitting a bid for a particular project, a contractor may be trying to expand into a submarket that is new to the firm, and by so doing gain experience in a type of construction that requires greater technical or managerial

expertise than the firm's usual projects. Alternatively, a firm may be trying to obtain a contract award from a particular private owner (for example, a large university or the local telephone company) with whom it would like to develop a continuing relationship. Whatever its motivations for expanding, and whatever dimension or combination of submarket dimensions it expands along (technical, geographical, industry branch, or project size), the contractor has a substantial incentive to attempt to be low bidder, in order to "buy its way into" the new submarket. The firm is likely to reduce its markup to the lowest possible level, hoping to offset the short-run general overhead and profit deficiencies with the long-term profits to be realized by gaining a firm foothold in the new submarket. The cost of buying in, of overcoming barriers to submarket entry, may initially be quite high and include the higher cost of bidding in an unfamiliar project area and the initial losses that the firm must incur to offset possible absolute cost advantages possessed by its more experienced competitors. It is likely that a firm will attempt to expand into unfamiliar technical or industry branch territory when it is prospering, so that it can cover the initial costs of entry into the new submarket. In contrast, a leaner economic climate is more likely to induce a firm's geographical expansion into submarkets requiring its proven technical capabilities.

2. A contracting firm may reduce its percentage markup on the assumption that it can reduce costs or increase revenues after having been awarded a project. Sometimes such bidding behavior may reflect a contractor's preference for risk or, alternatively, possession of superior knowledge. For example, a firm may believe that it can reduce material costs through volume purchases. In addition, some contractors buy their way into projects by submitting bids below direct costs, in order to make an ultimate profit on owner change orders or on charges to tenants who desire to have their suite custom-designed. The latter situation is said to arise frequently in the construction of large office buildings, permitting the owner to construct the building at a discount by passing along additional costs to the tenants. Unscrupulous tactics by some firms are also not unknown. For example, a contractor may plan on falling behind in contractual payments to subcontractors as a means of forcing subcontractors to settle for the payment of a lesser amount than originally agreed upon (say 80 percent of the funds owed).

The Applicability of the Analytic Framework
to Specific Industry Submarkets

The submarkets in the construction industry are quite diverse, and factors included in the analytic framework must be applied to each submarket only after paying careful attention to its particular institutions. To illustrate, the design of a $1 billion nuclear power plant is so complex, lengthy, and costly a task that the major design activity is undertaken by the contracting firm *after* it has won the contract award. On the other hand, the design for a $10 million college laboratory and classroom building is generally carried out by the owner's architects and engineers, with the contractor submitting a bid for the construction phase only. Hence, the model is more useful in explaining the bidding competitions for the award of *subcontracts* in a power plant project than in explaining the award of the general contract for overall design and construction.

Summary

The suggested analytic framework provides a basis for understanding the important dimensions of the adversary relationship among contractors competing for the great majority of construction projects. It may be considered a checklist, from which the analyst can select the subset of relevant factors that account for contractor pricing behavior in a particular industry submarket. The major factors in this checklist are as follows:

A. Factors Affecting the Estimation of Direct Project Cost
   1. *Precision of estimating procedures.*
   2. *Differences in contractor ability to assess the impact of cost-related uncertainties*: changes in prices and wages, changes in technology, strikes, difficult site conditions, unfavorable weather, community protests, inefficient or late subcontractor performance, political influence, and litigation arising from disputes among the actors in the construction process.
   3. *Errors of computation.*
B. Factors Affecting the Size of the Contractor's Markup
   1. *Internal firm considerations:* contractor willingness to accept risk, size of work backlogs, availability of key supervisory personnel, cash flow needs, minimum markup policies, and overhead rates.
   2. *Project and buyer characteristics:* previous contractor experience with a particular type of structure or equipment, or previous experience in a given locality; the probability of postaward price increases due to changes in specifications; buyer knowledge and technical expertise in assessing bid prices; and the quality of buyer or architect supervision.
   3. *Contractor assessment of competing firms:* the number of competitors, the size of competitor backlogs and the resulting hunger for work, any special technical expertise possessed by competitors that could be translated into cost savings, and competitor overhead structure.
   4. *Miscellaneous factors:* state of demand in the relevant submarket, contractor desire to enter a new submarket, and the prospect of post-award cost savings through volume materials purchases, utilization of materials and equipment left over from a previous job, or postaward bid shopping.

Notes

1. See William R. Park, *The Strategy of Contracting for Profit* (Englewood Cliffs, N.J.: Prentice-Hall, 1966), p. 43.

2. U.S., Department of Commerce, Bureau of the Census, *1972 Census of Construction Industries* (Washington, D.C.: U.S. Government Printing Office: Washington, D.C., 1975), pp. 1-8, 1-9.

3. Although a large builder usually offers only a few models of homes, if a buyer is found before the structure is started, the buyer can request minor design modifications in return for an increase in price over that of the standard "model home."

4. Sherman J. Maisel, *Housebuilding in Transition* (Berkeley: University of California Press, 1953), p. 60.

5. For works concerning optimal bidding strategies for contractors, see Park, *Strategy of Contracting*; Harry Rubey, *Construction Management* (New York: MacMillan Co., 1966); Richard H. Clough, *Construction Contracting*, 3d ed. (New York: Wiley-Interscience, 1975), app. L; and H.E. Kierulff and D.E. Robinson, "Probabilistic Forecasting for Contractors," *Management Science* 17 (August 1971): B-773. For works concerning the use of competitive bidding in the pricing of other goods, see Vernon L. Smith, "Bidding Theory and the Treasury Bill Auction: Does Price Discrimination Increase Bill Prices?" *Review of Economics and Statistics* 48 (May (1966):141; Vernon A. Mund, "Identical Bid Prices," *Journal of Political Economy* 47 (April 1960):150; Merton J. Peck and Frederic M. Scherer, *The Weapons Acquisition Process: An Economic Analysis* (Boston: Division of Research, Harvard Business School, 1962); Frederic M. Scherer, *The Weapons Acquisition Process: Economic Incentives* (Boston: Division of Research, Harvard Business School, 1964); Charles Christenson, *Strategic Aspects of Competitive Bidding for Corporate Securities* (Boston: Division of Research, Harvard Business School, 1965); J.J. McCall, "The Simple Economics of Incentive Contracting," *American Economic Review* 40 (December 1970):837; David P. Baron, "Incentive Contracts and Competitive Bidding," *American Economic Review* 42 (June 1972):384; Colin C. Blaydon and Paul W. Marshall, "Incentive Contracts and Competitive Bidding: Comment," *American Economic Review* 44 (December 1974):1070; David P. Baron, "Incentive Contracts and Competitive Bidding: Reply," *American Economic Review* 44 (December 1974):1072.

6. Two notable exceptions are the treatment of uncertainty in Baron, "Incentive Contracts," and the Bayesian analysis in Christenson, *Strategic Aspects of Competitive Bidding,* chap. 6.

7. Julian E. Lange, "The Bidding Process in the Construction Industry," (Ph.D. diss., Harvard University, 1973), esp. chaps. 4-5.

8. These minimum requirements are chiefly a function of a contractor's current cash flow position, in-house backlog, and whether or not general

overhead is adequately covered by present in-house projects.

9. This framework can be most readily applied to submarkets in nonresidential building construction and with some modifications to most construction submarkets in which competitive bidding plays a part.

10. Lange, "Bidding Process," chaps. 4-5. The nature of variation in direct costs deserves a fuller treatment than can be presented here. Such an examination must necessarily focus on the relative size and frequency of variations in the major components of direct cost estimates as well as the causes of the variations (that is, what portion is due to differences in estimating technique and what portion is due to differences in contractor treatment of uncertainty).

11. Park, *Strategy of Contracting for Profit,* p. 43.

12. Lange, "Bidding Process," chaps. 4-5 for empirical evidence in support of this contention.

13. Materials plus labor as a percentage of the total direct cost amounted to 48 percent for general contractors as compared to 67 percent for all construction contractors as a group. The low general contractor percentage is due to the fact that the value of subcontracted work equalled 51 percent of the direct cost. See U.S. *1972 Census of Construction* Vol. I, pp. 1-8, 1-9.

14. To illustrate, assume that the estimated direct project cost of a building is $100,000, with the markup being $6,000, for a total bid price of $106,000. If Contractor A submits a $106,000 bid and is performing all the work with his own forces, his profit and overhead contribution as a percentage of sales is 6 percent. If Contractor B subcontracts half the job, his percentage profit and overhead contribution, based on the value of services performed with his own forces (and therefore, the value of services which are subject to cost overruns), is approximately twice that of Contractor A.

15. Bid shopping and its implications are discussed in greater detail in chapter 3.

16. The names and résumés of the contractor's management team are important in power plant construction because the coordination of design and construction is an integral part of the service provided by the contractor.

17. This hypothesis is probably more relevant for submarkets whose high entry barriers result in an inelastic supply of contractors. In submarkets where entry barriers are minimal, an inflow of new firms might be induced in times of vigorous economic activity, thus counterbalancing somewhat the tendency of existing firms to bid on fewer projects.

18. For example, see Clough, *Construction Contracting,* pp. 439-444.

19. For example, a medium-size mechanical contracting firm may concentrate on the private commercial office building submarket in the metropolitan area of a large city. If jobs become more scarce, it may shift its attention without much difficulty to the construction of public office buildings, work for which it possesses the basic requisite technical skills.

20. The securing of plans and specifications requires only the posting of a

refundable deposit with the owner. Normally, for a variety of reasons, the number of contractors who actually submit bids is substantially less than those taking out plans and specifications (often less than 50 percent), and it is difficult to guess accurately the identities, let alone the number, of contractors who will emerge as serious bidders.

3 Pricing Public Construction

Julian E. Lange

Governments at all levels transact most of their procurement business on a competitive bidding basis, regulated by statutory requirements. These bidding statutes have several objectives, including: (1) the prevention of collusion among firms and wrongdoing by public officials; (2) the placing of all businesses desiring to sell goods and services to the government on an equal footing; and (3) the securing of goods and services at the lowest possible price consistent with acceptable quality. Since large amounts of public funds are controlled by officials of public agencies, sound public policy dictates that safeguards be instituted to avoid favoritism and fraud. In addition, since American society is committed in principle to a free enterprise system, governments have traditionally shied away from direct provision of goods and services in favor of private production. Further, economic theory teaches the efficacy of competition in reducing prices below those that would be charged by a monopolist or colluding oligopolists. From this theoretical cornerstone emerges a fundamental premise underlying the policy of giving all qualified firms an equal opportunity to secure government contracts: the belief that competition will result in the lowest possible price for the goods and services being provided. A Florida court opinion provides a succinct expression of this point of view, maintaining that competitive bidding statutes are designed

> to protect the public against collusive contracts; to secure fair competition upon equal terms to all bidders; to remove not only collusion, but temptation for collusion and opportunity for gain at public expense; to close all avenues to favoritism and fraud in its various forms; to secure the best values for the [public] at the lowest possible expense; and to afford an equal advantage to all desiring to do business with the [public] by affording an opportunity for an exact comparison of bids.[1]

These considerations apply generally to all government procurement activities, but because of the high dollar value of public construction (more than $45 billion in 1978[2]), the application of competitive bidding procedures to public construction projects is particularly important in its impact on the disbursement of public funds. This is especially true because the awarding of public construction contracts is potentially vulnerable to the political nature of governmental decision making. The legislative bodies that appropriate public funds and the executive agencies that disburse them are, of course, deeply involved in the political process, and it is common knowledge that political repercussions can result from the loss of a contract by one firm or the awarding of a large contract to another. Consequently, legislatures have made award procedures as automatic as possible (in that they follow a well-known set of rules), so that the claim of political favoritism or chicanery can more easily be put to rest.

Competitive bidding is not without its cost to the public. The preparation of bids imposes a cost on contractors which is passed along to the awarding authority and ultimately to the public. This cost takes the form of higher contractor overhead to cover bid preparation charges on *all* projects for which he competes, both the wins and the losses. The cost of bidding varies with the size and complexity of the project, ranging from a few hundred dollars for small projects to tens of thousands for multimillion dollar structures. From society's point of view, an argument can be advanced that an optimal number of bidders exists for projects of a given size and complexity. This optimal number would result from the interaction of two opposing influences affecting the cost of construction services: (1) the greater the number of bidders, the lower the bid price; and (2) the greater the number of bidders, the greater the *aggregate* cost of bid preparation (society's cost) for a given project. Theoretically at least, these two opposing forces neutralize each other at some point when the cost of preparing an additional bid exceeds the diminution of the winning bid price that results from an additional competitor.[3]

This argument is often cited in proposals either to limit the number of bidders in public competitions or to rely more heavily on negotiated pricing. Unfortunately, there is very little empirical data to shed light on the amount of the additional costs to the government (and taxpayers) imposed by the almost total reliance upon unrestricted bidding competitions in public construction. Indeed, because construction projects are in many ways unique, such data would necessarily apply to narrowly defined groups of projects, thus requiring a myriad of procedures in different situations and complicating the already onerous political task of creating statutes that are perceived as fair to all interests. Even if such data were available, legislatures in all likelihood would be reluctant to abandon the objective of opening the competition for public construction to the widest possible number of firms on an equal footing, even with the prospect of lowering somewhat the aggregate cost. It is not surprising therefore that most government jurisdictions rely almost exclusively on the competitive bidding mechanism as the best method of preventing political influence and corruption consistent with a reasonably low (if not always the lowest possible) price.[4]

The Process of Public Sector Bidding

In order to implement the objectives of competitive bidding for public projects, legislative bodies have enacted detailed statutes. These laws must in turn be implemented by means of comprehensive administrative regulations promulgated by a variety of executive agencies at all levels of government. Current practice in public sector procurement results from a complex interaction of forces. Legislative action attempts to balance the public interest with the special interests of architects, engineers, general contractors, specialty contractors, labor, suppliers, sureties, and institutional lenders. The executive agencies then set the rules for the day-to-day operation of the statutes. Finally, modifications of administrative regulations are effected by judicial interpretations that stem from disputes among the private actors in the construction process and between the private actors and the administrative agencies.

The statutes and regulations cover a wide range of topics, including definitions for projects which come under the jurisdiction of the bidding statutes; procedures to be followed in advertising for bids; conditions for acceptance or return of bid deposits; criteria for awarding contracts (in virtually all statutes, awards are made to the lowest responsible bidder, with *responsible* being subject to a variety of interpretations[5]); definition of the circumstances under which bids may be rejected; provision for bonafide errors made by bidders; requirement or waiver of surety bonds; provision for liquidated damages and penalties for delay; and payment procedures vis-à-vis contractors (including allowable retention percentages and rights of subcontractors).[6] In general, the governmental agencies responsible for administering bidding regulations during the contract award stage also monitor the progress of construction activity. Because of differences in the level of funding for such agencies and in the requirements set down by legislative bodies in various government jurisdictions, the quality of administration and supervision varies. Consequently, some contractors will compete only for those projects awarded by the most qualified administrative agencies, while other firms restrict their activities completely to the private sector.[7]

Although specific procedures and regulations vary widely among government agencies, there are certain common threads which transcend jurisdictional lines. In order to provide a frame of reference for assessing the differences among public bidding procedures, it is useful to survey briefly the major steps in a typical procurement, in this case the awarding of a contract for the construction of a public building in Massachusetts.[8]

Initiation of the Project

The need for the construction of a new facility is usually determined by a public executive agency. In Massachusetts, state agencies submit requests for new buildings and public works projects, which are then considered by legislative committees. Funds for specific projects are appropriated by the legislature. The state Bureau of Building Construction (BBC) oversees the bidding procedure for all public buildings in Massachusetts.[9] Once the legislature has authorized a building, the BBC commissions an architectural firm (and an engineering firm as needed) to design the structure,[10] paying heed to both the upper limit on funding set by the legislature and the requirements of the agency or agencies that will be using the building. In many cases, the actual design work may be begun before the total appropriation has been made for the building itself, funded by a small appropriation for design and engineering services only. The architects and engineers then develop detailed plans and specifications for the building, which in some cases include several alternatives to be priced separately by the contractors who bid on the project. This practice allows the awarding authority to make a final decision on the exact characteristics of the structure after the bid prices have been submitted.

After completing the plans and specifications, the BBC advertises for bids. Advertisements must appear for a specified number of days and must inform potential bidders of the type of project, the location at which plans and specifications can be secured, and the date, time, and place where bids must be received in order to be considered eligible for an award. The appendix to this chapter contains a facsimile of the "Notice to Contractors" for a typical project.[11]

In addition to reading advertisements, contractors also keep apprised of projects for which bids are being solicited by referring to the *Dodge Reports,* an information service available on a subscription basis from the McGraw-Hill Company. The *Dodge Reports* service continually updates a list of projects which are in the bidding stage in industry branches or geographical areas that are specified by the subscribing contractor. The service also updates the names of general and specialty contractors who have taken out plans and specifications for particular projects.[12] Contractors, therefore, have a basis for determining the nature of their potential competition, but since the number of actual bidders is often substantially lower than the number of firms who have taken out plans and specifications, a contractor is rarely certain of the identities of all his competitors until the bids are in.[13] It is often possible, however, to identify the serious bidders by noting which contracting firms are spending large amounts of time in the plans room of the awarding authority or at prebid conferences (held to clarify ambiguities in the plans and specifications), or by simply checking with the local "grapevine."

Qualification of Contractors

In some states, contractors cannot bid on public work unless they have demonstrated their ability to perform such work successfully. To qualify, they must submit evidence of their financial capacity to perform a project of a given dollar value, and in some cases, they must also demonstrate technical competence—usually by presenting a list of similar projects that they have success-fully completed. Such a procedure is called *prequalification* if it is a prerequisite for submitting a bid and *postqualification* if it occurs after a contractor has been selected as the low bidder. In Massachusetts there is no formal prequalification procedure for building construction.[14] However, the awarding authority re-quires, along with the bid documents, information about the bidder's previous completion of similar work and can request financial statements; subsequently, the authority can disqualify a bidder if the firm does not appear to possess the requisites for completing the project in accordance with the plans and specifi-cations.

Determining a Bid Price

The Massachusetts bidding statute stipulates that bids on public buildings must be in the form of lump-sum prices for which the contractor agrees to furnish the building described in the plans and specifications within a stipulated time period (usually expressed in calendar days).[15] Briefly stated, contractors attempt to estimate their direct costs in fabricating the structure (including materials, labor, payments to subcontractors, equipment rental or depreciation on owned equipment, and the costs that will likely be imposed by the occurrence of uncertain events, such as strikes or the discovery of adverse site conditions) and to a markup for contribution to profit and general (non-job-related) overhead.[16] Contractors compute their cost estimates on the basis of the plans and specifications and any additions or corrections supplied by the awarding authority. (Preaward briefings for prospective bidders are sometimes held by the awarding authority for the purpose of clearing up ambiguities and mistakes in the plans and specifications and issuing addenda.) Contractors are free to choose their own estimating procedures. The accuracy of the estimates will depend upon the precision of the estimating technique, the amount of time that each contractor devotes to bid preparation, and the expertise of the estimators, particularly their skill in anticipating the likely cost impact of uncertain events.

Award Procedure

On the announced date, at the place and time stipulated in the advertisements and notice to contractors, the awarding authority publicly opens all sealed bids. Late bids are not accepted. The awarding authority then announces the name of the "apparent low bidder," who in the overwhelming majority of cases is subsequently declared the "lowest responsible bidder."[17] After selection, contract documents are signed by the general contractor and the various subcontractors that he carried in his bid.

Postaward Price Modification

The price agreed to by the general contractor is legally binding. Changes in design requested by the awarding authority, however, ordinarily result in an increase in the price. The general contractor will submit a price quotation for the additional work (some of which may involve subcontractors as well), and if the awarding authority accepts the price, authorization will be given to proceed with the modification.

Public Sector Bidding and Social Policy

*Minimum Wage Requirements and Equal
Employment Opportunity*

In the awarding of public contracts, government agencies must make certain that their procedures coincide with the broad social policies promulgated by the legislatures. One example of the implementation of such a government policy in the awarding of construction projects is the "prevailing wage" requirements that appear as a condition of project awards in federal contracts and in many state contracts.[18] These requirements are in keeping with the dictates of the federal Davis-Bacon Act and the state statutes modeled after it.

The Davis-Bacon Act requires that the minimum wages of workmen on a government construction project shall be based upon the wages that will be determined by the Secretary of Labor to be prevailing for corresponding classes of workmen employed for similar work on similar projects in the "city, town, village, or other civil subdivision of the State, in which the work is to be performed."[19] Since prevailing wage rates are heavily influenced by union wage scales in most metropolitan areas, the Davis-Bacon Act and similar state laws have the effect of underwriting the payment of union wage levels on government projects.

In the same way, public awarding authorities can attempt to exercise leverage in the guarantee of equal employment opportunity on government construction projects. Effecting this goal is considerably less amenable to administrative fiat than the setting of prevailing wage rates, since the issue involves the availability of sufficient numbers of qualified minority craftsmen. Consequently, attempts to attain equal employment opportunity in construction require the cooperation of employers, unions, and government, and several different approaches to the problem are being pursued.[20] While it is not ordinarily the responsibility of awarding authorities to formulate or enforce such plans, they can exert considerable influence in encouraging contractor compliance. In this respect, public awarding authorities differ from private owners, who are not constrained to further the goals of public policy in awarding contracts despite governmental and community pressure to do so.

Barriers to Competition

In some cases, competitive bidding statutes and administrative procurement regulations create barriers to the entry of new firms into public construction submarkets. This is particularly true of minority firms and small firms. Entry problems for minority firms stem from two major causes: lack of experience and insufficient financial strength. These problems plague new entrant firms in the private sector as well, but in recent years, some legislatures have been the scene of spirited debates as to whether public awarding authorities have an obligation to encourage the entry and growth of such firms.

The encouragement of new minority firms creates a dilemma for public agencies that derives from an attempt to balance two important objectives of competitive bidding statutes. First, bidding laws grant all qualified contractors the opportunity to compete equally for the chance to perform public work. Second, these statutes are intended to facilitate the procurement of goods and services at the lowest possible price consistent with acceptable quality.

In order to implement these objectives, several practices have evolved. Most bidding statutes attempt to provide adequate safeguards for the participants in the construction process to assure that once started, a project will be completed to the satisfaction of the awarding authority, and that the various parties to the construction project (contractors, subcontractors, craftsmen, suppliers) will be paid. Contractors are required to post bonds and deposits of various sorts: bid bonds or deposits, performance bonds, and payment bonds. Each of these bonds guarantees that a particular party will be paid if another party fails to live up to his contract. The cost of performance bonds and payment bonds is passed along to the awarding authority by the winning contractor, but bid bonds or deposits must be posted by all competing contractors *prior* to the award, thus increasing a contractor's need for working capital. Each time a contractor bids on a proposed project he must submit a certified check as a bid deposit or obtain a bid bond from a surety.[21] It is also customary for most awarding authorities not to release the bid deposits of the *three* lowest bidders until a contract is signed, in case of difficulties involving the lowest bidder. If a contractor is bidding on several projects simultaneously, his working capital needs will increase markedly.

A second practice that increases a contractor's need for financial strength is retainage; funds are held back by the awarding authority pending final acceptance of the completed construction project. Retainage rates vary among government jurisdictions (usually ranging between 10 percent and 20 percent of contractor revenues) and often exceed the amount of contractor profits. It is commonly conceded, however, that some form of retainage is necessary to insure adequate contractor performance.

It is clear that while such practices represent a prudent legislative attempt to encourage contractors to fulfill their commitments, they also tend to raise entry barriers to new firms. Since the easing of such requirements for minority and other small firms creates protected markets, such action ordinarily can only be implemented by amending the statutes. Such proposed amendments generally take the form of lowering or eliminating bid bond, bid deposit, and retainage requirements in favor of posting some other form of security for contracts under a given dollar limit. Occasionally, it is suggested that projects in certain geographical areas or those that fall within a particular dollar figure be set aside for a competition restricted to small firms and minority firms.[22] Such proposals are usually opposed by entrenched contractor groups because they foster the creation of potential competitors and increase competition in certain sub-markets. It is for legislative bodies to decide whether the objective of nurturing minority enterprise and small contracting firms justifies placing limits on the principle of equal access. If so, they must decide whether this goal can be accomplished without unduly increasing the risk of default or substandard performance by inexperienced firms. At present, the issue continues to be the subject of vigorous debate.

The Division of Public Construction Profits

The difficulties of granting all firms an equal opportunity to compete for government contract awards are not limited to minority firms and small contractors. Since most construction projects involve the work of several specialty contractors in addition to the general contractor, the question arises whether government procurement agencies should try to ensure equal access to public construction work for specialty contractors as well as general contractors. Most statutes at all governmental levels provide only for single contracts—the awarding of construction contracts to general contracting firms.[23] In such statutes, no constraints are placed upon the general contractor in awarding the subcontracts, thus following common practice in the private sector. The only concern of the awarding authority is that the general contractor complete the project for the lump-sum price as stated in his bid.

In the case of single contracts, the general contractor reigns supreme. It is an interesting fact of commercial law that the general contractor can hold the subcontractors on whom he relied in preparing his bid to their quoted prices, according to the doctrine of promissory estoppel. The subcontractors, however, cannot force the winning general contractor to use them on the project.[24] The asymmetry of this situation leads to the practices known as bid shopping and bid peddling. Bid shopping occurs when a general contractor approaches subcontractors other than those he used in his winning bid and offers them a subcontract on the project if they will underbid the original subcontractor. Bid peddling is the other side of the coin. It occurs when a subcontractor goes to the general contractor and tries to replace a subcontractor carried in the winning bid by offering to do the work for less money. Since the general contractor normally has a fixed price contract with the awarding authority, any reduction in the price his subcontractors charge for their work represents extra profit.

The terms *bid shopping* and *bid peddling* carry the pejorative connotation of unethical contractor behavior, but there is considerable disagreement over the difference between bid shopping and prudent business behavior. Because of the time pressure and confusion surrounding most bid submissions, mistakes can occur. Consequently, it sometimes turns out that two of the subcontractors' bids were not comparable and that the apparent low bid was not, in fact, the lowest bid submitted. In such cases, the general contractor may feel quite justified in changing subcontractors, while the subcontractor being replaced may cry foul, claiming that his competitor adjusted his bid downward after the contract was awarded.

Filed Subbid Laws

Although single contract awards are the rule in most governmental jurisdictions, several state governments have taken a different approach. Ten states require the submission of filed subcontractor bids.[25] The objectives of most of these statutes are clearly spelled out in the following passage contained in California's filed subbid law:

> The Legislature finds that the practice of bid shopping and bid peddling in connection with the construction, alteration, and repair of public improvements often results in poor quality of material and workmanship to the detriment of the public, deprives the public of the full benefits of fair competition among prime contractors and subcontractors, and leads to insolvencies, loss of wages to employees, and other evils.[26]

Hence, a major intent of filed subbid laws is the prevention of bid shopping by general contractors as a means of increasing their share of the profits at the expense of subcontractors. The reasoning behind this policy is that: (1) the general contractor may succeed in reducing a subcontractor's price (through postaward bargaining or substitution of subcontracting firms) at the expense of quality of workmanship; and (2) if the general contractor could obtain a lower price from a subcontractor without sacrificing quality, the public should benefit by way of a lower project cost, rather than allowing an increase in the general contractor's profit.

The filed subbid laws differ in their provisions, permitting varying degrees of latitude on the part of the general contractor in choosing his subcontractors. Three distinctly different statutory bidding procedures can be identified. These alternatives may be represented by the bidding laws in the states of Massachusetts, California, and Rhode Island.

Massachusetts. Massachusetts has the most complex law, a two-tiered system requiring separate competitions for general contractors and specialty subcontractors. The statute lists eighteen different categories of subcontract work, including such specialties as painting; plumbing; heating, ventilation, and air conditioning; electrical work; masonry; roofing and flashing; metal window installation; lathing and plastering; acoustical tiling; marble work; and a catchall category consisting of "any other class of work for which the awarding authority deems it necessary or convenient to receive sub-bids."[27] The subbidders must submit their bids to the awarding authority approximately one week prior to the deadline for general contractor bids. The sealed subbids are opened publicly immediately after the announced deadline, and a list of the subbidders and their bids is furnished to the general contractors competing for the work.

A general contractor must choose one of the subcontractors on the list in each specialty category and carry him at the listed price. Ordinarily, one of the lowest three bidders is selected, but regardless of which specialty firms are chosen, the general contractor who wins the contract award *must* use the subcontractors that he has listed in his bid. Freedom of choice in selecting a contractor team is permitted by two additional statutory provisions. First, a subbidder is allowed to restrict his bid *from* use by a particular general contractor, or alternatively, to stipulate that his bid may be used *only* by the specific general contractors which he enumerates. This provision enables a subcontractor to guard against the possibility of working with a general contractor with whom he has had bad experiences in the past. It also permits him to enter into a special arrangement with one or more general contractors to whom he can give a lower price because of their previous work together or because of confidence in the contractor's superior technical or managerial expertise. In such cases, a general contractor may only select a subcontractor who has either submitted an unrestricted bid or has restricted his bid to that particular general contractor. Second, a general contractor can refuse to carry a particular subcontractor in his bid, simply because he does not wish to work with the firm even though that firm may be the low bidder. In cases where the lowest subbid has not been used, the awarding authority will attempt to bring pressure to bear on the general contractor to carry the lowest subbidder, but legally the general contractor can refuse to make the switch. In most cases, however, a general contractor has a substantial incentive to use the lowest subbidder in each subcontract category since by so doing, his chance of emerging as low bidder in the general contractor competition is enhanced.

The provision that allows the restricting of a subcontractor's bid *to* a particular contractor also permits (in fact, requires) a general contractor to submit a bid in the subcontractor competition if he wants to use his own forces for the work in a specific subcontractor category. In such a case, the general contractor's subcontracting bid is usually a dummy bid, since he does not wish to divulge to his competitors his actual price for any portion of the work before the general contractors' bid competition. To compensate for a dummy bid, a general contractor will make an upward or downward adjustment in his final bid for the entire project.

California. California's filed subbid law is somewhat simpler. Only one bidding competition is held, for general contractors. Each general contractor must list the subcontractors that are to perform work amounting to more than "one half of one percent" of his total bid.[28] If a general firm wishes to perform work in a subcontract specialty, it must be listed in the appropriate category. As in Massachusetts, the winning general firm must use the listed subcontractors, unless it can be demonstrated to the awarding authority that a subcontractor has subsequently become unwilling or unable to perform the work for the price listed in the general contractor's bid.

Rhode Island. Rhode Island's filed subbid statute is the simplest of all. It requires only that the general contractor submit a list of his subcontractors *after* he has received a contract award.[29]

The Separate Contract Statutes

Nine states require the awarding of separate contracts to a general contractor and several specialty contractors—usually including specialties such as plumbing, heating, and electrical work.[30] The separate contract statutes protect a few categories of specialty contractors against bid shopping and bid peddling by granting them prime contractor status, but the statutes allow the practices to continue with respect to all other specialty contractors. These laws vary in the particular specialty trades that are protected and in the categories of projects to which they apply.

New York's competitive bidding statute is illustrative of such laws. It requires four separate bidding competitions for building projects whose estimated cost exceeds $50,000. In addition to the general contractor's portion of the work, separate sealed bids are required for plumbing and gas fitting; heating, ventilating, and air conditioning; and electrical work. Four separate prime contracts are awarded by the state. Sometimes the awarding authority handles coordination of the contract, but ordinarily the general contractor takes responsibility. There is no requirement for the filing of the bids of subcontractors to the four prime contractors.[31]

New Jersey's bidding statute also deserves mention. It permits the awarding authority to accept bids under both the single and separate contract systems. The bids are then compared, and the decision to award a single contract or separate contracts depends upon which method results in the lowest overall project bid price.[32]

The Virginia Statute

For purposes of comparison, Virginia's bidding statute should be cited because it is typical of statutes in the governmental jurisdictions without filed subbid or separate contracts laws. For all state construction work costing over $2,500, the law calls for one competition for general contractors, with the award made to the lowest responsible bidder. The general contractor's choice of subcontractors is unrestricted, both before and after the contract award, as in the private sector.[33]

*A Comparison of the Several Forms of Public
Sector Competitive Bidding*

Because of the political nature of the legislative bodies that appropriate public construction funds and the executive agencies that disburse them, the prevention of fraud and favoritism by the use of competitive bidding procedures represents sound public policy. Given the desirability of competitive bidding in the public sector, it is important to examine the effects of the principal alternative forms of bidding legislation just described. These statutes differ mainly in their effects on (1) the cost to the consumer (the public awarding authority, but ultimately the taxpayer) and the maintenance of minimum quality standards and (2) the division of the "profit pie" between general contractors and subcontractors.

Little empirical data on the subject is available and generating such evidence is a complex task; the unique nature of construction projects and the enormous variation in institutional factors among different governmental jurisdictions make categorization difficult. Despite the scarcity of quantitative data, it is useful to propose hypotheses, however tentative, concerning the probable effects of different bidding statutes on contractor behavior. Such an exercise represents an attempt to organize what may reasonably be conjectured about the differential impact of various bidding statutes, and serves as a necessary first step toward the building up of empirical evidence.

Effects on the Consumer. The state statutes differ chiefly in the extent to which they inhibit bid shopping, both before and after the contract award. The Massachusetts statute effectively eliminates both preaward and postaward shopping, while the California statute does away with only postaward shopping. The New York law eliminates bid shopping in the four prime contract categories, but does not legally restrict shopping activities involving any other specialty subcontractors. The Virginia statute, by not addressing the issue at all, effectively permits both preaward and postaward bid shopping as does the Rhode Island law, which requires only a list of subcontractors after the award has been made. The New Jersey statute combines the New York and Virginia models.

Postaward bid shopping is only of benefit to the general contractor. Its elimination may well reduce the cost of construction to the awarding authority, because if subcontractors are certain that postaward shopping cannot take place, they will most likely submit as low a price as possible before the general contract award in order to enhance the chance of their bid being used by the general contractor. Further, the practice of postaward bid shopping may lead to a deterioration in subcontractor quality, since the price concessions extracted from subcontractors may prompt them to cut corners in order to shore up their profit again.

In contrast, preaward bid shopping is not detrimental to the public interest and may well be beneficial since preaward shopping amounts to nothing more than old-fashioned competition. Contractor associations frown on the practice because it tends to exert a downward pressure on subcontractor bid prices, and contractor associations quite naturally are interested in maintaining healthy profit margins for their members.[34] However, preaward price reductions by subcontractors are ordinarily passed along to the awarding authority in the form of a lower general contractor bid price, since each general contractor is eager to emerge as low bidder. Further, preaward bid shopping is less likely than postaward shopping to result in the deterioration of subcontractor quality standards. The general contractor is in a more powerful position to extract subcontractor price concessions *after* the contract award, when he is offering a firm offer of employment, than *before* the award, when he is offering only the possibility of employment. Before the award, a subcontractor will be more likely to resist making price concessions that would reduce his profit margin to unacceptable levels. After the contract award, when a subcontractor is faced with the choice between losing assured employment or reducing his profit margin, he may well opt for the latter and let quality and labor standards slide.[35]

The subcontractor competition called for in the Massachusetts law is likely to result in somewhat higher subcontractor prices than would obtain under the California filed subbid procedure, assuming projects of similar size and complexity. The Massachusetts statute requires subcontractors to submit a single price for use by all general contractors. Unless a subcontractor will accept the relatively high risk of restricting his bid to only one general contractor, the subcontractor will be unable to adjust his price to reflect the efficiency of a particular general contractor; that is, he cannot submit different prices to different generals based on perceived variations in firm efficiency. Further, if a subcontractor submits an unrestricted bid, he must include in his price enough of a cushion to hedge against the possibility of working for a general contractor who operates at only average levels of efficiency. The California law seems preferable in this respect since under it (as in the unregulated private sector), subcontractors may quote different prices to individual general contractors and thus take into account differences in contractor efficiency.

From the point of view of the consumer, the Massachusetts and California laws seem superior to the Virginia statute, which does not prohibit postaward bid shopping. Under the Virginia system, subcontractor bids before the award may be somewhat inflated in order to provide for the possible necessity of making postaward price concessions to the general contractor.

The New York law poses special problems. First, it elevates a few categories of specialty subcontractors to equality with the general contractors while ignoring the practice of bid shopping with respect to other categories of specialty contractor. Second, since the general contractor is a coequal with the three principal specialty contractors, part of the responsibility for project coordination (especially involving control of the flow of funds) falls to state contracting officials. This organizational arrangement makes the general contractor's job management task more difficult and increases the likelihood of litigation arising from conflicts among contractors. The rigid enforcement of the separate contract procedure for all contracts, regardless of the relative amounts of work being performed by the general and the three principal specialty contractors, seems unlikely to promote efficient management of the work and may well result in the elimination of any apparent cost savings over single contract procurement.

In both New York and Virginia, where bid shopping is not prohibited, deterioration of quality standards appears to be an ever present threat. In the private sector, a buyer can take steps to ensure the maintenance of quality by limiting the list of bidders to firms possessing a high level of technical competence. Exclusion of prospective bidders on grounds of poor past performance is much more difficult in the public sector, given its commitment to maintaining equal opportunity for competing firms.[36] One possible remedy for this might be to amend statutes to permit awarding authorities to set up stringent prequalification standards for contractors competing for *major* project awards, although this course of action may well be politically unacceptable.

Division of Profits between General Contractors and Subcontractors. Postaward bid shopping, in general, constitutes a transfer of profits from the subcontractors to the general contractors without in any way benefiting the taxpayers through price reductions. In contrast, price reductions brought about by preaward bargaining between general contractors and subcontractors are more likely to be passed along to the awarding authority.

Each of the statutes outlined earlier results in a somewhat different bargaining situation for general contractors and subcontractors. The Massachusetts statute is the most favorable in its treatment of subcontractors. In addition to protecting subcontractors' profit margins from postaward bid shopping, the separate subcontractors' competition enables subcontractors to withstand preaward bid shopping pressures as well, and, indeed, provides incentives to raise prices somewhat because of uncertainty about the identity of the winning general contractor. The statute represents a political compromise between the general contractors and subcontractors. Consequently, it is not surprising that both the general contractors' association and the subcontractors' association introduce bills into the legislature each year in a continuing attempt to alter the bidding law in favor of their separate constituencies.

The California statute also protects subcontractors' profits from being reduced by postaward shopping, but in contrast to Massachusetts, it encourages hard bargaining between general contractors and subcontractors prior to the contract award. The Virginia statute offers no special protection to subcontractors, and any protection offered by the Rhode Island law is more apparent than real. Finally, the New York law only grants favored status to three categories of specialty contractors and no protection against bid shopping to any other subcontractors.

Recommendations for Public Policy. The California statute would seem to represent the best compromise among the conflicting goals of securing the benefits of price competition, maintaining minimum quality standards, and providing equitable treatment to both general contractors and subcontractors. Although in some cases negotiated pricing could result in lower procurement costs, the use of competitive bidding in awarding the great majority of public construction contracts appears necessary to prevent corruption and favoritism. Given their commitment to competitive bidding, it is important that legislative bodies design bidding procedures that are likely to produce genuine price competition among contracting firms.

Since postaward bid shopping encourages the erosion of subcontractor quality standards while benefiting only the general contractors, it should be eliminated. Of the principal alternatives, only the California and Massachusetts statutes accomplish this goal for all major subcontractors' categories. Before the contract award, general contractors and subcontractors should be permitted to bargain freely and determine subcontractor prices through open competition. The smooth functioning of preaward general contractors' and subcontractors' price bargaining, however, hinges upon the elimination of postaward bid shopping if subcontractors are to be discouraged from inflating their bids to protect themselves in the event of postaward price concessions. Only the California statute encourages preaward price bargaining while simultaneously prohibiting postaward bid shopping. Given the dearth of data, and in the absence of empirical evidence to the contrary, statutes based on the California model appear to satisfy best the objectives of public policy.

Notes

1. Webster v. Belote, 138 So. 721 (Fla., 1931). Cited in Henry A. Cohen, *Public Construction Contracts and the Law* (New York: McGraw-Hill, 1961), p. 3.

2. *Construction Review* 25 (February 1979):12.

3. For an interesting attempt to measure the effect on bid price of additional firms in the competition among bond underwriters for new issues, see Reuben Kessel, "A Study of the Effects of Competition in the Tax-exempt Bond Market," *Journal of Political Economy* 79 (July-August 1971):706.

4. The periodic convictions of public officials and private business firms and individuals for wrongdoing connected with construction procurement justifies the concern of legislatures with preventing fraud in the awarding of construction contracts. In addition, price-fixing schemes are not unknown in construction; for an interesting account of collusion among contractors, see "Road Paving in Ontario" (Ottawa: Canadian Restrictive Trade Practices Commission, 1970).

5. See Cohen, *Public Construction Contracts,* chap. 4.

6. Ibid., chap. 1.

7. Of a total of 437,941 contracting firms with employees in 1972, 304,995 restricted their business to the private sector. Only 19,668 firms dealt exclusively in the public sector, with the remaining firms performing both public and private work. See U.S., Department of Commerce, Bureau of the Census, *1972 Census of U.S. Construction Industries* (Washington, D.C.: Government Printing Office, 1975), p. 1-19.

8. While most of the steps in the Massachusetts awarding procedure are common to most government jurisdictions, the treatment of general contractors and subcontractors is substantially different. Consequently, a detailed treatment of the filed subbid process, as it is known to construction professionals, is deferred until later in this chapter.

9. The Department of Public Works has jurisdiction over state road construction and other non-building structures.

10. The awarding of such design work in Massachusetts (and elsewhere generally) is not, at present, covered by competitive bidding statutes. In fact, the professional societies involved have traditionally prohibited their members from competing solely on a price basis. In the recent past, however, courts have taken a dim view of such prohibitions, and the current trend would appear to be in the direction of increased price competition.

11. The information contained in the first five paragraphs usually appears in local newspapers and trade journals. The notice appears in its entirety in the volume containing the specifications, which is available from the BBC for a $150 deposit.

12. At this point, it is useful to clarify the meaning of three terms which are commonly used in construction work: general contractor, subcontractor, and specialty contractor. These designations are most easily understood in terms of the "chain of command" on a particular project. The general contractor deals directly with the owner or awarding authority and is responsible for overall project supervision. The general contractor, in turn, employs and supervises

subcontractors to perform the specialized tasks associated with the construction process (such as the installation of plumbing, heating, and electrical systems). Because they perform specialized construction tasks, these subcontractors are known as specialty contractors.

It is sometimes the case that general contractors perform specialized tasks and specialty contractors act as their own general contractor. For example, a particular project may involve only one specialty (such as painting or plumbing), with the result that the specialty contractor deals directly with the owner. In a like manner, a general contractor for a large project involving several specialty subcontractors may choose to perform a particular specialized task (for example, the masonry work) with his own forces rather than hire a specialty subcontractor. The general contractor may then be said to be acting as his own subcontractor for that particular task.

13. It is not unusual for only half of the contractors who take out plans and specifications actually to submit a bid.

14. Prequalification is required for non-building public works projects. See *Massachusetts General Laws Annotated,* chapter 29, section 8B.

15. The factors that contractors take into consideration when preparing their bids are discussed in chapter 2. Public works projects (such as roads) are generally bid on a unit price basis, since the exact amounts of materials used cannot be known at the outset of the project. See *Massachusetts General Laws Annotated,* chapter 149, section 29. See also chapter 2 of this volume for a discussion of unit pricing.

16. Under the Massachusetts filed subbid statute, general contractors do not obtain price quotations directly from subcontractors, but instead select subcontracting firms from the official list, containing subcontractor bid prices, that is distributed by the awarding authority after the subcontractors have filed their bids. See pp. 45-47 of this chapter for further discussion. The contractor must also make certain that his wage-rate estimates are in accordance with the minimum wage rates as determined by the Commissioner of Labor and Industries under the provisions of *Massachusetts General Laws Annotated,* chapter 149, sections 26-27D. These provisions in the Massachusetts bidding law are similar in aim and content to the Davis-Bacon Act, which provides for the setting of minimum wage rates in federal construction by the U.S. Secretary of Labor. See *United States Code Annotated,* title 40, section 276a et. seq. See also discussion of the Davis-Bacon law on p. 42 of this chapter.

17. Only in rare cases does the awarding authority challenge the competence of the low bidder. If the low bidder is disqualified on grounds of not being "responsible," he can bring suit against the awarding authority. In that event the burden of proof lies with the awarding authority, which must demonstrate that there is substantial doubt as to whether the firm in question can perform the work in accordance with the plans and specifications. See Cohen, *Public Construction Contracts,* chap. 4, esp. pp. 80-92.

18. See the appendix to this chapter.

19. *United States Code Annotated*, title 40, section 276a et seq. For a discussion of the statute, see Cohen, *Public Construction Contracts,* pp. 286-290.

20. See Daniel Quinn Mills, *Industrial Relations and Manpower in Construction* (Cambridge, Mass.: MIT Press, 1972), esp. pts. 3, 4.

21. In most governmental jurisdictions, bid deposits amount to approximately 5 percent of the estimated value of the project.

22. See, for example, Massachusetts, House of Representatives, "An Act Relative to the Manner of Awarding Certain Contracts for Public Construction," House Bill 2739, Spring 1971. This bill has not been enacted into law.

23. See Roy Meilman, "State Regulation of Public Construction Awards," unpub. seminar paper, Harvard Law School, 1972.

24. See John D. Calamari and Joseph M. Perillo, *Contracts,* 2nd ed. (St. Paul: West Publishing Co., 1977), pp. 212-213.

25. See Meilman, "State Regulation."

26. *California Government Code,* section 4101 (West).

27. See *Massachusetts General Laws Annotated,* chapter 149, section 44C, for a complete listing of the enumerated subcontractor categories.

28. See *California Government Code,* sections 4100-4113 (West).

29. See *General Laws of Rhode Island,* sections 37-13-1–37-13-16.

30. New Jersey is included again here, since its statute combines a filed subbid type statute with a separate contracts law.

31. See *New York State Finance Law,* sections 135-145 (McKinney).

32. See *New Jersey Statutes Annotated,* sections 52:32-1–52:32-16 (West).

33. *Code of Virginia,* sections 11-17–11-23.

34. Many associations press for the adoption of standardized bidding and cost accounting procedures by their memberships with the objective of keeping profit margins up.

35. In discussions of preaward bid shopping, the argument is often advanced that such activity is unfair to subcontractors because of the expense they have incurred in bid preparation. However, it must be emphasized that in preaward shopping the crucial element of coercion is missing, since a specialty contractor can refuse to reduce his price and attempt to ally himself with another general contractor. But even if the last minute nature of the shopping activity prevents some subcontractors from finding another general contractor who will use them, they are only running the same risk to which they are exposed in private sector bidding, and the identical sanction is available to them, that is, refusal to deal subsequently with offending general contractors.

36. See Cohen, *Public Construction Contracts,* chap. 4, esp. pp. 80-92.

Appendix 3A
Notice to Contractors

NOTICE TO CONTRACTORS

COMMONWEALTH OF MASSACHUSETTS

BUREAU OF BUILDING CONSTRUCTION

MASSACHUSETTS STATE COLLEGE SYSTEM

Sealed proposals will be received by the Commonwealth of Massachusetts, Bureau of Building Construction for Mass.
State Project No.___E71-8___Cont. No.___1_____

Title: CLASSROOM BUILDING, MASSACHUSETTS MARITIME ACADEMY, BOURNE, MASSACHUSETTS

In general the project includes:
Three story building, concrete structure, concrete foundation, masonry exterior, metal decking, misc. ornamental iron, waterproofing, roofing, metal doors & frame, elevator, carpeting, building specialties, plumbing, HVAC, electrical and site development including several building trades.

All bids will be received at the office of the Bureau of Building Construction, Room 1519, fifteenth floor, One Ashburton Place, Boston, Mass. 02108 no later than the time and date specified below and be publicly opened and read aloud in Room 1519. Any bid received after the time and date specified will not be considered.

Sealed bids for the General Contract submitted on a form furnished by the Awarding Authority will be received not later than 2:00 P.M., Eastern Standard Time or Eastern Daylight Time, whichever is in effect in the Commonwealth on ___SEPTEMBER 8, 1978_____.

Each general bid proposal must be secured by an accompanying deposit of $_50,000_____ in the form of a bid bond, in cash or certified or treasurer's or cashier's check issued by a responsible bank or trust company payable to the Commonwealth of Massachusetts. (Insert check on Page 6 of Contract Form.)

Each proposal must be enclosed in a sealed envelope clearly endorsed with the name and address of the bidder, the project number, contract number and title.

Source: Massachusetts State Project No. E71-8, Contract No. 1, (Boston: Massachusetts Bureau of Building Construction, August 1978). For an explanation of the Massachusetts filed subbid system, see the section on filed subbid laws in chapter 3.

All bids for this project are subject to the provisions of either or both Mass. G.L., Chapter 30, Section 39M as amended and Mass. G.L., Chapter 149, Section 44A-44L inclusive. Attention is directed to the minimum wage rates to be paid on the work as determined by the Commissioner of Labor and Industries under the provisions of Mass. G.L., Chapter 149, Section 26 to 27D inclusive. The Awarding Authority reserves the right to waive any informalities in or to reject any and all bids if it be in the public interest so to do.

All bid deposits of general bidders, except those of the three lowest responsible and eligible general bidders, shall be returned within five days, Saturdays, Sundays, and legal holidays excluded, after the opening of the general bids. The bid deposits of the three lowest responsible and eligible general bidders shall be returned upon the execution and delivery of the general contract or, if no award is made, then at the expiration of thirty days after the opening of the bids therefor, Saturdays, Sundays, and legal holidays excluded, unless forfeited by failure to sign the contract as hereinafter provided. All bid bonds shall be retained by BBC unless accompanied by a stamped self-addressed envelope.

Sealed bids for Filed Sub-Bids submitted on a form furnished by the Awarding Authority will be received before 12 Noon, Eastern Standard Time, or Eastern Daylight Time, whichever is in effect in the Commonwealth on ___AUGUST 31, 1978___ .

Each sub-bid for the trade specified below must be accompanied by a bid deposit in the form of a bid bond, in cash or certified or treasurer's or cashier's check issued by a responsible bank or trust company payable to the Commonwealth of Massachusetts in the amount specified for the respective sub-trades. All sub-bid bid bonds shall be retained by BBC unless accompanied by a stamped self-addressed envelope.

The contract time commences immediately from the date that the executed copy of the contract is mailed to the contractor, or within such other period as the Bureau shall authorize in writing. The work shall be completed on or before ___600___ calendar days from said date. In case the work embraced in this contract shall not have been completed due to the failure of the contractor to complete the work or any part of the work within the time specified, the Bureau shall recover said sum or sums of money, equal to the cost of engineering, inspection of work, and any additional and other expenses incurred, from the contractor, from the surety or from both. The amount of these deductions shall be assessed as liquidated damages, and are not to be considered as penalties. For administrative purposes $___100___ per day for every day beyond the contract completion date or completion date as extended will be withheld as a special reserve to be applied as liquidated damages, if any, the amount of said damages to be determined as per the above mentioned method.

No prepaid delivery of documents including U.S. Postage is possible. Messenger and other type of pick-up and delivery services are the agent of the bidder and the Bureau of Building Construction assumes no responsibility for delivery or receipt of the documents. Bidders are encouraged to take advantage of a rotating credit plans and specifications deposit program initiated by the BBC to encourage the easy accessibility of documents to contractors.

No *personal, corporate checks nor cash can be accepted as deposits.* The bidding documents may be examined at the office of the Bureau of Building Construction and copies obtained by depositing a certified, treasurer's, cashier's or official bank check in the sum of $____150.____ payable to the Commonwealth of Massachusetts. Refund will be made to those returning the documents in satisfactory condition on or before _____OCTOBER 23, 1978_____ otherwise the deposit shall be the property of the Commonwealth. The documents may also be seen but not removed or taken out of the locations listed elsewhere in this notice.

BUREAU OF BUILDING CONSTRUCTION

SECTION	SUB-TRADES	BID DEPOSITS
4A	MASONRY	$21,000.
5A	MISC. & ORNAMENTAL IRON	2,600.
7A	WATERPROOFING, DAMP-PROOFING & CAULKING	800.
7B	ROOFING AND FLASHING	4,500.
8A	METAL WINDOWS	4,500.
8B	GLASS & GLAZING	3,200.
9B	TILE	1,300.
9E	ACOUSTICAL TILE	2,600.
9F	RESILIENT FLOORS	1,300.
9G	PAINTING	2,000.
11A	FIXED EQUIPMENT	5,000.
14A	ELEVATOR	1,500.
15A	PLUMBING	7,500.
15B	HVAC	30,000.
16A	ELECTRICAL	25,000.

SUB-BIDS SUBMITTED UNDER CHAPTER 149, SECTION 44H, WHICH ARE RESTRICTED TO THE USE BY ONE GENERAL CONTRACTOR, OR SUB-BIDS FILED PURSUANT TO CHAPTER 149, SECTION 44J, WHICH ARE DEEMED TO BE UNREALISTIC IN THAT THE PRICE PROPOSED IS, IN THE JUDGEMENT OF THIS AWARDING AUTHORITY, *SUBSTANTIALLY*

LESS OR MORE THAN THE ACTUAL COST TO COMPLETE ALL OF THE
WORK SPECIFIED IN THAT SECTION OF THE SPECIFICATIONS WILL BE
CONSIDERED AS NOT RESPONSIVE TO THE INVITATION TO BID AND
SHALL BE REJECTED. (DEPARTMENT OF LABOR AND INDUSTRIES
RULING #136 and #169).

4 Labor Relations and Collective Bargaining

Daniel Quinn Mills

The Labor Force

The labor force in the construction industry is composed of workers in more than twenty crafts and a much larger number of specialties. Most contractors, who are also specialized, hire directly from only one or a few of these crafts. The number of persons and crafts hired directly will depend on the type of work and the geographic area in which the contractor operates.

The volume of construction in process fluctuates, often within brief periods. In addition, certain types of construction work are seasonal. Sometimes large projects are begun in an area that has seen little major construction for years before, and will see very little for years after. Other areas, large cities especially, experience a sizable and continuing volume of work, but even in these, some types of work may decline in importance while others increase. In an unstable economic environment, employers place great value on their flexibility—the ability to hire and lay off men at a predetermined wage scale, so that the wage changes negotiated after a bid price has been established do not consume the profit of a job. The flexibility that the contractor requires for profitable operation, however, is often translated into insecurity for the working man. Labor organizations attempt to limit the effects on the employee of the changing economic conditions in which he and the contractor must operate.

Because of the peculiar economic conditions and characteristics of employment in construction, employers and unions are placed in a much more intimate relationship than in many other industries. Contractors and unions must negotiate not only wages and working conditions but also hiring and training practices as well. In an unstable industry, the need to develop and retain a skilled labor force requires that employers and unions agree on practices to preserve the job opportunities of craftsmen. The problem, of course, is to adopt policies that effectively protect employment opportunities but do not restrict needed expansion of the labor force or promote uneconomic practices.

Not all crafts, sectors of the industry, or geographic areas are unionized to the same degree, or even unionized at all. But all contractors, union or nonunion, are influenced by the labor relations policies of other contractors. Wages in the union sector influence what nonunion contractors must pay. Frequently, nonunion scales are below union scales, but union men are often considered better mechanics. Many contractors feel that the wage rate paid employees is less important than the productivity they exhibit. Because of the

59

higher productivity of their workers, union employers can sometimes pay higher wage rates but nonetheless may have lower labor costs than nonunion contractors.

The Open-Shop Segment of the Industry

The portion of the construction industry that remains outside collective bargaining agreements has usually been pictured as a fringe around the larger unionized sector; however, this nonunion segment has apparently been growing rapidly in relation to the industry as a whole. Furthermore, significant parts of this segment are developing their own structure, with formal industrial relations procedures—not under labor agreements, but under policies adopted by nonunion employer associations.

The industrial relations and manpower arrangement of the construction industry now operate in three forms that compete for future dominance: (1) the system under collective bargaining agreements; (2) open-shop (that is, nonunion) agreements under the national or local policies of a contractors' organization, the "merit shop"; and (3) the sector of individual enterprises pursuing policies apart from either collective bargaining or a formal organization of contractors— the truly "unorganized" sector. In a sense, the merit shop associations have adopted many of the substantive industrial relations policies and procedures of collective bargaining, but decision making is under the control of a local or national employers' association without union involvement or participation.

Several major associations are composed of nonunion contractors and are designed to facilitate relations with the labor force. Most of the associations that include both union and nonunion contractors as members have separate labor committees for the two groups. The National Association of Homebuilders, for example, which has a predominantly nonunion membership, has conducted separate labor policies for a long time. The Associated General Contractors of America (AGC), with a very large nonunion membership, established separate labor committees in 1975. In the 1960s and early 1970s, the AGC seemed to confirm the assertion that an association trying to conduct a single labor policy covering both groups of contractors would appear irresolute and erratic in behavior. It can be offered as a general proposition that an association cannot continue to represent union and nonunion interests unless it makes a formal separation of the two groups in the labor area.

Among the primarily nonunion associations of contractors, Associated Builders and Contractors (ABC) has emerged as the most prominent. Significantly, the form of organization or structure being developed by the ABC applies in an undifferentiated way to all branches of the construction industry. Thus the apprenticeship and training plans, health and welfare plans, pension plan, and still-to-come credit union plan, apply to all the employees and crafts of a contractor regardless of whether they fall under the heading of housing or heavy construction, highway, commercial, or industrial construction. This pattern differs, of course, from that in the unionized sector of the industry. These plans are also national in scope, except for the local or state apprenticeship and training plans. Within these plans, workers possess full rights to move throughout the nation among member firms of the association. Thus much of the previously unorganized nonunion segment of the industry is being organized by employer associations that also tie various sectors of the industry into an integral part of the construction industry as a whole.

We do not know the proportion of open-shop construction activity or employment. Reliable statistics on the degree of organization in construction are unavailable,[1] but a number of partially relevant measures of the importance of the nonunion sector do exist. Government surveys taken in May of each year of a sample of the American workforce indicate that some 37 percent of construction workers in 1976 reported themselves as union members. A relatively greater proportion of contractors than of employees are in the nonunion sector (that is, the average size of nonunion contractors by number of employees is smaller than that of union contractors). In the housing industry, for example, a major employers' association estimates that more than half the employers are nonunion, but because union builders construct a majority of the housing in most large metropolitan areas, more than 50 percent or so of all housing is constructed by union builders. (There are, of course, exceptions, including, especially the Washington, D.C. area.)

Some discussion of the degree of union organization by branch of the industry may be helpful. Most industrial and utility construction is union, but there are several major nonunion industrial and utility contractors, including especially Brown and Root Construction and Daniels Construction companies. The degree of participation by nonunion employees in this type of work is difficult to assess, however, because large nonunion contractors subcontract substantial proportions of their projects to union contractors. Finally, highway construction is primarily nonunion, but urban transportation systems are primarily union.

In the large commercial and small industrial sectors of the industry, nonunion contractors have made specially significant advances in recent years, but the unions have made important advances in other areas. For example, the pipeline and gas distribution construction sectors have been almost completely organized by the unions in recent years. Thus despite the advances of the nonunion contractors, it cannot be concluded that the unionized sector of construction as a whole is in permanent decline. Rather, the relative future of these two competing segments of the industry will depend largely on the developing character of the response unions make to the nonunion challenge.

The Unionized Segment

Contractors who operate in the unionized segment of the industry are ordinarily party to legally binding collective bargaining agreements with one or more of the unions of the building and construction trades. These agreements obligate the union contractor to observe in one way or another the work jurisdictions of the various unions. In some branches of the industry, agreements also obligate an employer to hire employees through a union operated referral system. These two aspects of the unionized sector are absent in the unorganized sector, and constitute major differences between the two.

Labor organizations are permitted to operate systems of job referral, but only when certain conditions are met. First, referrals must not involve discrimination against an employee because of his relationship to the union. The union is legally required to refer all qualified mechanics to jobs, without regard to union membership. Second, the employer reserves the absolute right to hire or refuse to hire, on the basis of qualifications, any employee referred to him by the union. Third, the referral plan, including any priorities of referral or standards of qualification, must be posted for all to see. The old closed shop, in which the union hall would dispatch only union members to the job, is illegal, and any plan that has as its purpose the reestablishment of a closed shop is illegal.

Referral mechanisms operated by labor organizations in the construction industry differ widely. In extreme cases, many locals operate no referral system at all, while others maintain an "exclusive" hall. An exclusive hiring arrangement obligates the contractor, by virtue of his collective bargaining agreement, to hire journeymen only through the union hiring hall, unless after a period of twenty-four to forty-eight hours the union has been unable to furnish journeymen. At this point, the contractor is free to hire from any source. Nonexclusive hall arrangements may obligate the contractor to inform the union of job opportunities and give preference in hiring to union referrals. In many cases, contractors may contact the union as a central source of job applicants, even when no hiring provision exists in the collective bargaining agreement. Unions may establish criteria for the referral of men to jobs, based on such factors as length of service at the trade, length of service in the immediate area, area residency, and competence to do the work.

Regardless of the formal nature of the hiring hall, the union is often a rapid and dependable source of mechanics for the contractor when he moves from the territory of one local into another, and where his labor requirements on a project vary from day to day.

The Building Trades Unions

The International Union. In the organized building trades sector of the construction labor force, the primary unit of organization is the international union, which is an association of local American and Canadian unions. Groups of locals in various trades participated in the foundation of internationals some sixty to eighty years ago in order that the standards of the organized portions of the trade not be undercut by unorganized areas. The internationals were founded with the power to issue charters, to organize locals, to combine locals (under normal provisions), and to remove charters. The chartering of locals by the international indicates the primacy of the national organization. In many cases, however, bitter power struggles that began during the early years of the union between international union officers and the larger locals have continued to this date.

An international labor organization is headed by a general president and a general executive board. Regional vice-presidents (executive board members) and the general president are elected by the convention of the labor organization, which meets at periods of two to five years. The international organization is governed by a constitution adopted and amended by the convention (which is the supreme body of the international union). Between conventions, the general president runs the labor organization, subject to (in one form or another) the approval of the general executive board, which is made up of general vice-presidents, normally selected to represent the various regions of the country. The general president is normally in charge of the work jurisdiction of the union. General presidents rarely take part in collective bargaining apart from their participation in developing national agreements, and they rarely intervene in the operation of local unions except where matters of general policy are in question. In many cases, such authority is used by international presidents with extreme discretion, because they are well aware of the policital danger to themselves of alienating local unions (the representatives of whom must reelect the general president in the national convention).

In many international unions, an intermediate structure exists between the international union and the local union. Normally, there are regional vice-presidents, and perhaps regional councils, and district councils in metropolitan areas, which may exercise authority in the affairs of the local unions. In some trades and in some areas, regional or district councils exercise those collective bargaining functions and other prerogatives that in most trades, or in other areas, rest with the local unions. Representatives of the international unions are stationed in the regions to represent the national officers and to assist locals in collective bargaining and other functions. The international representatives are appointed by the general president of the international union and report regularly to him. They also regularly visit local unions and district councils in their region. Some unions maintain staffs of international organizers and other representatives. In recent years, an expansion of organizing activities by the internationals has taken place.

The international unions have recently been drawn more closely into the problems of locals in many areas. The general president and his representatives have been called to local bargaining and grievance situations other than jurisdictions, especially to those that involve national contractors.

Local Unions. Local unions, which are closest to the rank-and-file membership, owe their existence to charters from the international union, despite the fact that many local unions antedate the formation of the international union. The charter of the local union defines both a geographic and work jurisdiction for the local. In some of the larger cities, for example, a single international union will have chartered several locals with different work jurisdictions.

Local unions in the building trades have preserved, for the most part, a considerable degree of autonomy in the conduct of their affairs. The negotiation of collective bargaining agreements, their provisions, and the enforcement of the segments are largely matters of local authority, subject only to general supervision from the international union. There are, of course, exceptions to this rule.

The local union usually elects a president and vice-president and other officers, some of whom are salaried, and a business agent, who is almost always a full-time salaried representative of the local union. In the case of very large unions, there may be a business agent and several assistants. The roles of the president and vice-president of the local union are generally restricted to internal parliamentary matters. Their roles are less important to industrial relations than that of the business agent, who has perhaps the most critical external administrative role at any level of the building trades union organization. The business agent is a full-time, salaried official of the local union, but he must stand for election every one, two, or three years, depending on the local union. Most business agents do not work with the tools of the trade, although they are members of the trade, have worked as journeymen themselves, and are familiar with site conditions. The functions of the business agent are as many as can be imagined of a representative of an institution in the labor market. The business agent, along with other officers or an elected committee, represents the labor organization in negotiations with employers and their representatives. He represents the labor organization before legislative bodies, before public officials of all sorts, and assists legal counsel in the courts. He handles grievances on the job site, representing the views of his membership and the interests of the labor organization. He directs strikes, boycotts, or whatever concerted activities are undertaken by the local union; he watches and defends the jurisdiction of the local union from encroachment by other labor organizations or by employers. Business agents attend the international union convention and are to a large extent the constituency of the general president and executive board of the international union.

The business agent is an elected official of the local union. He is therefore a political man in what is essentially a political office. Often the agent has offices to dispense, or other favors (such as referral to jobs) to support his position. Business agents may be voted out of office. Opponents of a business agent in the local union will watch his steps carefully and may bring any alleged deficiencies in his leadership before the membership at the election. Generally, an agent who is out of touch with the views of his membership does not remain an agent long.

In many respects, the most important function of both business agents and international union officials and representatives is what may be called policing the trade. Once agreements, practices, and customs of the trade are established, both by general agreement among the union membership and by explicit or tacit agreement with employers, the process of enforcing of these arrangements becomes extremely important. Enforcement of agreements and regulations in construction may often be a most difficult task. The industry is characterized by dispersed and continual shifts among sites, and by very rapid turnover of both employees and employers. A local area may at any given time have a large number of contractors from outside of its jurisdiction working within the jurisdiction of the local union. Further, the local union may have a number of men working temporarily in the jurisdiction "on permit," without membership in the local. It may even have a number of employees working who are union in some trades and nonunion in others. In this complex and shifting environment, the business agent and the representatives of the international union must seek to maintain the standards of the trade.

Collective Bargaining in Construction

Contractors' Associations

Collective bargaining agreements in construction are characteristically negotiated between a local union (or district council) in a single craft and the employers of that craft as represented by an association. There are, however, many exceptions to this pattern. In some branches of the industry nationwide agreements exist (especially in pipelines, sprinkler systems, and elevator construction). In others, regional agreements (embracing many states) have been established (for example, covering the boilermakers, dredging work, and some ironworkers). In highway and heavy construction, agreements are usually regional in coverage or specific to major projects. In some cases, local unions are so large that entire states or regions of states are covered by a single contract with a single local. The structure of bargaining also varies greatly among the different regions of the country. In the West, bargaining on a regional or a metropolitan-wide basis has become the normal case for most crafts. In the rest of the country, local bargaining is still the rule, although wider area bargaining is on the increase.

Contractors' associations vary widely in composition and structure. In the East, negotiations are frequently conducted by a building trades employers' association in a metropolitan area, or by a builders' exchange. Negotiations with each craft are conducted by a committee including: (1) contractors and/or the representatives of the trade association (for example, if negotiations are with the painters, the local association of the painting and decorating contractors will be included) and (2) representatives of the Building Trades Employers' Association or the builders' exchange. The association or exchange plays a central coordinating role when several negotiations are in progress at once, or follow one another closely. In the rest of the country, negotiations usually are limited to the individual trades and their employees, but the general contractors' associations (especially the AGC member groups on the local level) will often attempt to provide some central leadership (and may actually negotiate contracts themselves with many of the trades).

Depending on its size, a contractors' association may employ an executive director who devotes full time to the affairs of the association. Large associations may have staff personnel assigned directly to labor relations. Smaller associations may lack these resources, and a small group of contractors may conduct the labor relations of the association themselves.

A strong association usually provides considerable advantages. Because the union possesses a central, unified organization, it is capable of exerting selective pressures on individual contractors when an association is ineffective.

In order to strengthen local contractors' associations, an association may affiliate on a national level, much as a local union is usually affiliated with an international organization. The national contractors' organization represents the local chapters of the international unions, and may supply information and assistance to local associations. Examples of such national contractors' associations include the Associated General Contractors of America, the Mechanical Contractors Association of America, the Mason Contractors Association, the Painting and Decorating Contractors of America, the National Electrical Contractors Association, and the National Association of Homebuilders. In general, local contractors' associations are considerably less well organized and less professionally staffed than the union with which they deal. In some areas, state level associations are well staffed and play a prominent role in local bargaining.

An employer is included in a multiemployer bargaining unit if he unequivocally intends to be bound by joint action, rather than by individual bargaining. The employer's intention to be bound may be indicated by the fact of membership in an association that bargains for all of its members or by written authorization. Frequently, an employer who is not a member of a bargaining association simply goes along with the association, intending to be bound by the negotiated agreement. If, upon joining an association, an employer states unequivocally that he will not be bound by the joint negotiations, he cannot be so bound. Further, an employer may withdraw from a multiemployer unit at his own discretion on appropriate notice for any reason, except that he cannot withdraw after negotiations have begun (except by joint consent or in unusual economic circumstances). If he attempts to withdraw, he will still be legally bound by the association's agreement. There is one major exception, however. If the union involved in the negotiations agrees to the withdrawal of the employer from the association's bargaining unit, then the employer may withdraw at *any* time. Further, the contractor cannot make his participation in multiemployer negotiations contingent upon a desirable outcome of the negotiations. Finally, in the event that other contractors withdraw from the association during negotiation with union consent, other members of the association remain bound by an agreement reached by the association.

A contractor may remain outside the association and negotiate independently with the union. In so doing, he cannot generally obtain a better agreement than the association. In some cases, collective bargaining agreements between associations and unions include a clause saying that if the union grants conditions more favorable to any other contractor, it will extend those conditions to the association.

The Geographic Area of an Agreement

The geographic area included in a collective bargaining agreement does not necessarily coincide with the territory of the union and contractors' organizations in the negotiations.[2] In some cases, union or contractor groups from several localities negotiate a single agreement together, so that the scope of the agreement is wider than that of any single organization. In other cases, a contractors' association or union may negotiate different agreements for different parts of their geographic jurisdiction or territory. On the union side, the geographic area of a single agreement may therefore cover part of a local union, the full territory of an individual local union, or several locals bound together into a district council, a grouping of councils, or a statewide or regional association. Similarly, employers' associations may organize themselves, formally or informally, to cover geographic areas not coincident with a single association. At times, employers utilize interlocking representation to include the influence of contiguous areas, and affected contractors, in a local negotiation. Associations may be grouped together formally or informally within a single locality or among different localities. These contractors' associations may encompass a single branch of the industry or larger groupings, including in some few localities at some periods the whole industry. An employers' association may sometimes negotiate an agreement narrower in geographical scope than its full geographic territory. Further, because some contractors are independent (not members of an association) and because in some localities there are competing contractors' associations, a union may (but often does not) negotiate separate arrangements with each. Finally, visiting contractors operating in very large geographic areas may also be included in local contractors' negotiations. The geographic scope of the operations of certain contractors is much broader than that of any single agreement; the same contractor may on occasion be signatory to many different local agreements and, in some instances, to agreements applicable to many branches of the industry.

Wages and other conditions established by a single agreement may differ within geographic zones encompassed within the agreement. Alternatively, bargaining over a broad area (for example, statewide or regional may establish general conditions with separate wage rates established in subsequent negotiations for smaller units. Wages and conditions may also be made uniform across several negotiations by cooperation of the parties. In this way, separate agreements may conceal a much wider uniformity in wages and conditions. Separate negotiations are often tied together, and uniformity is established by the device of common expiration dates among different contracts. Project agreements, applicable to a large project of considerable duration, may be negotiated by national parties independent of the parties to the area agreements, or at other times the project agreement may be negotiated with the full cooperation of the local parties. Thus, the geographical scope of agreements in the construction industry is complex and may be quite variable from locality to locality and from branch to branch in the industry. The area covered by an agreement is not necessarily coterminous with the geographic jurisdiction of a local union or the territory served by a contractors' association.

Most agreements are negotiated locally, but regional agreements embracing a number of states have been established (for example, among the boilermakers, for operating engineers on dredging work, and for electricians on transmission lines). In some areas, local unions encompass so much territory that entire states or several states are covered by a single contract with a single local. The structure of bargaining also varies greatly in different regions of the country. In the West, bargaining in a regional or metropolitan-wide area has become the standard procedure for many crafts. In the rest of the country, particularly in the East, bargaining is much more localized and fragmented. In some cases, special geographic areas have been established for the coverage of pension plans, medical care, and work jurisdiction.

The role of national union negotiators and contractors' representatives in local collective bargaining is limited. For the most part, wages and conditions of work are negotiated without the participation of national unions or associations. When work stoppages threaten, national representatives may be involved. Currently, most of the eighteen international unions have authority in their constitutions to approve local strikes (and thereby the issues over which the strike may occur), but in many, the authority exists only when strike benefits are requested. The power of an international union to intervene in local negotiations is infrequently exercised even when it exists, although considerable differences exist among international unions. National contractors' associations have little power to intervene in local disputes and, with some exceptions, are poorly staffed to do so. In consequence, the concern of national offices with the broader context of the industry is not often reflected in local bargaining.

The National Agreement

Most international unions have negotiated or adopted a standardized agreement for the national contractor. These short documents usually state that the contractor will use union men, subcontract all work to other union contractors, and meet local wages, fringe benefits, and other conditions of construction. In return, the contractor is given assistance from the international union in manning his job and in settling disputes that may arise in the course of its completion. Agreements of this type are to be distinguished from those that establish conditions in sectors of the industry that lack local bargaining, such as in pipeline construction. Further, national agreements are more important in some branches of the industry than in others. In industrial construction, the national agreement is of very great significance. For example, the agreement between the National Constructors' Association (NCA) and the United Association (UA), plumbers and pipefitters, includes specific wage scales and working conditions which may differ from those in local agreements. The Ironworkers have steel erection agreements at the national level with the National Constructors' Association and the National Erectors' Association (NEA). In some instances, national agreements have been used as a device to establish preferred working rules and conditions, which can also be used as a standard for local parties to include in their agreements.

The national agreement normally binds the contractor to the conditions of the local agreement, but not to the local contractors' association and bargaining unit. In consequence, contractors who have national agreements sometimes work through local strikes or lockouts. In this and other ways, national agreements may appear to undermine the position of local contractors' associations.

Because of criticism of national agreements, a trend has grown toward modifying the no-strike, no-lockout provisions of the agreements. For example, the UA-NCA agreement now permits the union to strike, or the employer to lock out after five days notice to the other party. But if national employers avail themselves of the right to lock out in support of the negotiating position of local contractors, they may no longer take advantage of other provisions of the national agreement.

Project Agreements

Collective bargaining agreements are sometimes negotiated to cover only a single large construction project. Often, these agreements are signed by a group of building trades unions and a contractor or contractors. In some instances, the owner of the project is party to the agreement and binds its contractors as well.

For example, in 1974, Alyeska Pipeline Service Company, the consortium of six oil companies which built the Trans-Alaska Pipeline, signed an agreement with some twenty national unions and thirty or so local unions to cover construction on the pipeline for the duration of the project (approximately 1975-78).

Project agreements usually incorporate some provisions of the local agreements of the various trades. In particular, wage rates and fringe benefits are ordinarily established from the local agreements. Working conditions, such as overtime premiums and holidays, may be set by the project agreement itself. The agreements also provide for a procedure to settle disputes and often include a no-strike, no-lockout commitment.

Project agreements may be negotiated by the national union or the local unions or both together. Prior to the 1970s, project agreements were rare. They have become common in the 1970s. By 1978 the Building and Construction Trades Department of the AFL-CIO (to which the various national unions belong) was party to more than one hundred eighty such agreements on behalf of the national unions.

Jurisdictional Disputes

Jurisdictional disputes are an inevitable element of an industry in which wage rates and other conditions of work differ by occupation, in which mechanics are organized into labor unions on craft lines, and in which production processes and materials are continually changing. The objective of contractors and the industry has been to adopt means of handling these disputes and mechanisms for dispute resolution that minimize the disruption of production and efficiency occasioned by jurisdictional disputes.

Jurisdictional strikes are an unfair labor practice under the Labor-Management Relations Act, and procedures for the handling of such cases by the National Labor Relations Board (NLRB) are spelled out in section 10(k) of the act. Section 10(1) provides injunctive relief and opens the way for damage suits under section 303. The NLRB is required, in adjusting a jurisdictional dispute, to make a positive assignment of work to a particular craft. Unfortunately, the NLRB has little expertise in dealing with jurisdictional disputes, and its procedures are lengthy and cumbersome. As a result, contractors and unions have sought to establish a voluntary mechanism within the industry to adjust these disputes. Federal law explicitly recognizes the value of private dispute settlement and allows the NLRB to dismiss charges of an unfair labor practice when voluntary adjustment is attempted. The most important mechanism for voluntary adjustment currently existing is the Impartial Board for the Settlement of Jurisdictional Disputes. Most collective bargaining contracts in construction specify that disputes over work assignment are to be submitted for resolution to the Impartial Board, which is composed of three neutral members and is located in Washington, D.C.

Disputes with contractors may be bound over to the Impartial Board in many ways, including the following: under clauses in collective bargaining agreements; as a result of action by those national contractors' associations that have the power to bind their members; by signing an individual stipulation to the board; and under the terms of a project contract. Local unions are bound by action of their international unions.

The criteria under which the Impartial Board awards work assignments include the following: decisions and agreements of record, area practice, contractor's assignment, and economy and efficiency of operation.[3] There is considerable dispute over which criterion should be applied first (that is, which has priority). The Impartial Board has used decisions and agreements of record (precedents) as its first criterion. The NLRB, in contrast, appears to have followed the contractor's assignment in virtually all cases.

Decisions and agreements of record are the awards of the American Federation of Labor (AFL) and its Building and Construction Trades Department (BCTD), the awards of earlier dispute settlement plans (the first national plan dates from 1897), and jurisdictional agreements between the international unions themselves, provided the latter have been "attested" by the Board. Decisions and agreements of record are binding on contractors who are stipulated to the Board, and are published in the "Green Book." Under the Impartial Board plan, these rules serve as the basis for the contractor's assignment of work. In recent years, the practice of writing the jurisdictional claims of a union into collective bargaining contracts has become increasingly widespread. However, the Board takes no notice of these contractual clauses in its deliberations.

Problems of Collective Bargaining in Construction

The following problems in collective bargaining can be identified without offering a detailed analysis of each issue.

1. In many localities and branches of the construction industry the geographical scope of collective bargaining is too narrow. Workers and contractors operate over wider areas than ever before because of modern transportation systems and more widespread business competition. Work stoppages in one locality have an impact on neighboring localities. Settlements of disputes in one area are used for tactical bargaining purposes in nearby localities. It is generally recognized that a wider geographical scope for bargaining in these cases would prove to have a stabilizing effect on all parties, contribute to industrial peace, and promote the public interest.

2. In some localities and branches of the construction industry, it would be beneficial to all parties, and be in the public interest, to provide separate wages (and in some cases working conditions) for different branches of the construc-

tion industry, such as housing, heavy and highway, and pipeline. Such differences prevail in some localities and not in others.

3. The machinery for the settlement of collective bargaining disputes in the industry is inadequate. It cannot meet the requirements of the decentralized and localized structure of bargaining, nor resolve the complex issues that bargaining confronts today. Effective machinery for the settlement of national disputes exists in only a few trades (electricians have the oldest and most comprehensive system), and in most areas there is no local mechanism to assist the disputing parties in resolving the conflict.

4. The succession of contract termination dates, coupled with traditional rivalries among the crafts, has created a pattern of "leapfrogging" settlements, which is especially serious in the context of high employment. Each craft may seek to better the settlements achieved by the other. In some cases, unions that have previously reached an agreement demand either that further increases received by other trades apply to them retroactively, or that their own agreements be reopened. Such demands may lead to long and bitter disputes over wages. During inflationary periods, this problem is acerbated by the wage leadership exercised by very small bargaining units. Some crafts usually negotiate with an association of employers from many small shops that often specialize in commercial and industrial work. The relative price inelasticity of this type of work, coupled with the relative ineffectiveness of the contractors' association at the bargaining table in these circumstances, exerts a significant upward pressure on wages generally. Other crafts are under pressure to achieve settlements large enough to maintain traditional earnings differentials with whichever crafts obtain the highest settlements. Resistance to change is increased by the common procedure of submitting proposed contracts to union membership for ratification. Some employer groups are in a position to negotiate conditions or wages that have little direct effect on their operations, but that can have substantial adverse effects on rival or competitive contractor groups engaged in negotiations with the same trade.

5. The information available to negotiating parties and their national leaders is often inadequate to the needs of effective problem solving through collective bargaining. For example, it is often difficult for one trade to obtain *accurate* information regarding the rates paid (both currently and in the past) to other trades or to the same trade in other areas, although wage negotiations normally depend a great deal on the comparison of rates. This problem has been largely overcome since 1973 by the development of a national wage data bank in the U.S. Department of Labor. Even greater difficulty continues to exist in determining the conditions of work in other trades and areas. Guidelines for common practices in the provision of fringe benefits and costs are often lacking. Finally, accurate information about manpower availability and future needs is often nonexistent. In the absence of information, collective bargaining may become no more than an argument over matters that could largely be resolved by the presentation of factual evidence.

Directions for the Future

Many solutions have been offered for the problems that confront collective bargaining in construction, but only two of the major areas covered by reform proposals will be discussed here: reform of the structure of collective bargaining and improvements in the procedures for settling disputes. The two are not, as we shall see, fully separate. The intent of these pages is not to decide upon the best direction for the industry, but to contribute to the thinking of those who are concerned.

Reform of the Bargaining Structure

No aspect of collective bargaining in construction has received as much attention as the bargaining structure itself. The various approaches to reforming the structure of bargaining can be grouped into three categories: (1) proposals for regional bargaining; (2) proposals for multicraft bargaining; and (3) reorganization of the employer side of the table.

Regional Bargaining. In the late 1960s, a substantial trend developed among employers' associations, especially among those of general contractors, to organize themselves into regional organizations for the purpose of expanding the geographic scope of negotiations with the unions. Much of the motivation for this activity came from the belief that the decentralized structure of bargaining, particularly characteristic in the East and upper Midwest, facilitated the unions' successful use of the strike weapon by dividing employers against themselves.[4] Covering a wide area in bargaining was already common on the West Coast, particularly in California, but it offered little support in recent years for the proposition that bargaining covering a wider area would result in a lower rate of wage inflation.[5] Nonetheless, organizations of employers' associations on a regional basis have begun to take shape. For example, the Contractors' Mutual Association in 1975 listed twenty-five coordinated employer bargaining units that covered a wide area. Among the more significant of these units are the Construction Employers Labor Relations Association of New York (CELRA), the Mid-America Regional Bargaining Association (MARBA), and the Regional Council of Construction Employers (RCCE) in Minnesota. These associations have sought to bind their members firmly to the broader bargaining unit and have begun to negotiate contracts over a wide area when the unions will agree to do so.

In many instances, broadening the geographic area of an agreement in a given trade seems a useful reform of the structure of collective bargaining. Since 1969, regional agreements covering several local unions have been negotiated in Massachusetts, Connecticut, New York, Ohio, Indiana, Illinois, and Oklahoma. In some cases, the agreements cover the entire state, in others only large portions. In some, a single rate is negotiated for building work; in others, different zones create different wage rates. The laborers are also developing multistate agreements for pension plans and for certain specialties in their jurisdiction (tunnel workers, for example). The carpenters have been negotiating some agreements covering larger areas and currently are moving in that direction in several states. The painters have merged locals, expanded district councils, and widened the coverage of agreements in many areas. Ironworkers' locals in several areas have been cooperating to widen negotiations to areas involving many locals (for example, the Delaware River Valley, including parts of Pennsylvania, New Jersey, and Delaware, and the Ohio River Valley, including sections of Ohio, Kentucky, Indiana, and Illinois). In fact, there has been steady progress for several years in widening the geographic scope of bargaining in the basic trades, but there has been less progress in the mechanical trades. Recently, in some metropolitan areas, a trend to consolidation of locals has begun. But area-wide bargaining brings its own problems, some of which are significant.

Among the more difficult problems to be confronted in regional bargaining are the likelihood of a large strike and the difficulty of determining the appropriate coverage of wage rates. In some areas, regional bargaining (often combined with multitrade bargaining) has replaced the likelihood that one big strike would shut down all construction in a wide area. Whether the employers will have a greater capacity to withstand the pressures of a large strike, rather than the pressures of several smaller strikes, remains to be seen. The answer is not self-evident.

Second, the substitution of an agreement of wider geographic extent for several of more limited jurisdiction raises the issue of where wage rates should apply. In the past, the several agreements involved a range of wage rates, but their replacement by a single agreement may result in the application of a single rate to the entire area involved. If the primary consequences of regional bargaining should then turn out to be, on one hand, the substitution of large, crisis-creating work stoppages for several separate and more tolerable stoppages and, on the other hand, the extension of the highest wage rate in an area to all adjacent areas (rather than a range of rates from high to low), then regional bargaining will hardly be judged a contribution to the stability of the industry.

There are means of avoiding the application of a single high wage rate to all work in an expanded geographic area. It is necessary to consider these alternatives carefully, because it is, in practice, all too easy for union representatives and the employers' negotiators (who generally represent the larger contractors) to agree to extend the highest wage rate in an area to all adjacent areas. This practice presents the union with a minimum of political problems in the extension of the geographic coverage of a single agreement and is also consistent with the practice of large employers, who usually are located in the major metropolitan areas and who usually pay the higher metropolitan rates on all their jobs, even those in suburban or rural areas. But the extension of high rates over broader geographic areas threatens the union sector of construction in two ways. First, it applies to noncommercial work rates, which can only be sustained in the large cities, with the result that either the volume of work is reduced, or trade is given to nonunion contractors. Second, even commercial work, except for those large jobs bid by the larger contractors, may be lost to the union sector. There are two possible alternatives to extending a single rate across a broadened geographic area. First, wage zones could be established in a single agreement, applying a range of rates on a geographical basis, although working conditions might be common throughout the geographic jurisdiction of the agreement. Second, a single agreement could provide separate rates of pay for different types of work, rather than for different geographic zones. For example, an agreement might provide a high rate for new commercial and industrial construction, a lesser rate for highway and heavy construction, a lesser rate still for residential work, and the lowest rate for maintenance work. In some instances, a single agreement with different rates for various types of work within a wide geographic area has replaced a group of agreements applying varying wage rates to different geographic areas, but without differentiation in the rates paid within a geographic area by type of work. Finally, considerable flexibility in the adjustment of wage rates to economic circumstances could be obtained by including both geographic zones and differences on rates by type of work in a single wide-area agreement.

Proposals for the establishment of regional bargaining often confuse several separate issues. One aspect of the proposals involves widening the geographic area of bargaining within a single trade, which we have discussed above. Other aspects sometimes included, however, are the establishment of multitrade bargaining, the elimination of national agreements, the control of local independent (that is, nonassociation) contractors, and the shift of negotiating authority among contractors' associations (especially from the subcontractors to the general contractors). We now turn our attention to a selected group of these additional factors.

Multicraft Bargaining. Dealing with interrelationships among the trades presents one of the oldest and most complex issues in the collective-bargaining process in construction. The problem involves a paradox, and is therefore probably without any best resolution: the collective-bargaining process must somehow consider the interrelationships among the trades, but it also must recognize that each trade has peculiar problems and circumstances. There must be some coordination of negotiations among the trades, but a large degree of flexibility is also necessary to permit the resolution of problems specific to an individual trade or group of trades. Present practice in the industry with respect to the coordination of bargaining varies considerably. In some few areas, virtually all trades negotiate together, so that there is now multitrade bargaining. More commonly, a large group of trades, particularly the basic ones, negotiate together and sometimes set a pattern, at least with respect to wages, for the trades (often the mechanicals) which negotiate separately. This is the practice, for example in Detroit, New Orleans, and Dallas-Fort Worth. In many areas, some branches of the industry— for example, the highway construction sector—negotiate in a multitrade framework. In most areas, however, negotiations occur on a trade-by-trade basis with such informal coordination as seems desirable.

The extension of multitrade negotiations is often suggested as a means to resolve some of the major problems of collective bargaining in construction. The proponents of this suggestion believe it will help resolve two major difficulties of separate trade bargaining: (1) the leapfrogging of wages in successive settlements and (2) the sequence of strikes by trade after trade that so often disrupts the industry in an area. But there are also certain problems inherent in multitrade bargaining, which, if pursued for a long period, may make it very difficult to adjust wage differentials to changing economic circumstances. First, there is a strong tendency in multitrade negotiations for each trade to receive the same cents-per-hour increase. This practice, continued for several years, can prevent the industry from adapting to changing economic conditions that affect the various trades differently. Second, multitrade negotiations are extraordinarily fragile arrangements, subject to disruption at any point by a single trade or employers' association. Further, since in an increasing number of branches of the industry both management and labor want to conduct their own collective bargaining separately from other branches, localized multitrade bargaining arrangements are increasingly vulnerable.[6]

Two forces at work in the industry may clash in the coming years. On one hand, many local employers' associations (and in a few instances local unions) are seeking to establish multitrade bargaining arrangements that emphasize local needs in negotiations. On the other hand, several national unions and employers' associations are seeking to pursue a more consistent national policy with respect to collective bargaining among various localities in a single trade. In the first instance, collective bargaining would attempt to resolve issues in the framework of the relationship of the trades in a locality. In the second, collective bargaining would attempt to resolve issues in the framework of national policies within a given trade. The potential for conflict in specific negotiations is obvious, although conflict is more likely with respect to some issues of bargaining than others.

This is not the place to attempt to suggest which path is more likely, or more appropriate, for the industry in the future. It is important, however, that the proponents of either approach be aware of the potential for conflict within the industry. Those who emphasize national policy in a single trade should recognize the disruptive potential among the trades in local areas of a national policy at variance with local conditions. The proponents of multitrade bargaining on a local basis should, in their turn, be aware of the inherent instability of the solution they propose to the industry's bargaining problems.[7]

Employer Certification. To many observers, the problems of employers have been peculiarly responsible for the poor performance of collective bargaining in construction in recent years.[8] A number of proposals for reform have been advanced. One set involves various procedures for the certification of employers' associations as exclusive bargaining agents. These proposals received considerable discussion in the fall of 1970 and in 1971. But during 1972-1974, the success of the government controls program in restraining wage settlements in construction and in restructuring bargaining resulted in a declining interest in the proposed reforms. The termination of comprehensive controls in 1974 has revived interest in some new arrangements.

In 1970, several schemes were advanced for reform of the employers' collective bargaining arrangements. John Garvin, for example, proposed that Congress establish ten or fifteen regional employers' associations to do all negotiations in construction with all trades.[9] Several major national contractors' associations proposed a bill that required the National Labor Relations Board to certify a local contractors' association as the exclusive bargaining agent for contractors in a given area with a particular trade or trades.[10] Thereafter, the Construction Industry Collective Bargaining Commission and the Administration separately considered proposing legislation to Congress.[11] The Administration's discussions were focused not only upon certifying contractor associations as exclusive bargaining agents but also upon a mechanism to reform the geographic structure of bargaining. In September 1971, Congressman John B. Anderson of Illinois proposed a bill to establish a tripartite commission to study a proposed change in the industry's bargaining structure. Changes approved by the Secretary of Labor would become binding on employers and unions. The commission could recommend multitrade bargaining units in some situations, but not where a multitrade unit would "severely jeopardize the interests of any particular craft."[12] The proposed bill failed to receive the support of all contractors' associations, and, by 1972, concern for legislation had lapsed in the industry and in the government.

In the United States, interest in legislation to restructure collective bargaining and to certify employers' associations has been influenced to a large degree by the experimentation with such legislation that is taking place in Canada. Legislation providing for employers' association accreditation as an exclusive bargaining agent has now been provided in at least four Canadian provinces. The first act was passed in British Columbia in April 1970, and has been followed by similar legislation in Alberta, Ontario, and New Brunswick. The Ontario legislation (enacted in February 1971) is the most elaborate, and worthy of review here. It provides for a government board that could hold hearings and establish an appropriate bargaining unit by geographic area or sector of the industry, on a single-trade or multitrade basis. The device for establishing the bargaining unit is the accreditation of an employers' association as the exclusive bargaining agent in the established unit. The legislation explicitly distinguishes the following sectors as potentially appropriate to separate bargaining units: industrial, commercial, and institutional building; residential building; sewers, tunnels, and watermains; roads and heavy construction; pipelines; and electrical power systems. An employers' association can be accredited only if a "double majority" can be shown to exist: that is, the association must represent a majority of the contractors, who must employ a majority of the workers in a designated unit. The certifying board must also satisfy itself that the employers' association seeking certification is properly constituted, has enough authority to negotiate, and is free of union influence. Finally, an employer is prohibited from signing an *agreement* with the union which requires him to work through a strike or lockout involving a certified association, but a saving clause permits any employer to decide to continue work during a stoppage if he so desires.[13]

Thus far, there is insufficient experience for evaluating the various pieces of Canadian legislation. An American observer might note, however, that certain elements that are critical to the effective performance of employers' associations in collective bargaining are not, or cannot be, addressed by the legislation. These include the provision of an adequate financial basis for an association, improvements in the quality of its leadership, and the involvement of the national leadership of the organization in local negotiations. Nonetheless, the certification of employers' associations and the attendant restructuring of bargaining may prove valuable in improving the performance of collective bargaining.

Events in recent years have provided particularly interesting material for a comparative analysis of American and Canadian public policy. Faced with a collective bargaining crisis in the late 1960s and in 1970, the United States successively applied direct wage controls. The United States is now considering policies for the restructuring of bargaining. The Canadians, however, faced with similar problems, did not use controls, but rather sought to strengthen the employer side of the table in negotiations. A careful comparison of the effectiveness of the two approaches would be of great academic and practical interest. Certainly American observers will be interested in the Canadian experience as we consider proposals for the certification of employers' associations and the restructuring of bargaining.

The period from March 29, 1971 until May 1, 1974 saw formal wage and price controls in construction. The controls were administered by the Construction Industry Stabilization Committee, a board made up of union, management, and government representatives. During the period of controls, wage and fringe benefit increases fell from a 17 percent annual rate in 1970 to 6.2 percent in 1973. Strikes also declined. Some progress was made in reorganizing bargaining units in the industry. The expiration of controls caused concern that collective bargaining in construction might revert to the unstable situation of the late 1960s and of 1970. In 1975, the Ford Administration proposed a bill to Congress designed to reform the collective bargaining structure in construction. Title I of the bill permitted a broader role for picketing by building trades unions at construction sites. Title II provided for a national joint labor-management-government committee to oversee local collective bargaining in construction. The bill was formerly titled, "Equal Treatment for Construction Workers," but was generally referred to, because of Title I, as the "situs picketing bill."

There was considerable opposition to the bill from employers. Early in December 1975, the legislation had passed both houses of Congress and was sent to President Ford. Later that month, the President vetoed the bill.

The unions reintroduced the situs picketing bill in the spring of 1977, after the Carter Administration had taken office. The bill was again opposed by management. The bill failed to pass the Congress. Thus, some ten years of efforts by national leaders of unions, management, and the government to find a common ground from which to reform collective bargaining in construction ended in bitterness and division.

Procedures for Settling Disputes

Collective bargaining in construction could be reformed by still another method: the development and extension of the procedures used for settling disputes in each of the trades. Such procedures could provide the assistance of national parties in resolving disputes that arise in the context of local contract negotiations. In some cases, the procedures could extend to provide a decision by the national parties with respect to issues in a local dispute. The Council on Industrial Relations of the Electrical Construction Industry is the oldest (operating since the 1920s) and has the most comprehensive such plan for dispute settlement.[14] Other national plans exist in the sheet metal construction industry and in the plumbing and pipeline industry. The value of having a national machinery for settling disputes is not limited to providing assistance for the achievement of increased industrial peace, but extends as well to other objectives. Except in exceedingly tight labor markets or otherwise unusual circumstances, the machinery for handling disputes is likely to serve as a device by which unreasonably ambitious local demands can be restrained.

There have been earlier attempts to develop procedures for settling disputes in the basic trades that are somewhat analogous to those now existing in some of the mechanical trades. In 1961, for example, the AGC and seven basic trades reached agreement on a National Joint Appeals Board with an impartial chairman to settle disputes over the terms of collective bargaining among local affiliates of AGC and the unions if the local associations and local unions voluntarily agreed to the submission of the dispute for resolution. Unfortunately, the plan has hardly been used. In 1971, at the time of the establishment of craft boards by a Presidential Executive Order, unsuccessful attempts were made to create a single board or a coordinated group of boards for the basic trades. Unfortunately, no agreements were reached between labor and management for the continuation of a craft board beyond the expiration of controls (except that in some trades an already existant machinery was extended to a much larger number of localities). The absence of procedures by which the wider perspectives of national union and employers' association leadership can be made influential in the resolution of local disputes is a major unfinished element in the needed reform of bargaining in construction.

Construction Labor Relations in the Future

Since the failure of the proposed situs picketing legislation, the government's relationship with the construction industry can be most usefully characterized as that of an interested party, rather than as one of involvement. The government has retained considerable interest in the results of the collective bargaining process in construction, but this has taken various forms, some of which are not regulatory in nature, but rather in the nature of assistance. Data regarding the level of wage rates, past patterns of relative wages, and the amounts of negotiated increases are maintained by the government for the use of national and local unions and employers' associations. The government provides information regarding health, welfare, and pension plans, and also renders assistance in improving economic practices in the industry.

Whether with government support of these activities the unionized segment of the industry can contain the nonunion challenge remains to be seen. There have been dramatic developments. The national unions and the larger employers have negotiated agreements to cover large-scale construction in which provisions have been made for enhanced efficiency in construction. One such agreement became effective April 1, 1978, to cover nuclear power plant construction. Another, the National Industrial Construction Agreement was executed on May 12, 1978, to cover the construction of such facilities as oil refineries, chemical processing plants, paper mills, and breweries. The National Industrial Agreement commits the employers to union recognition on the projects, and the unions to furnish skilled employees to the projects. The agreement prohibits strikes or lockouts, except under certain conditions involving the negotiation of a local collective bargaining agreement by a local union and a local employers' association. Mechanisms are provided for dispute resolution, and there are stringent penalties for work stoppages in violation of the agreement. In an apparent attempt to meet the competitive pressure from nonunion contractors, the agreement established working conditions that were very favorable, by the measure of past practice, to the employers. Thus the agreement provides for *no* paid holidays; for overtime at time and one-half (not double time); for *no* limit on production by workmen nor restrictions on the use of tools or equipment; for *no* rest periods, organized coffee breaks, or other nonworking time during working hours; and for *no* recognition or application of seniority to employees working on projects under the agreement.

Thus, the 1970s have seen the emergence of a strong open-shop challenge to the unionized sector of construction. By the late 1970s, the union sector had begun to adjust its practices in response. The 1980s will show whether the union sector's emerging response will be successful.

Notes

1. ABC estimated that in 1978 nonunion contractors performed 51 percent of all new construction activity. For 1979, ABC predicted that nonunion contractors would do 60 percent of all construction, with 71 percent of new private construction and 20 percent of new public construction being nonunion. These figures are undoubtedly overestimates, although to what degree is uncertain.

2. See, for example, John T. Dunlop, "The Industrial Relations System in Construction," in *The Structure of Collective Bargaining,* ed. Arnold Weber (Chicago: University of Chicago Press, 1971), pp. 255-278.

3. John T. Dunlop, "The Settlement of Jurisdictional Disputes," *New Jersey Building Contractor* (April 1955).

4. Some employers cite, for example, the generally successful experience of regional, multitrade bargaining in West Coast shipbuiding as a model to be emulated.

5. See, for example, Gordon W. Bertram, *Consolidated Bargaining in California Construction* (Los Angeles: Institute of Industrial Relations, University of California, 1966).

6. The mechanical trades, for example, have for several decades been jealous of their separate identity, and there has been an increasing desire for separate agreements in some of the other trades in recent years.

7. One useful contribution to a means of coordinating potentially conflicting national and local policies has been made by the Building and Construction Trades Department of the AFL-CIO. At its 1971 convention, the department authorized its executive council to merge or amalgamate local councils where appropriate. The department might, thereby, assist in widening the geographic areas of multitrade cooperation in various localities without engendering conflicts among local and national policies.

8. In 1970, for example, Frank J. White, executive vice-president of the Connecticut Associated General Contractors, was quoted as saying that in construction "multi-employer bargaining cannot work, because of the economic diversity of the industry, rather than because of union power" (*Engineering News-Record,* May 21, 1970, p. 125).

9. John Garvin, "A Plan for Regional Bargaining in the Construction Industry," Address to the Builders Exchange of Greater Lansing, Michigan, text in Bureau of National Affairs, *Daily Labor Report* 189 (September 29, 1970):DL 77.

10. "Multi-Employer Certification Legislation," mimeo., undated. The reader should be aware that there has been only limited use of NLRB election and certification procedure in construction. In some instances, representation elections have been held on a single employer basis, but in very few instances have there been representation elections covering the employees of member firms of an employers' association. In fact, the only NLRB election covering a major association was not a representation election at all, but an election to determine if the employees wanted a union shop conducted under a provision of the federal labor statutes that has since been deleted. The election involved carpenters, piledrivers, laborers, operating engineers, and teamsters employed in heavy and highway construction in western Pennsylvania, and was conducted during April-June 1948.

11. See, for example, speech by John T. Dunlop to the AGC Mid-Year Board meeting, Minneapolis, October 14, 1970, text in Bureau of National Affairs, *Daily Labor Report* 236 (December 7, 1970):E1 77.

12. See "Construction Acts Areawide Bargaining Bill," *Engineering News-Record*, September 23, 1971, p. 45.

13. See Joseph B. Rose, "Accreditation and the Construction Industry," mimeographed report (New Brunswick, Canada: Department of Labor, 1972).

14. Donald J. White, "The Council on Industrial Relations of the Electrical Contracting Industry." *Proceedings of the Industrial Relations Research Association,* 1971, pp. 16-24.

5 Is Construction Technologically Stagnant?

Steven Rosefielde and
Daniel Quinn Mills

A Review of Statistical Definitions

Some economists claim that little technological change occurs in the construction industry. It is often said that buildings are constructed the same way they were centuries ago, and that construction is a handicraft industry. Labor productivity is said to be low, and the industry is generally held to be costly and technologically stagnant.

But is this the case? Persons familiar with the industry know of many changes in construction techniques, machinery, and equipment. Indeed, it is such changes that generate jurisdictional disputes (disputes over work assignments) between various trades, for instance. New techniques allow new and different designs in facilities and permit contractors to make profits by cutting costs. Even the individual examples cited by critics of the industry are often erroneous. Bricklaying, for example, is said not to have changed in thousands of years; perhaps in the literal placing of brick on brick it has not. But masonry technology has changed a great deal. Motorized wheelbarrows and mortar mixers, sophisticated scaffolding systems, and forklift trucks now assist the bricklayer. New expoxy mortars give stronger adhesion between bricks. Mortar additives and cold-weather protection eliminate winter shutdowns. Each of these advances has made masonry a more modern and efficient industry and has enabled it to compete on a cost basis with such indisputably modern technologies as steel and glass construction. Masonry has not developed an assembly line technique, but it has adapted to its peculiar industrial needs in many efficient ways. After all, one could assemble masonry buildings at a manufacturing plant, but who could pay for their transportation to a given site?

Construction does not use assembly lines. Is it therefore technologically stagnant? Government statistics suggest that the answer is yes. They seem to show rapid cost inflation, a slow rate of productivity growth, and limited growth in the industry's output. Are these statistics accurate, or could they be misleading?

Analysis of government statistics involves three questions: (1) Are the statistics accurate? (2) Do the statistics measure what they claim to measure? (3) What interpretation is appropriately given to the behavior of the statistics? To answer these questions, we must examine the definitions used in compiling statistics, the ways in which statistics are collected, and their technical meaning. In the end, our analysis of the statistics will show that construction is not a technologically stagnant sector of the economy. It is, instead, a unique sector that has undergone important technological changes in recent years.

The United States collects a variety of economic information about construction activity. The major types of data are:

1. Expenditure data—estimates in current dollars of how much was spent by owners (through contractors or on their own account) on construction in a given time period.
2. Shipments data—estimates in tons or other units of the amounts of construction materials shipped by producers, such as tons of cement, board feet of lumber, and so on.
3. Cost data—estimates of changes in price to the contractor of construction materials and labor; the increase in the wages and fringe benefit rates of laborers, for example, or the increase in the price of cement to a builder. These are not output price indexes; they are input cost indexes.
4. Output price data—estimates of the price that an owner pays to buy a constructed facility. There are only two carefully prepared indexes of this type: the Bureau of Public Roads index of the price to state highway agencies of a standard mile of highway construction and the Census Bureau index of the prices of single-family homes. These are very close to a true price index of the type that exists for manufactured products (for example, automobiles), in that the product is defined to be a standard item, and the measure is of its price to the buyer (not the cost of its inputs to the producer).
5. Employment data—estimates of the number of employees and of man-hours worked by employees are collected from contractors on a monthly basis.

Using these five types of statistics, a number of relationships can be determined. For example, if one takes gross expenditures in dollars on construction (type 1) for a given year and divides it by the index of construction prices (type 4), the result is a measure of fixed dollar expenditures (called real output). Examining a series of real output estimates over a sequence of years indicates its growth rate.

Unfortunately, such a price index exists only for two sectors of the industry. As a second-best measure, current dollar expenditures may be divided by an input cost index. But the resultant estimate of so-called real output is biased; that is, it does not behave like an accurate real output series. We will examine the consequences of this later. Table 5-1 shows the cost and price indexes used to deflate major categories of construction expenditures data.

A measure of labor productivity can be obtained, theoretically, by dividing real output by the man-hours of labor used by contractors. But when the so-called real output series derived from an input cost index is used, the resultant labor productivity measure is also biased, as we shall see later.

Table 5-1
Indexes Used for Individual Categories in Deriving Constant Dollar
Estimates of the Value of New Construction Put-in-Place

Type of Construction	Applicable Deflating Index		
	Source of Index	Availability	Type of Index
Residential bldg. (incl. farm)	Bureau of Census: New One-Family House	Quarterly	Price
Industrial bldgs.	Turner Construction Co.	Quarterly	Cost
Commercial	Unweighted average of:		
	American Appraisal Co.	Monthly	Cost
	George A. Fuller Co.	Quarterly	Cost
Religious	American Appraisal Co.	Monthly	Cost
Educational bldgs.	American Appraisal Co.	Monthly	Cost
Hospital and Institutional bldgs.	American Appraisal Co.	Monthly	Cost
Other nonresidential bldgs.	American Appraisal Co.	Monthly	Cost
Other farm const.	Other farm const. index	Annual	Cost
Railroads	Unweighted average of:		
	Federal Highway Admin.	Quarterly	Cost
	Bureau of Reclamation		
Telephone & telegraph	Bell System telephone plant indexes ("buildings" index and "outside plant" index weighted by relative value of expenditures)	Annual	Cost
Electric light & power (private)	Weighted average of: *Weight*		
	Handy-Whitman Electric[a] 9	Semiannual	Cost
	Handy-Whitman Utility bldg. 1	Semiannual	Cost
Gas	Weighted average of: *Weight*		
	Handy-Whitman Gas plant 9	Semiannual	Cost
	Handy-Whitman Utility bldg. 1	Semiannual	Cost
Petroleum pipe lines	Unweighted average of:		
	Handy-Whitman Electric plant	Semiannual	Cost
	Handy-Whitman Gas plant	Semiannual	Cost
	Handy-Whitman Utility bldg.	Semiannual	Cost
	Interstate Commerce Comm. Railroad	Annual	Cost
Military facilities[b]	Unweighted average of:		
	American Appraisal Co.	Monthly	Cost
	Bureau of Public Roads	Quarterly	Price
	George A. Fuller Co.	Quarterly	Cost
	Turner Construction Co.	Quarterly	Cost
Highways	Bureau of Public Roads	Quarterly	Price
Sewer and water systems[c]	Unweighted average of:		
	Associated Gen'l. Cont.	Monthly	Cost
	Engineering News Record Construction	Monthly	Cost

Table 5-1 continued

Type of Construction	Applicable Deflating Index			
	Source of Index		Availability	Type of Index
Conservation and development[c]	Unweighted average of: Associated Gen'l. Cont. Engineering News Record		Monthly	Cost
	Construction		Monthly	Cost
All other private[c]	Unweighted average of: Associated Gen'l. Cont. Engineering News Record		Monthly	Cost
	Construction		Monthly	Cost
Miscellaneous public construction[c]	Weighted average of:	Weight		
	A Handy-Whitman Electric plant	9	Semiannual	Cost
	Handy-Whitman Utility bldg.	1	Semiannual	Cost
	B Associated Gen'l. Cont.	9	Monthly	Cost
	Engineering New Record Construction	1	Monthly	Cost

Source: U.S., Department of Commerce, Bureau of the Census.
[a]Whitman, Requardt, and Associates.
[b]As of first quarter 1972, Fuller discontinued indexes.
[c]AGC suspended between August 1971 and present.

Thus, despite the apparent wealth of economic statistics we possess regarding construction, the measures of real output and labor productivity that we have are surrogates for more accurate measures and are, in fact, biased measures at best. Yet is is from the study of these statistics that economists derive their conclusions regarding the rate of technological advance in construction.

A recognition of the inadequacies of our construction data has led in recent years to an increasing scrutiny of the official American indexes of construction growth and labor productivity. Critics have contended that the behavior of the official output series is inconsistent with the growth pattern suggested by various economic models. That is, when one looks at the growth of the total real gross national product (GNP) in the United States and compares it to the official measures of real construction, there does not appear to have been enough construction to generate the actual level of GNP. Why is this? the critics ask.

Two types of answers may be given. One asserts that the statistics themselves are in error and attempts to make adjustments in the statistics to get a true picture of real construction output and productivity. The second answer (which represents our approach) entails a more fundamental inquiry: it accepts the statistics at face value, but asks, What do they really mean? Do the statistics demonstrate that construction is technologically stagnant, as has been the common interpretation, or do they, in fact, tell a very different story when analyzed carefully?

Are the Statistics in Error?

Several economists and statisticians have studied official construction data in recent years (see table 5-2). In some cases, they have concluded that the statistics are erroneous and misleading. In order to derive more useful figures, two economists, Douglas C. Dacy and Robert J. Gordon,[1] developed methods of making adjustments in the official series in an effort to make the series more realistic. The fundamental adjustments they made can be summarized here. Dacy used the material shipments data by making real construction output proportional to material shipments. Thus,

$$O = \frac{E}{P} = \gamma(M), \text{ for each year;} \qquad (5.1)$$

where　O　is real construction output,

　　　　E　is current dollar expenditures on construction,

　　　　P　is a price index for construction products,

　　　　M　is an index of material shipments, and

　　　　γ　is a proportionality coefficient

Dacy used the official statistics for E and M. With M and an estimate for γ, it was possible to determine O and, using O and E, to calculate P. The calculated P would be compared to the official input cost series ordinarily used as deflators. Dacy found that his calculated P showed a considerably slower rate of inflation than the official cost index (specifically, the Department of Commerce's Composite Construction Cost Index). As a result, the government appeared to have been overestimating inflation in construction, underestimating real output, and underestimating labor productivity.

By how much had the underestimates been in error? Gordon extended and improved Dacy's analysis and showed that, in a period of seventeen years, real construction output was underestimated in official statistics by a total of $40 billion. Further, the adjusted series for labor productivity showed annual rates of increase in construction labor productivity roughly equal to the national average of productivity growth for all industries, not substantially less, as the official statistics had suggested.

Unfortunately, the government has not adopted the Dacy-Gordon procedures, but instead it continues to publish the unadjusted official statistics, which show low rates of real output growth and of labor productivity. Why has the government not modified its statistical procedures? In part, because there are questions about the legitimacy of the Dacy-Gordon procedures. The procedures are reasonable and effective for practical purposes, but they lack theoretical justification. The Dacy-Gordon adjustments are, in fact, a kind of rough adjustment of the existing data, not a fundamental realignment of the statistical

Table 5-2
Various Measures of the Average Annual Rates of Increase in Productivity in the Construction Industry and in the National Economy of the United States

Sources	Construction Industry			National Economy
	Pre-World War II	1945-1960	1960-1970	
A. Construction (Total)				
1. Kendrick (1961)[a]	1.1 (1899-1953)	1.1 (1899-1953)	—	2.0 (1899-1953)– private domestic economy
2. Gordon (1968)[b]				
a. Final price of structures	1.43 (1919-1929) 0.56 (1929-1948)	2.75 (1948-1965)	2.75 (1948-1965)	—
b. Official commerce index	1.12 (1919-1929) 0.42 (1929-1948)	1.36 (1948-1965)	1.36 (1948-1965)	—
3. Dow Service (1949)[c]	−0.8 (1924-1939)	—	—	—
4. Alterman & Jacobs (1961)[d]	—	2.5 (1947-1955)	—	3.6 (1947-1955)– total private economy
5. Dacy (1965)[e]	—	3.0 (1947-1963)	3.0 (1947-1963)	—
6. Cassimatis (1969)[f]				
a. Labor productivity i. Output per man	—	1.5* (1947-1967) 2.5† (1947-1967) 2.8‡ (1947-1967)	1.5* (1947-1967) 2.5† (1947-1967) 2.8‡ (1947-1967)	—
ii. Output per man-hour		1.6* (1947-1967) 2.6† (1947-1967) 2.9‡ (1947-1967)	1.6* (1947-1967) 2.6† (1947-1967) 2.9‡ (1947-1967)	
b. Total factor productivity	—	1.5 (1952-1965)	1.5 (1952-1965)	—
7. Sims (1968)[g]	—	2.3 (1947-1966)	2.3 (1947-1966)	—
8. Council of Economic Advisors (1968)[h]	—	1.9 (1947-1966)	1.9 (1947-1966)	2.8 (1947-1960)
9. Domar et al. (1964)[i]	—	2.0 (1948-1960)	—	3.4 (1948-1960)

10. ECE				
a. (1964)[j]	—	1.8 (1949-1959)	—	2.1 (1949-1959)
b. (1970)[k]	—	0.48 (1953-1967)	0.48 (1953-1967)	3.6 (1953-1967)
11. Clague & Greenberg (1962)[l]	—	2.7 (1948-1953)	—	2.8 (1953-1959)
B. Residential construction				
1. Grebler et al. (1956)[m]	0.1 (1890-1934)	—	—	—
2. Haber & Levinson (1956)[n]	1.5 ("recent decades")	1.5 ("recent decades")	—	—
C. Building				
1. Chawner (1935)[o]				
a. Turner index	0.3 (1910-1934)	—	—	—
b. Am. appraisal index	0.6 (1913-1934)	—	—	—
c. RR buildings	0.6 (1915-1933)	—	—	—
2. Colean & Newcomb (1952)[p]	0.02 (1913-1951)	0.02 (1913-1951)	—	—
3. Haber & Levinson (1956)[n]	2.0 ("recent decades")	2.0 ("recent decades")	—	—
D. Heavy Construction				
1. Chawner (1935)[o]				
a. Heavy RR	1.6 (1915-1933)	—	—	—
2. Bureau of Public Roads (1954)[q]				
a. Excavation	4.2 (1923-1953)	4.2 (1923-1953)	—	—
b. Surfacing	2.3 (1923-1953)	2.3 (1923-1953)	—	—
c. Structures	0.6 (1923-1953)	0.6 (1923-1953)	—	—
d. Composite highway	2.9 (1923-1953)	2.9 (1923-1953)	—	—

Source: E.J. Howenstine, "Productivity Trends in the Construction Industry," in "Measuring Productivity in the Construction Industry," a conference sponsored by the National Commission on Productivity and the Construction Industry Collective Bargaining Commission, Washington, D.C., September 14, 1972.

*Implicit deflator.
†Composite cost index.
‡Derived deflator.

Table 5-2 continued

aJohn W. Kendrick, *Productivity Trends in the United States* (Princeton, N.J.: Princeton University Press, 1961), pp. 148, 149, 498.

bRobert J. Gordon, "A New View of Real Investment in Structures, 1919-1966," *Review of Economics and Statistics* 50 (November 1968):423.

cDow Service, *Construction Cost Survey* (April 1949), quoted in Anglo-American Council on Productivity, *Building* (New York, 1950), pp. 14-15.

dJack Alterman and Eva E. Jacobs, "Estimates of Real Products in the United States by Industrial Sector, 1947-1955," in National Bureau of Economic Research, *Output, Input and Productivity Measurement* (Princeton, N.J.: Princeton University Press, 1961), p. 248.

eDouglas C. Dacy, "Productivity and Price Trends in Construction Since 1947," *Review of Economics and Statistics* 47 (November 1965):408.

fPeter J. Cassimatis, *Economics of the Construction Industry* (New York: National Industrial Conference Board, 1969), pp. 76-88.

gChristopher A. Sims, "Efficiency in the Construction Industry," in President's Committee on Urban Housing (Kaiser Committee), *The Report of the President's Committee on Urban Housing*, Technical Studies (Washington, D.C.: Government Printing Office, 1968) II, pp. 168-175.

hCouncil of Economic Advisers, *Economic Report of the President* (Washington, D.C.: Government Printing Office, 1968), p. 123.

iEvsey D. Domar, Scott H. Eddie, Bruce H. Herrick, Paul M. Hohenberg, Michael D. Intriligator, and Ichizio Miyamoto, "Economic Growth and Productivity in the United States, Canada, United Kingdom, Germany and Japan in the Post-War Period," *Review of Economics and Statistics* 46 (February 1964):36.

jUnited Nations Economic Commission for Europe, *Some Factors in Economic Growth in Europe during the 1950's* (Geneva, 1964), chap. III, p. 57.

kIbid.; *Economic Survey of Europe in 1969*, part I: *Structural Trends and Prospects in the European Economy* (New York: 1970), pp. 3, 92.

lEwan Clague and Leon Greenberg, "Employment," in American Assembly, *Automation and Technological Change* (Englewood Cliffs, N.J.: Prentice-Hall, 1962), p. 120.

mLeo Grebler, David M. Blank, and Louis Winnick, *Capital Formation in Residential Real Estate* (Princeton, N.J.: Princeton University Press, 1956), pp. 342, 343, 351, 357, 358.

nWilliam Haber and Harold M. Levinson, *Labor Relations and Productivity in the Building Trades* (Ann Arbor: University of Michigan Press, 1956), p. 203.

oLowell J. Chawner, "Construction Cost Indexes as Influenced by Technological Change and Other Factors," *Journal of the American Statistical Association* 30 (September 1935):561-576.

pMiles L. Colean and Robinson Newcomb, *Stabilizing Construction: The Record and Potential* (New York: McGraw-Hill, 1952), pp. 67-74, 246-248.

qM.B. Christensen, "Highway Construction Costs Reduced through Greater Productivity of Labor-Equipment Combination," mimeographed (Washington, D.C.: Bureau of Public Roads, 1954), pp. 5-8.

concepts or methods. The government, concerned with consistency among its statistical operations in various industries, and essentially unconcerned with the practical uses or interpretations of its statistical output, has chosen to do nothing.

What Do the Official Statistics Mean?

The failure of Dacy and Gordon to generate reform in the development and presentation of official construction statistics means that the thoughtful student of construction must still rely on the unadjusted official statistics, but must be even more careful about interpretation. Dacy and Gordon have established that the statistics as usually interpreted conceal considerable growth in real output and labor productivity. But is it possible that the official statistics are consistent with a different explanation of construction growth and change than is ordinarily given? To answer this question, it is necessary to examine the technical basis of statistical indexes.

The next section of this chapter is devoted to a careful exploration of the meaning of indexes of output, price, and productivity in construction. First, we will determine how indexes are compiled. There are two major methods, each named for a statistician: the Paasche index and the Lespeyres index. Both the official series and the available adjusted variant (that is, the work of Dacy and Gordon) are derived from Paasche indexes, which generally understate the true rate of growth. Construction output measures should be adjusted for design and other aspects that we will refer to as quality. According to our estimates, a quality-adjusted Lespeyres indicator would significantly augment measured growth and productivity. Compared with quality-adjusted Paasche growth, Lespeyres growth, which includes the effect of structural change, could increase the observed growth rate from 3.3 percent to 6.6 percent, with the total of all factors of production rising disproportionately from 0.5 percent to 3.7 percent per annum. Thus, instead of characterizing construction as a backward sector, we should view it as a quality-intensive industry in which the heterogeneity of the final product obscures and biases conventional quantitative estimates of factor productivity.

The analysis that supports these conclusions is highly technical, and some readers may wish to skim this next section and turn directly to p. 105. However, the reader should study tables 5-3 to 5-5, which illustrate adjustments in the method of computing indexes. The reader will note that the differences between the resulting indexes are substantial.

Table 5-3
Index Number Relativity in the U.S. Construction Real Output Series
(1957-1959 = 100)

Year	Quality-Adjusted Paasche OC/OC"	Unadjusted Paasche OB/OB"
1957	99.6	99.1
1958	97.6	97.4
1959	102.8	103.4
1960	103.6	102.0
1961	106.0	100.5
1962	110.0	102.0
1963	114.1	102.8
1964	120.8	109.3
1965	129.6	110.2
Compound growth 1957-1965	3.3%	1.3%

Source: Peter J. Cassimatis, *Economics of the Construction Industry* (New York: National Industrial Conference Board, 1969), p. 128.

Indexes of Growth and Productivity in the Construction Sector

The Construction Product

The conventional view that productivity in the American construction industry has been stagnant throughout much of the postwar period is based on the simple quantitative observation that, compared with other sectors of the national economy, the growth of labor productivity (output per unit of labor) has been dismally sluggish, only slightly greater than zero, while capital productivity (output per unit of capital) has actually declined (−5.9 percent per annum). These statistics imply that the overall rate of technical progress in the construction industry, after making allowance for increased employment of labor and capital, is almost certainly negative, the exact magnitude depending on the precise functional specification used to assess the productive contribution of both factor inputs. By comparison, technical progress in the industrial sector as a whole is almost always positive, and usually substantially so.

What accounts for this glaring disparity? Some have suggested that, owing to the nature of the construction process itself, new machine tools, new bonding agents, and new materials contribute little to the volume of output that can be produced from a given supply of capital and labor. Likewise, it is argued that the scope for improving the aggregate quality of labor is relatively circumscribed. In short, the construction process is perceived as fundamentally different from the technical processes prevailing in the rest of the industrial economy, and it is this

Table 5-4
Trends in Labor Productivity and Capital Productivity in the
U.S. Construction Industry, 1957-1966

Year	Q/L Labor Productivity Real Output/Man-hour (1957-1959 = 100)	Q/K Capital Productivity (1957-1959 = 100)
1957	98.5	108.1
1958	105.3	99.3
1959	102.4	93.6
1960	106.4	94.8
1961	111.1	78.0
1962	112.6	82.1
1963	115.6	82.2
1964	112.3	81.3
1965	115.3	77.7
Compound rate of change 1957-1965	2.0%	−4.0%

Source: Peter J. Cassimatis, *Economics of the Construction Industry* (New York: National Industrial Conference Board, 1969), pp. 87, 128.

eccentricity that purportedly explains the technical stagnation of the construction sector.

Although this appeal to technological determinism may be superficially persuasive, the argument is largely impressionistic and perhaps even tautological. A better grasp of the issues involved can be obtained by approaching the problem in a different way. Instead of focusing on technique, attention should be paid to the specific character of the construction product.

Most construction durables are locationally immobile. Unlike ordinary mass-produced goods, they cannot be used interchangeably or moved about at will. As a consequence of this immobility, construction durables are usually designed not only to achieve some particular function at some specific site but

Table 5-5
Trends in Factor Productivity in the U.S. Construction Industry,
1957-1966: Alternative Index Measures

Factor Productivity (Annual Compound Rates of Growth)	Unadjusted Paasche (OB/OB")	Quality-Adjusted Paasche (OC/OC")	Quality-Adjusted Lespeyres (OA*/OA)
Labor	0	2.0	5.2
Capital	−5.9	−4.0	−1.0
Total ($K + L$)	−1.5	0.5	3.4
Output	1.3	3.3	6.6

also to meet the constraints and variable opportunities afforded by changing economic conditions. Good construction design therefore stresses functional flexibility. It facilitates the production of diverse outputs and the employment of capital and labor over a broad range of combinations of inputs in various proportions. Moreover, it governs the durability of the construction good itself, since durability is a crucial element of long-run marginal cost.

All these considerations taken together imply that construction durables are almost inevitably heterogeneous to the extent that they effectively use relevant locational opportunities. The measurement of growth and productivity in the construction sector therefore poses special difficulties. Quantitative calculations of the numerical increase in growth and productivity tell us very little about their qualitative growth; growth in quality is expressed by the contribution these durables make to the final volume of goods and services produced elsewhere in the economy. To put the matter as succinctly as possible, the immobility of design intensive construction durables and their heterogeneity are such that the impact of these characteristics upon estimates of economic growth is substantially more important in the construction sector than in other sectors of the economy. Any calculation of construction productivity, therefore, that omits measurement of growth and change in location and design is likely to result in a manifest underestimation of technical progress. From this perspective, it is not the peculiar nonindustrial character of construction that accounts for the low levels of observed factor productivity, but the omission of certain aspects of growth from the conventional measurement of productivity. Indeed, the apparent stagnation of construction productivity can be almost entirely attributed to neglecting to measure these factors. For convenience in exposition, let us refer to the factors other than volume as the *quality* of the product.

Quality

Before examining the available quantitative evidence, some further consideration of the concept of quality is in order. Two aspects of qualitative growth need to be distinguished, one relating to level or scale, the other to structure. Suppose that construction durables could be ranked on an ordinal scale of quality. Initially some goods may be relatively inferior (those ranked 1 to 5), while others are superior (those ranked 6 to 10). The distribution of construction durables among the ranks determines the qualitative structure of construction outputs. The ordinal scale governs acknowledged levels of achieved quality. Over time, then, qualitative growth can take two forms. The ordinal scale can increase (say from 3 to 14) and the distribution of inferior and superior goods may shift.[2] Typically, both types of qualitative growth occur concomitantly, and their combined effect determines the magnitude of productivity growth usually ignored by conventional computations.

As the quality scale increases, however, new goods are produced that were not previously available. This complicates matters because growth necessarily takes place in an environment where the quality assortment of construction durables is changing in both composition and type. Given the great heterogeneity of construction products, the measurement of quality growth becomes especially difficult, since changes in structure are not easily distinguished from changes in the quality scale.

These complexities usually encourage analysts to disregard the issue altogether. A more prudent approach might be to presume that structural change and the level or scale of quality are positively correlated. This implies that if the data suggest that the mix of construction durables changes significantly over time from inferior to superior goods, it is sensible to assume that the quality level has increased as well. If this assumption is allowed, index number theory can be used to demonstrate the range over which productivity has been understated in the construction sector. In the next two subsections, index theory is used for this purpose. Since the analysis is complex, a brief summary of the argument is useful here.

Unique and unambiguous measures of economic growth cannot be computed. Under normal conditions, an index employing base-year price weights (Lespeyres index) overstates growth, while one with end-year price weights understates growth (Paasche index).[3] The disparity between the Paasche and Lespeyres indexes of growth constitutes a measure of structural quality change, which must be added to any independent growth in the scale or level of achieved quality. Using data on inputs and outputs, supplemented with available evidence on the time rate of quality improvement in construction, we establish the following important facts:

1. The conventional measure of productivity is based on a Paasche index that understates growth.
2. The conventional quality adjustments do not systematically account for changes in the quality structure of outputs.
3. Left unadjusted, total factor productivity in the construction sector 1957-1966 was actually negative (−1.5 percent per annum).
4. Available data on the scale of quality growth increase the annual productivity rate to a positive level (0.5 percent per annum).
5. If the magnitude of structural quality growth is equal to the increase in the scale of the achieved quality increment, then quality-adjusted Lespeyres growth in the construction sector rises to 3.4 percent, well within the normal range of all industrial sectors.

We conclude that if productivity indexes of American construction durables were computed on a correct theoretical basis, such as a quality-adjusted Lespeyres index, the apparent stagnation of construction productivity would vanish.

Structural Change, Quality, and
Index Number Relativity

Productivity growth, as we have suggested, depends on the relationship over time exhibited between outputs and inputs, adjusted for changes in quality. To facilitate exposition, let us assume initially that the volume and structure of input remain fixed, so that productivity growth is determined simply by output growth in all the senses previously identified.

Figure 5-1 provides a geometric representation of all three types of output growth: volumetric, structural, and qualitative.

Two production possibility frontiers (*PPF*) are depicted, describing all feasible transformation ratios in the initial and current period, PPF_0 and PPF_1. Every point on each locus illustrates the amount of either good that must be sacrificed to obtain an increment of the other. The curves are drawn to indicate that productivity has increased only for q_2 good, so that every unit of q_1 can be exchanged for more units of q_2 in the current period. Point A on PPF_0 represents the mix of q_1 and q_2 prevailing initially. If growth were exclusively volumetric (quantitative as opposed to qualitative), production at time 1 would occur at A' where the constant proportion vector v_0 cuts the production frontier PPF_1. Measured growth would be OA'/OA, which would accurately reflect the volumetric change, even though the marginal rate of transformation of A' differed from A. Figure 5-1 demonstrates, however, that the realized output mix in period 1 is B, not A'. A structural change has occurred. Since structural transformations are conventionally given a volumetric interpretation according to equation 5.2,

$$Q = \frac{\alpha_0 \beta_{11} q_1 + \beta_{12} q_2}{\alpha_0 q_1 + q_2}, \tag{5.2}$$

where Q = the quantity index,

   α_0 = the marginal rate of commodity transformation in the base year,

   β_{ij} = the quantity produced of the jth good in the ith year, and

   q_j = any jth good, $j = j(1, \ldots, n)$,

B must somehow be converted into its equivalent expressed in terms of the original mix v_0. If we employ a Lespeyres index variant of equation 5.2 where the transformation (price) weights refer to the initial period (α_0),

$$L = \frac{\alpha_0 \beta_{11} q_1 + \beta_{12} q_2}{\alpha_0 q_1 + q_2}, \tag{5.3}$$

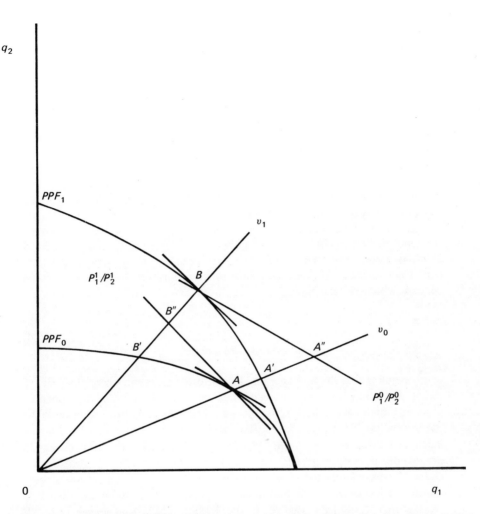

Figure 5-1. Product Growth and Intrasectoral Transformation in the Construction Industry

the index form indicates that B can be converted into A along the linear transformation function implied by the marginal conditions of the initial year (this is also the price line P_1^0/P_2^0).[4] Because the linearity assumption embedded in the marginal condition overstates the true transformational possibilities of PPF_1, the Lespeyres formulation exaggerates achievable volumetric growth, $OA''/OA > OA'/OA$. But the product mix v_0 is no longer desired by the community. In an important sense, the exaggeration is partially fictitious, since structural growth has been implicitly given a volumetric expression. This point is verified by measuring volumetric growth in terms of current preferences. Utilizing the taste of period 1 represented by the product mix vector v_1, volumetric growth computed as the linear distance separating the two transformation loci is OB/OB', a magnitude substantially greater than OA'/OA. In every case where production potential and the average commodity share increase in the same direction, the volumetric measure of growth will be greater along the expansion vector of the current period.

Further inspection of figure 5-1 brings out another crucial point. Whenever the price of the more rapidly growing good falls relative to the slower growing substitute, a Lespeyres index, although overstating the growth of the original mix, actually provides a reasonable approximation of the volumetric growth of the late period bundle, $OA''/OA \approx OB/OB'$. This implies that if the structural aspect of growth is taken into account, the Lespeyres measure provides a fair estimate of the total growth effect.

One might suppose that the cumbersome inferential approach described above is unnecessarily circuitous. Why not evaluate the growth of the later period mix directly, using current transformation weights? The calculation could be made with a Paasche index,

$$P = \frac{\alpha_1 \beta_{11} q_1 + \beta_{12} q_2}{\alpha_1 q_1 + q_2},$$
(5.4)

which requires that the base-year mix be converted to its equivalent along the v_1 vector. Assuming that the marginal rate of transformation at B represents prevailing marginal conditions, the desired value is obtained by moving along the transformation line (price line P_1^1/P_2^1) from A to B''. Notice that the Paasche index measuring growth as OB/OB'' actually understates the true change in production potential OB/OB'. If we adopt the ostensibly straightforward method of calculating the growth of the late period output mix with current transformation weights, growth is underestimated, approximating the volumetric increase that would have occurred in the absence of structural change, OA'/OA. This anomalous result indicates that a perfunctory approach to growth in the construction sector is perilous indeed and brings us back to the subject of quality. As was suggested earlier, quality growth manifests itself in index number analysis through the conversion of new goods to their equivalent value in terms of the original output. If the q_2 good is quality augmented, the volumetric expression of interperiod physical growth is $\gamma \beta_{12} q_2 / q_2$, where γ represents the marginal rate of transformation of the quality-improved q_2^* good into its initial q_2 variant, and β_{ij} represents the output levels of each good. Geometrically, the γ parameter affects the observed production mix B $(\beta_{11} q_1, \beta_{12} q_2)$, by vertically increasing the q_2 activity level from $\beta_{12} q_2$ to $\gamma \beta_{12} q_2$ at point C. This adjustment, however, is not structurally neutral, unless q_1 is adjusted in the same proportion, $\gamma \beta_{11} q_1$, an assumption not embodied in figure 5-1. Therefore, in our example quality growth alters the slope of the v_1 vector, changing the measured composition of the aggregate product. How this structural variation affects measured growth depends largely on the mechanical conventions forming the index. Several possibilities exist. Figure 5-2, which duplicates figure 5-1 with certain self-evident revisions, illustrates some important alternatives. The basic analytical problem involves the choice of transformation weights to be applied in comparing output bundles A and C. One approach might be to utilize the price relatives associated with point B to transform the C mix to its equivalent along the v_1 vector, B^*, computing quality-adjusted Paasche growth as OB^*/OB''. This procedure is justifiable if both q_2^* and q_2 are currently being produced, with q_2 the predominant component. Alternatively, q_2 may have been completely replaced by q_2^*, in which case conversion of C to its B equivalent is no longer warranted. Interest should now focus properly on the new product variant q_2^* and the marginal conditions ruling at point C on the implicit frontier joining q_2^* with q_1 (drawn as $-\,-\,-$ in figure 5-2). This means that volumetric growth must be measured along the vector v_1^*, representing the quality-adjusted output mix, which is achieved by applying the transformation relative (the tangency) at C to point A, converting A to C''^*. Growth then is computed as OC/OC''^*. This volumetric magnitude, like most Paasche measures, understates the true change in production potential OC/OC', where C' lies on the hypothetical base period transformation curve that would have existed had q_2^* actually been produced at that time. If neither v_1 nor v_1^* precisely reflects the mix of q_2 and q_2^* currently being produced, a linear combination of the growth along both vectors employing component shares to weight the transformation ratios can also be attempted. The Lespeyres alternative is not precluded either. In figure 5-2, base-year price weights indicate growth OA^*/OA along the vector v_0 which overstates the volumetric increase even more than the non-quality-adjusted value OA''/OA.

All of the qualitative adjustments just mentioned have one common characteristic: they measure growth in terms of both volumetric and transformational change. As we saw earlier, structural growth exhibits precisely the same attributes. Can we therefore conclude that structural change and quality improvement are merely different labels for the same phenomenon? No, treating qualitative change as a special case of structural transformation overlooks one important consideration. Whenever qualitative improvement entails increased factor costs, the marginal rate of transformation will increase in the sense that more units of the substitute could be produced from the factors embodied in the quality-improved good than could have been produced from its less quality-intensive counterpart. Structural growth as we have described it has the opposite effect because it is assumed that technology induced productivity gains are associated with the faster growing commodity. Looked at from another angle, quality growth is embodied in the improvement of the final product, which serves the needs of others. Structural growth, however, derives from quality improvements in the inputs purchased by the expanding segment of the construction sector. As a consequence, structural change and qualitative growth

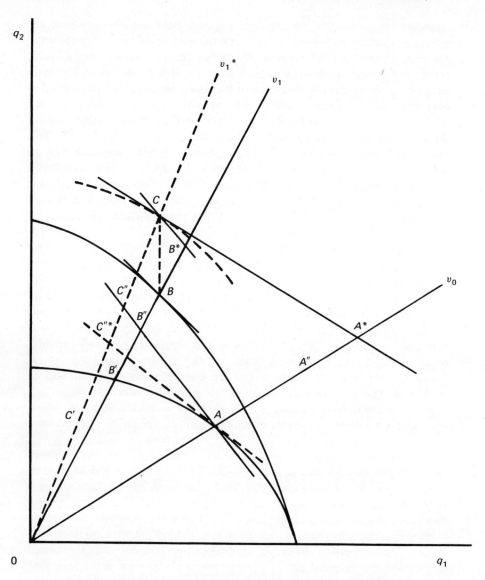

Figure 5-2. Qualitative Growth in the Construction Industry

affect current-year transformation weights, and therefore Paasche values, differently. Structural growth, which contributes to the understatement of current production potential and the overstatement of initial production potential, maximizes the divergence between Paasche and Lespeyres growth because the change in output composition is inversely correlated with prices. Quality growth in outputs, however, diminishes the effect of compositional change by making current price relatives more similar to those of the initial period, thereby minimizing the divergence between Paasche- and Lespeyres-measured growth. While quality growth might still generate index number relativity, the magnitude of the phenomenon is likely to be substantially less than that associated with structural growth. To summarize, each aspect of growth has a special geometric representation corresponding to its particular behavioral characteristics. Index measures that incorporate these diverse effects necessarily obscure the underlying growth process. Accurate appraisal of the scope, magnitude, and character of growth therefore requires that the analyst fully comprehend every convention employed in forming both the Paasche and Lespeyres indexes. Only on the basis of such a comprehensive approach can the growth process really be understood.

Input Cost Deflators, Quality Adjustments,
and Measured Growth in the
American Construction Sector

In light of the preceding discussion, one might suppose that official indexes of American construction growth would be predicated on elaborate computations designed to capture all aspects of the growth process. Such a supposition is erroneous. The government publishes neither a systematic quality-adjusted series nor the alternative Paasche and Lespeyres indexes that are essential to the appraisal of structural change. The single index provided is a hybrid quantity form that, although an intermediate process, is transformed from a Lespeyres to a Paasche type. This results in a double underestimation of construction growth, since both structural and qualitative changes are excluded from the official indicator. Rough adjustments for quality growth can be made, but as we noted before, this cannot compensate for unmeasured changes in input productivity. At best, quality adjustment enables us to compute OB^*/OB'' or OC^*/OC'' in figure 5-2 rather than OB/OB'' and OC/OC'', which still understates the true volumetric change OB^*/OB' or OC^*/OC'.

The systematic downward bias in the official construction growth index, while not intentional, is, in part, the result of compromises made necessary by the heterogeneous character of construction output, and is nonetheless correctable.

Consider the interrelated problems of deflation and heterogeneity. Up to now, prices or transformation rates have been described in real terms. Interperiod comparisons, however, are also sensitive to changes in the money price level. If money prices have doubled from their initial values because the money supply has increased twofold, current prices misleadingly imply that utility (value) of the aggregate product has doubled, when in fact only the unit of measurement has changed. To calculate real as opposed to nominal growth, therefore, the influence of money-price inflation must be removed. This objective is achieved in standard practice through the use of money price level deflators of the form

$$M = \frac{\mu(\alpha_1 q_1 + q_2)}{\alpha_0 q_1 + q_2},$$ (5.5)

where the parameter μ represents the price change attributed to variations in the price level. Typically, the current value of output is deflated by M, and a volumetric growth index is formed by relating the deflated value to base-year output.

$$P = \left[\frac{\mu(\alpha_1 \beta_{11} q_1 + \beta_{12} q_2)}{\frac{\mu(\alpha_1 q_1 + q_2)}{\alpha_0 q_1 + q_2}}\right] \div \alpha_0 q_1 + q_2.$$ (5.6)

By rearranging the terms this can be expressed as the ratio of a current product to a Lespeyres price index

$$P = \frac{\mu(\alpha_1 \beta_{11} q_1 + \beta_{12} q_2)}{\alpha_0 q_1 + q_2} \div \frac{\mu(\alpha_1 q_1 + q_2)}{\alpha_0 q_1 + q_2},$$ (5.7)

which with some additional elementary algebraic manipulation can be transformed into a Paasche quantity index

$$P = \frac{\mu(\alpha_1 \beta_{11} q_1 + q_2)}{\mu(\alpha_1 q_1 + q_2)} = \frac{\alpha_1 \beta_{11} q_1 + q_2}{\alpha_1 q_1 + q_2}.$$ (5.8)

As we have argued, though, Paasche quantity indexes understate volumetric growth. Does money-price deflation therefore mean that we cannot measure true volumetric growth along the vector v_1? No, a Lespeyres quantity index is easily computed by substituting a Paasche price deflator for the Lespeyres variant of equation 5.5.

$$L = \left[\frac{\mu(\alpha_1 \beta_{11} q_1 + \beta_{12} q_2)}{\frac{\mu(\alpha_1 \beta_{11} q_1 + \beta_{12} q_2)}{\alpha_0 \beta_{11} q_1 + \beta_{12} q_2}}\right] \div \alpha_0 q_1 + q_2 = \frac{\alpha_0 \beta_{11} q_1 + \beta_{12} q_2}{\alpha_0 q_1 + q_2}.$$ (5.9)

Thus, the choice of the slow growth estimator is avoidable. The heterogeneous character of construction output, however, is in part responsible for obscuring the real choices available to the statisticians. Heterogeneity makes it extremely difficult to compile output price deflators of either the Paasche or Lespeyres type. As a consequence, the Department of Commerce does not employ output deflators at all. Instead, input cost deflators are used as a surrogate:

$$F = \frac{\mu(\rho_1 x_1 + x_2)}{\rho_0 x_1 + x_2}.$$ (5.10)

Equation 5.10 illustrates a Lespeyres type input cost deflator, where μ represents the money price level, ρ_1 the marginal technical rate of factor substitution in the ith year, and x_1 and x_2 represent materials and labor respectively. If factor costs are similar to their respective output values

$$\rho_1 x_1 + x_2 \approx \alpha_1 q_1 + q_2$$ (5.11)

and

$$\rho_0 x_1 + x_2 \approx \alpha_0 q_1 + q_2,$$ (5.12)

then the measured Paasche quantity index should not be too badly distorted by input cost deflation.

$$P = \frac{\alpha_1 \beta_{11} q_1 + \beta_{12} q_2}{\alpha_1 q_1 + q_2} \approx \frac{\dfrac{\mu(\alpha_1 \beta_{11} q_1 + \beta_{12} q_2)}{\alpha_0 q_1 + q_2}}{\dfrac{\mu(\rho_1 x_1 + x_2)}{\rho_0 x_1 + x_2}}.$$ (5.13)

The assumption that the weighted commodity rate of inflation is very similar to the weighted factor inflation rate is hard to evaluate in the abstract. If the inflation of factor prices exceeded that of output prices, the Paasche growth would be underestimated. In the reverse instance, the Paasche index would more closely approximate the true Lespeyres value. But in the absence of independent evidence, a priori appraisal is not likely to be very helpful. It should be clear, however, that insofar as input cost deflation has obscured the latent problem of index number relativity, our perception of the structural aspect of construction growth has been impaired.

Much the same can be said about quality growth. Adequate quality adjustment is impeded by the heterogeneity of construction goods. As a consequence, the cost of acquiring information on quality change in the detail required is especially high and has not been systematically attempted. Private organizations and the Bureau of Public Roads do collect some component series on quality growth, and the statistics in table 5-3 illustrate how construction growth differs in quality-adjusted and non-quality-adjusted Paasche series.[5] From 1957 to 1965 the quality-adjusted Paasche series rose from 99.6 to 129.6, compared with 99.1 to 110.2 for the unadjusted Paasche measure. This is equivalent to 3.3 percent and 1.3 percent respectively in compound terms.[6] Assuming that the quality adjustment defined a new output vector v_1*, volumetric growth in figure 5-2 is OC/OC'' for the quality-adjusted variant and OB/OB'' for the unadjusted Paasche indicator. The ratio of adjusted to unadjusted growth, $(OC/OC'')/(OB/OB'') = 3.3/1.3$, implies that 60 percent of the growth increment can be imputed to the improved quality of outputs. Without a Lespeyres series, however, uncaptured structural growth OC''/OC' cannot be estimated as the ratio $(OA*/OA)/(OC/OC'')$, which in terms of the specific geometric example under consideration would add 3.3 percent to the total annual compound rate of growth, increasing the quality-adjusted Paasche value for 1965 from 129.6 to 166.7. Obviously, the omission of the structural growth component that can be imputed to enhanced factor (including neutral technical change) productivity could be of immense significance for any complete appraisal of the relative growth performance of the construction sector.

Table 5-4 reports productivity data that emphasize this deduction. The first column refers to labor productivity with output measured in terms of the quality-adjusted Paasche index taken from table 5-3. Capital productivity analogously defined appears in the second column. From 1957 to 1965 labor productivity (output per unit of labor) rose at about half the quality-adjusted Paasche rate of output growth, indicating that increased use of labor inputs explains almost as large a share of total growth as augmented productivity: Capital productivity on the other hand declined continuously throughout the period from 108.1 to 77.7, at a compound annual rate of −4 percent. Clearly, the rate of new capital formation in the construction sector was increasing far more rapidly than the growth of the labor force or volumetric productivity. Normally, theory teaches that capital is substituted for labor when its relative price falls and/or its marginal productivity increases. The sharply diminishing rate of capital productivity growth evidenced in table 5-4 contradicts that explanation.

It is possible that rapidly rising wage costs and the fear of further increases were in part responsible for capital-augmenting growth in the face of precipitously falling marginal capital productivity. Given the rather large impact quality growth has on the unadjusted Paasche index, it seems plausible to suggest that the trend toward capital-intensive construction may also be associated with enhanced quality of construction output. For example, substitution of the unadjusted Paasche output series for the adjusted Paasche output series used in calculating the productivity ratios in table 5-4 shows labor productivity at 98 in both 1957 and 1965, while capital productivity declined from 107.6 to 66.1, or at a compound annual rate of −5.9 percent. Thus, other things being equal, had the 1957 quality level been maintained, the productivity of both factors would have fallen. The same conclusion also can be drawn using the total input (capital plus labor) approach to productivity growth. The quality-adjusted Paasche measure rises on an interperiod basis from 100 to 104, or 0.5 percent per annum, compared with an unadjusted Paasche rate of −1.5 percent.

Of course, figure 5-2 suggests that the *ceteris paribus* assumption is invalid. If structural growth were accounted for, the anomalously low level of construction productivity might be reversed. For example, adding structural change (3.3 percent) to volumetric growth (1.3 percent) and quality growth (2.0 percent) yields an aggregate compound rate of 6.6 percent. Substituting this output measure for the Paasche indicators increases labor productivity from 2.0 percent (quality-adjusted Paasche) to 5.2 percent and capital productivity from −4 percent to −1 percent. Total factor productivity likewise rises from 0.5 percent to 3.7 percent. These changes, summarized and contrasted with their Paasche counterparts in Table 5-5, are well within the bounds of reason suggested by the productivity performance of other sectors of the economy. A modest fall in capital productivity associated with a rapid capital accumulation policy seems plausible, especially if the new capital represents technological innovations that render a portion of the old capital stock obsolescent. Although our estimate for structural growth is only conjectural and not predicated, as it should be, on a quality-adjusted Lespeyres volume index, it does reverse the anomalous results generated by the official unadjusted Paasche series. The question then arises whether other types of evidence support or invalidate the view that structural change constitutes a quantitatively significant omission from the total measure of growth in the American construction sector.

Structural Change and the Augmentation of Factor Productivity in the Construction Sector

Supplementary evidence bearing on the type and magnitude of change in the construction sector can be obtained from several sources. Informed observers of the construction sector can readily detail the constituent elements of its rapid transformation, in terms of both the final product and the changing technological processes of production. Included in the list that observers offer of changes in the industry are the growth of relatively new products such as nuclear power plants; new techniques of construction, such as panelization and precasting; and new types of equipment, such as power handtools, tower cranes, and concrete pumps. Table 5-6 presents some data on final product composition, breaking down total construction activity among broad categories of output for the United States over the period 1958-1973. As can be seen, the structure of final consumption demand fluctuates considerably between residential and nonresidential buildings, while the construction of utilities exhibits a slow but steadily increasing trend. Since each major product class involves a largely different combination of input factors and technology, the rapid structural changes to which the aggregate is subject are apparent. Moreover, each general classification of output is quite heterogeneous. The category of industrial construction, for example, involves such technologically divergent facilities as textile plants, complex automotive plants, and very sophisticated petroleum refineries. Alternatively, utilities construction would include fossil-fuel power plants, nuclear facilities, or simply transmission stations or transmission lines (steel derricks to carry cables). The impact of compositional changes, both among and within categories, on the relative magnitude of inputs and on the technology of their combination is great. Prices and wages in the industry and shortages or surpluses of materials and manpower are mostly the consequences of these compositional changes, not changes in the aggregate volume of construction.

The second major aspect of transformation in the construction industry involves the changing technology of the construction process itself. There are three major elements of change. First, there has been considerable mechanization of construction operations in recent years. Generally this mechanization has been laborsaving. It has taken the form of improved cranes, hand-held but power-operated machinery (for example, power-operated nail drivers, sanders, saws, drills, and wheelbarrows), improved lifting and moving machinery (such as larger backhoes, loaders, earth movers and graders, forklifts) and such other devices as power-operated scaffolds, mortar mixers, masonry saws, and so on. Second, new materials and processes are constantly being developed that affect production methods, but which have sometimes required substantial capital investments for production. For example, high-strength epoxy mortars have made masonry construction of prefabricated panels possible. Gypsum wallboard has replaced plaster for most wall covering, and movable metallic partitions have replaced masonry or cement block interior partitions. In many instances, material improvements have survived economically because they are laborsaving or timesaving in nature. Third, there is considerably more prefabrication off the jobsite. Often prefabrication has required substantial investments in plant and equipment on the part of construction firms. Where plants are located away from the jobsite, the production process becomes closely akin to a traditional manufacturing operation, with products shipped from a central location to dispersed points of use. Prefabrication of the manufacturing type has been especially rapid in the residential construction industry and in the use of precast concrete in building, suggesting, in conjunction with other direct evidence, that the construction sector has been undergoing significant technological transformation.

If this impressionistic evidence even remotely reflects the true magnitude of change, quality-adjusted Lespeyres growth should substantially exceed the Paasche measure. Given the relatively low rate of annual growth in total factor productivity, 0.5 percent, even a small augmentation of construction output attributable to change, say half the amount suggested by our geometric example, would produce Lespeyres growth of 5 percent and raise total factor productivity

Table 5-6
Percentage Distribution of New Construction Expenditures by Type,
United States, 1958-1977

	1958	1961	1963	1965	1967	1969	1971	1973	1975	1976	1977
Total new construction[a]	100	100	100	100	100	100	100	100	100	100	100
Residential buildings	42	41	42	37	32	34	40	43	35	41	48
Nonresidential buildings	27	29	28	33	36	37	30	28	31	28	27
Industrial	(5)	(4)	(5)	(7)	(9)	(7)	(5)	(4)	(7)	(5)	(5)
Commercial	(7)	(8)	(8)	(9)	(11)	(10)	(10)	(12)	(12)	(9)	(9)
Other (religious buildings, schools, etc.)	(15)	(17)	(15)	(17)	(16)	(20)	(15)	(12)	(12)	(14)	(13)
Utilities	9	8	7	8	10	10	11	11	14	14	12
Highways, streets, dams, and conservation facilities, etc.	13	16	17	18	20	17	16	11	11	9	8
Other (sewer systems, water-supply facilities, military construction, etc.)	9	6	6	6	4	2	2	3	9	8	8

Source: U.S., Department of Commerce, Bureau of Census, C-30 Series (Construction), *Value of New Construction Put in Place* (Washington, D.C.: Government Printing Office, 1978).
[a]Not all columns add up to 100 percent because of rounding.

growth to 1.9 percent per annum. Since the average rate of neutral technological change in the American industrial sector tends to be approximately 2 percent, the potential underestimate of Lespeyres growth may be of a startling order of magnitude.

Some Implications for Public Policy

The analysis presented above suggests that construction is not a technologically stagnant sector of the American economy, but one characterized by continuous and large-scale change. The changes occur in the composition of total construction output among general types of structures, the characteristics of particular structures within a general type, and the technological processes of production (including new materials, tools, and methods of production). Yet these changes, generally of a socially beneficial nature, surprisingly result in low measured rates of advance in labor productivity and actual decreases in capital productivity. In part, the declining productivity of capital appears to result from the increasingly specialized nature of construction goods, which limits the productivity of the existing capital stock in construction when the pattern of construction demand undergoes continuous change. In part, and perhaps in the main, it also reflects changes in output structure omitted from the quality-adjusted Paasche indicator.

These propositions have several implications for public policy in the United States. First, many of the perceived economic problems of construction arise not from technological stagnation, but from a too rapid rate of change in output and technology. Public policy might appropriately be directed at attaining a more stable rate of change in the industry and at helping business and labor to adjust to the actual rate of change.

Second, public initiatives to promote even more rapid economic change in construction, in the mistaken belief that the industry is technologically stagnant, are likely to be counterproductive to a substantial degree. Rather than promote higher productivity in construction, such policies may increase capital consumption and lower capital productivity, without correspondingly increasing output per man-hour. For example, the attempt of the Department of Housing and Urban Development in 1969 to 1973 to initiate major technological advances in residential construction through the so-called Operation Breakthrough is seen in light of our analysis to have been ill-advised at best, and its failure to have been largely predictable in advance.[7] In large part, the failure of Breakthrough occurred because the program's sponsors, misled by productivity statistics, underestimated the vitality and technological sophistication of the existing residential construction industry.

Third, the rapid expansion and construction of various branches of construction activity in the United States have unfortunate consequences for economic stability. Rapid variations in output composition and technology create bottlenecks in the supply of various types of materials, labor, and machinery, with consequent inflationary pressures.[8] Through the mechanism of independent product and labor markets, bottlenecks in construction frequently have an inflationary impact not only on construction but also on wages and prices generally.[9] This mechanism suggests that society has an interest in regulating the pattern of construction demand in order to minimize the economic losses sustained through unnecessary shortfalls in construction employment, construction capital productivity, and inflation. Instead of attempting to stimulate or suppress construction activity in general, specific incentives might be used to assure that output and technological transformation in construction occur in the smoothest way possible. This may entail a significant research commitment to the study and detailed forecasting of future construction requirements. If such efforts enhance productivity and help control inflation, they will be well worth their cost.

Notes

1. Robert J. Gordon, "$45 Billion of U.S. Private Investment Has Been Mislaid," *American Economic Review* 59 (June 1969):221-238; Robert J. Gordon, "A New View of Real Investment in Structures, 1919-1966," *Review of Economics and Statistics* 50 (November 1968):417-428; Douglas C. Dacy, "Productivity and Price Trends in Construction since 1947," *Review of Economics and Statistics* 47 (November 1965):406-411.

2. Strictly speaking, structural change can only be described as a component of growth when the production frontiers move outward in the activity space, owing to an increase in factor utilization or factor productivity.

In figure N-1, although a structural change occurs when the production point shifts from A to B along a specific production frontier, production potential is in no way augmented. A movement from A to B' is more ambiguous. If the structural change is correlated with real income, then it is certainly growth related, but this of course is not a necessary causal relationship. The clearest case of structural growth is exhibited by the transition from A to B'', because it is associated with q_2, augmenting technological change. As the marginal rate of transformation $\Delta q_2/\Delta q_1$ rises, the relative price of q_2 falls, inducing the movement from A to B''. Even in this case, other autonomous factors could be at work. For didactic purposes, however, we shall employ the term *structural growth* for the latter two cases, excluding the first, always assuming that the reader understands that some part of structural growth may really reflect only a change in the configuration of the social preference field, unrelated to the process of economic development.

3. The interested reader wishing to familiarize himself with index number theory is directed to R.G.D. Allen, *Index Numbers in Theory and Practice* (Chicago: Aldine, 1975).

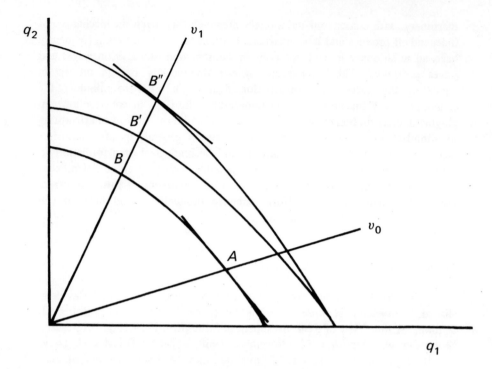

Figure N-1.

4. Throughout this chapter we shall use the notion of marginal transformation rates instead of prices to emphasize the objective aspect of index number measurement.

5. The E.H. Boeckh index of residential construction and the Turner Construction Company building cost index are two important private sources that calculate quality growth. The Bureau of Public Roads also publishes a quality-adjusted series for highway construction.

6. Peter Cassimatis, *Economics of the Construction Industry* (New York: National Industrial Conference Board, 1969), pp. 80-84.

7. See, for example, various publications of the Department of Housing and Urban Development (HUD) regarding Operation Breakthrough. The Advisory Committee to HUD of the National Academy of Sciences is now completing a detailed evaluation of the experience of the program. Breakthrough may be described as a failure in the sense that it has not resulted in major changes in construction technology, as its supporters had claimed it would do.

8. John T. Dunlop and Daniel Q. Mills, "Manpower in Construction: A Profile of the Industry and Projections to 1975," Paper in *The Report of the*

President's Committee on Urban Housing, Technical Studies, (Washington, D.C.: Government Printing Office, 1968), v. 2.

9. Daniel Q. Mills, *Industrial Relations and Manpower in Construction* (Cambridge, Mass.: MIT Press, 1972), esp. chaps. 3, 10.

Appendix 5A

The principal thesis of this chapter has been that a proper accounting of qualitative and structural change in the American construction industry would reveal that construction is a technologically progressive sector of the economy, rather than a stagnant one. A full empirical verification of this hypothesis unfortunately required resources beyond those at our disposal. However it is worthwhile noting that available data from another economic system support our view that quality improvement in construction capital durables is an important feature of a modern construction sector.

Consider the evidence from the Soviet experience. Table 5A-1 presents data on the Soviet construction capital stock along with capital-output tables. Notice that volumetric, structural, and quality input growth have been quite rapid. The physical volume of the capital stock has increased from 5.4 to 11.3 billion rubles, or at a compound rate of 11.8 percent per annum (the U.S. rate is 7.7 percent). Equally impressive has been the apparent change in the composition of the capital stock. In 1959, specialized machinery and equipment comprised only 5.2 percent of the stock. By 1966, however, the specialized machinery component of total construction capital had risen to 38.6 percent, implying a truly prodigious rate of expansion in excess of 48.7 percent per annum. Judging from the behavior of the transport machinery and equipment category, some of this growth must be attributable to changes in nomenclature. Even if we supposed, however, that transport machinery and equipment grew at the average capital rate and subtracted that estimate (3,606) from the 1966 specialized machinery and equipment value, specialized equipment would still be increasing at a 19.1 percent rate and would constitute 8 percent of the stock.

Given all the perplexities that surround the use of Soviet capital stock data as a norm for appraising the underlying process of construction growth in the United States, we are loathe to press these findings too hard. It does seem clear, and eminently plausible, however, that Soviet capital stock data support the proposition that the development of the Soviet construction industry has been structurally, and perhaps quality, growth intensive. This impression is buttressed by intermediate input evidence demonstrating a strong trend away from lumber towards other types of construction materials.[a] Moreover, recalling that both the capital and labor productivity trends in construction are nearly identical in America and the Soviet Union, it may not be too implausible to suppose that the trend toward substituting specialized for less specialized machinery and equip-

Table 5A-1
The Soviet Construction of Capital Stock

Capital Type	Capital Output Coefficients (Rubles of Capital per Ruble of Gross Output) Year		Capital Stock in the USSR (In Millions of Rubles) Year	
	1959	1966	1959	1966
1. Total capital	0.1868	0.2730	5,456	11,838
2. Buildings and structures	0.0692	0.0872	2,020	3,780
3. Power machinery and equipment	0.0076	0.0035	223	153
4. General machinery and equipment	0.0356	0.0537	1,038	2,329
5. Specialized machinery and equipment	0.0097	0.1054	283	4,569
6. Transportation machinery and equipment	0.0569	0.0161	1,662	696
7. Other machinery and equipment	0.0078	0.0071	230	310

Sources: Vladimir Treml, *The Structure of the Soviet Economy: Analysis and Reconstruction of the 1966 Input-Output Table* (New York: Praeger, 1972), pp. 465, 509; and Vladimir Treml, "New Soviet Interindustry Data" in U.S., Congress, Joint Economic Committee, *Soviet Economic Performance: 1966-67* (Washington, D.C.: Government Printing Office, May 1968), pp. 146-148.

Definitions

Buildings and structures: Buildings and structures, including all auxiliary and all fixed heating and sanitation equipment.

Power machinery and equipment: Stationary prime movers, including turbines, boiler equipment, electrical generators, and all electrical systems.

General machinery and equipment: (a) Metalworking machinery and equipment, including tools and forging-pressing equipment, (b) pumps and compressors, (c) measuring and control instruments, (d) hoisting, lifting, and conveyor machinery and equipment.

Specialized machinery and equipment: Specialized machine tools, machinery and equipment.

Transportation machinery and equipment: Transportation and draft machinery and equipment including tractors, railroad rolling stock, road construction equipment, and trucks.

Other capital: Cattle (productive herd) and other.

ment is an important aspect of the growth process in the U.S. construction sector. If this supposition is correct, it not only illuminates recent developments in the American construction industry but also suggests that other cross-systematic comparisons may be useful, insofar as technology rather than social systematic factors govern industrial activity.

[a]See D. Chudnovskii, I. Schapiro, and S. Baranova, "Nekotorye metodicheskie voprosy issledovania stroitel'stva v mezhotraslevom balanse," *Vestnik Statistiki* 6 (1971):14-23.

6 Cyclical Fluctuations in Residential Construction and Financing

Kenneth T. Rosen

Residential construction is a vital sector of the national economy, accounting for 5 percent of the GNP, 30 percent of fixed investment, and 3 percent of the national labor force. Housing, the product of the residential construction industry, is the single most important item in the average household's bundle of goods and services and capital assets.

The extreme cyclical volatility of new home construction is a pervasive characteristic of the industry. Because of this, residential construction plays an important role in efforts to stabilize the national economy. It has become the balance wheel, tempering excess demand during periods of expansion, and often leading the economy-wide recovery from recession.

These periodic cyclical declines in new housing construction are not, however, without cost to society. They produce widespread shutdowns, as much as a 25 percent decline in production and employment in the building industry, a swelling of the unemployment rolls, and idle plant and capital equipment in a number of related industries. They also create sharp rises in the inventory of unsold homes and building related products.

In addition to the short-run macroeconomic impacts, cyclical instability has long-term consequences for the efficiency of the home-building industry itself. In adapting to instability, the industry is forced to use a technology that may be inefficient at any particular time. It is forced to adopt a flexible technology that may be efficient over a wide range of outputs but inefficient at any particular output level. Capital and labor resources are less specialized than in a more stable environment. Start-up and shutdown costs, which often involve bankruptcy, may be substantial. Sharp declines in activity increase inventory holding costs throughout the housing production system. While it is difficult to quantify these costs, it can clearly be said that the short-run housing cycle increases the cost of housing production and in turn increases the prices consumers pay for housing services.

The realization that the housing cycle is costly to both the industry and to society has stimulated substantial research into the nature and causes of the short cycle in housing construction. Most of the research has been conducted since 1960 and represents a distinct break from the previous concentration of study on the long cycle.[1] The major findings of this research attribute these short-run fluctuations to the overwhelming dependency of housing on mortgage credit and to deficiencies in the housing finance system that provides mortgage credit. Grebler and Maisel, in a study for the Commission on Money and Credit, summarize their review of previous analyses, "While these analyses differ on matters of emphasis and detail they agree in the conclusion that short-run fluctuations in residential building have resulted mainly from changes in financial conditions labeled borrowing, availability of mortgage funds, and supply of mortgage credit."[2]

The conventional wisdom regarding the primary cause of fluctuations in housing construction is best summarized in a statement from a study undertaken by the Federal Reserve Board: "There is general agreement that one of the primary, if not the primary, determinant of this cyclical pattern is the similar pattern that holds with respect to a critical input in the residential construction process: the supply of mortgage credit."[3]

Nearly all the recent research emphasizes the role of the supply of mortgage credit rather than the price of mortgage credit. Emphasizing availability rather than price reflects the view that the mortgage interest rate is an inadequate indicator of the state of the mortgage markets. This implies that the supply of mortgage funds does not generally equal the demand for mortgage funds at the market interest rate. This rationing or disequilibrium characteristic of the mortgage market is responsible for the difficulty in obtaining mortgages during periods of financial restraint. During these periods, many households are not able to obtain any mortgage at the quoted interest rate. During these periods, rationing techniques are employed, such as requiring very large downpayments or limiting loans to large depositors of long-standing.

The research emphasis on the characteristic disequilibrium of the mortgage market has, in turn, led to a primarily institutional explanation for short-run housing cycles. Basic defects in the housing finance system are generally used as the major explanation for the rationing phenomena and the housing cycle. The poor portfolio balance of the major mortgage lenders (savings and loan banks); state usury ceilings on mortgage interest rates; Regulation Q, which places interest rate ceilings on accounts at thrift institutions and commercial banks; and Federal Housing Administration (FHA) and Veterans Administration (VA) ceilings on mortgage interest rates are all usually cited.

These studies have also recognized the influence of the cost of mortgage funds on the housing cycle. Housing and mortgage demand have traditionally been viewed as the most interest sensitive sector of the economy. Thus, although the mortgage rate may not clear the market, its movements do influence demand and, in turn, affect the cycle.

The mortgage availability and, to a lesser extent, mortgage cost explanations of the short-run housing cycle have had a major influence on public policy toward housing markets. Since 1968, the federal government has made a substantial attempt to moderate the fluctuations in new residential construction.

A number of governmental and quasi-governmental mechanisms have been devised in an effort to moderate the volatility of the housing industry. The Federal National Mortgage Association, the Federal Home Loan Bank Board, the Federal Home Loan Mortgage Corporation, and the Government National Mortgage Association play a major role in protecting housing from the periodic episodes of general financial restraint. While the specific techniques vary, these agencies and organizations all work through the mortgage market in their attempt to stabilize housing construction. Since they accept the explanation based on supply of credit for the cycle, they attempt to stabilize the flow of funds to the mortgage market. Whether or not this attempt by the federal government to fashion a sector-specific macroeconomic policy has been successful is the subject of this chapter. First, however, the connection between fluctuations in residential construction and the housing finance system must be analyzed, as well as the relationship between the housing finance system and governmental intermediaries.

Residential Construction Cycles

Since World War II, activity in new residential construction has undergone seven short-term cycles, occurring approximately every three and one-half years.[4] The average decline (or rise) in activity, as measured by percentage change in new housing from peak to trough (or vice versa), has been approximately 40 percent. Table 6-1 provides a tabular analysis of the seven postwar short-term cycles in housing construction. A peak in a cycle is a quarter in which the seasonally adjusted number of housing starts was greater than in the two quarters on either side of it. A trough is a quarter in which the number of housing starts was less than in the two quarters on either side. The data in table 6-1 indicate that the present decline in housing construction, while more severe than previous drops, merely continues the well-known pattern of economic instability in the building industry.

Additional information can be gained by examining the cycle of starts in the single-family and multifamily sector. Looking first at the total amplitude (peak to trough change) of the cycle, multifamily cycles have an amplitude that is a little more than twice that of single-family cycles. The single-family cycle, while not as severe, tends to be a little more than twice as long as the multifamily cycle. In terms of the timing of the cycle, single-family starts show more rapid expansions and contractions, while the multifamily sector contraction tends to be far more intense. The sharper contractions in the multifamily sector are due to inventory accumulation and the longer production period, which results in a sharp cutback in starts or production and in a relatively slow recovery in activity.

A number of other industries reflect the periodic declines in new housing

Table 6-1
Short-Term Cycles in New Residential Construction

Turning Point Dates	All Housing Starts in Number of Units (000)[a]	Percentage Change[b]	Average Percentage Change Quarter to Quarter
1953:3 Trough	1235		
		+32.4	+6.48
1954:4 Peak	1732		
		−49.9	−3.84
1958:1 Trough	1074		
		+41.4	+13.8
1958:4 Peak	1647		
		−51.9	−6.49
1960:4 Trough	987		
		+48.3	+3.22
1963:3 Peak	1676		
		−17.3	−4.33
1964:3 Trough	1422		
		+18.7	+3.74
1965:4 Peak	1735		
		−68.3	−15.8
1966:4 Trough	910		
		+53.3	+6.66
1968:4 Peak	1602		
		−18.3	−4.58
1969:4 Trough	1346		
		+57.4	+6.38
1972:1 Peak	2430		
		−83.9	−6.45
1975:2 Trough	994		

	Total Magnitude	Average Percentage Change Quarter to Quarter	Duration
Average peak to trough	−47.4	−6.9	7.7 quarters
Average trough to peak	+39.9	+6.7	7.5 quarters

Source: Kenneth Rosen, "Preliminary Measures of Cyclical and Seasonal Fluctuations in Residential Construction," Harvard-MIT Joint Center for Urban Studies, Paper no. 18 (Cambridge, Mass.: 1973).

[a]Excluding mobile homes. Seasonally adjusted annual rate.

[b]Adjusted for time trend before computing percentage change. Percentage change = change in starts/(Peak + Trough)/2.

activity. In particular, the output of nearly all building materials fluctuates in a similar direction. Both output and prices of materials tend to fall during contractions and rise during expansions of housing activity. The material output and price turning points often lag several quarters behind housing-start turning points, and the material output series all tend to fluctuate less than housing activity. This smaller fluctuation is a result of inventory accumulation, diversification of markets, and the nature of the material distribution system. In addition to fluctuations in the output of building materials, there is also a cyclical fluctuation in the use of labor, the other major input to the construction process. Over the course of a residential building cycle, unemployment rates in the construction industry show substantial volatility. The exact relationship between the housing cycle and construction unemployment depends not only on the magnitude of the change in housing activity but also on the level of nonresidential construction activity and the state of the general economy. These alternative sources of employment can mitigate the impact of the housing cycle on the industry's work force.

The relationship between the housing cycle and the cycle of general economy-wide activity is not clear. Conventional wisdom attributes remarkable contracyclical characteristics to the housing industry. Housing is normally thought to be most active when the economy is weak and is said to be weak when the economy is strong. A closer examination of this hypothesis reveals that housing is not quite the balance wheel that it is assumed to be. It appears rather to be a leading indicator of economic activity because of its greater sensitivity to monetary policy changes, preceding rather than counterbalancing general economy-wide slowdowns and booms. Figure 6-1 illustrates this lead relationship between housing starts and general economic activity. Housing starts are plotted against the GNPGAP, a measure of economic activity that shows the difference between potential and actual GNP. Housing starts appear to lead changes in the GNPGAP by several quarters.

Sources of Mortgage Credit

The residential mortgage loan provides the prime source of financing for the housing market. A mortgage loan represents funds borrowed by the purchaser of a parcel of real estate in order to cover a portion of the purchase price of the real estate. In return for extending the loan, the mortgage lender receives a pledge of an interest in the particular property purchased, as collateral for the loan. In addition, the lender receives a schedule for the payment of interest and the repayment of the principal value of the loan. Nearly all residential mortgage loans made today are fully amortized. This means that the entire interest and principal amounts of the loan are paid off in installments (usually monthly) over time, with the entire debt discharged by the time of debt maturity. This fully amortized residential mortgage loan is of relatively recent vintage. While there was some use of this type of mortgage prior to the 1930s (especially by savings and loan associations), widespread use of the fully amortized residential mortgage loan is primarily a postdepression phenomenon. In the 1920s, only 15 percent of home mortgages were fully amortized, with about half of home mortgage loans partially amortized.[5] The remainder of nonamortized loans were due and payable in a lump sum at the time of maturity. In practice, however, nonamortized loans were automatically refinanced and repayment of the principal could be delayed indefinitely.

The housing or mortgage finance system has undergone three major changes over the past seventy-five years. First, a large increase has occurred in the use of debt financing for the purchase of new and existing housing. Second, the housing finance system has become largely institutionalized, with financial intermediaries rather than households extending the vast majority of loans.

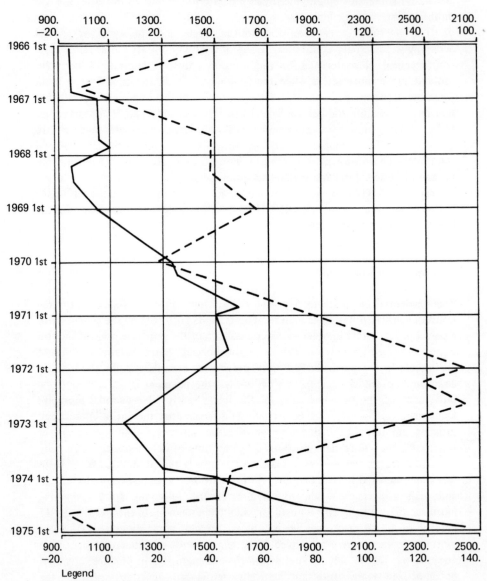

Figure 6-1. Relationship of Housing Starts to General Economy Activity

Third, what was once a largely private system of lending has been transformed into a system where the federal government plays an integral and essential role, both through the indirect insurance of loans and through direct loans and advances of government agencies.

Debt financing is central to the housing market because of the high capital costs and the extreme durability of the housing product. A house has a fairly long, useful economic life, and as a result, the services a housing unit provides in any one year are small compared to the total services the unit provides in its entire economic life. This in turn causes the total asset value (or cost) of the unit to be large in comparison to both the annual flow of services from the unit and the household's annual income. The household, therefore, must rely heavily on borrowing to purchase housing.

The reliance on mortgage borrowing for the acquisition of housing has increased substantially. In 1915, the average American household borrowed only about half the value of its dwelling unit. Since then, a long-term decline in the use of equity financing has taken place, so that at the present time 75-80 percent of the cost of the housing unit is financed through a mortgage loan. This secular increase in the use of mortgage debt is probably the result of two factors. First, consumer and lender attitudes toward the assumption of all types of debt have changed considerably; there has been widespread acceptance of the borrowing philosophy for the purchase of goods and services desired now and affordable only in the future. This has been especially true for durable goods like housing. Second, through the FHA and VA mortgage insurance and assistance programs the government has encouraged the use of borrowing to purchase housing. The low (and at times, as in the case of the VA, negligible) downpayment requirements of these government plans have influenced not only the recipients of these loans but also the remainder of the mortgage market as well. These demand and supply forces have increased the use of debt financing in home purchases.

The second major alteration in the housing finance system has been the virtually total institutionalization of the provision of mortgage loans. In the early 1900s, nearly half of all mortgage loans were provided by the noninstitutionalized segment of the market, representing primarily individual households. By 1974, however, only 2.4 percent of outstanding residential mortgages were provided by the household sector. Today financial intermediaries—savings banks, commercial banks, and life insurance companies—provide the great bulk of mortgage financing. (See table 6-2 for the distribution of mortgage funds by sector.) This trend toward institutionalization is not confined to the mortgage market; on the contrary, it is primarily because of the tremendous increase in the institutionalization of all personal savings that the financial intermediaries have become so large a component of the mortgage market.

Several additional factors also account for the increasingly important role of financial intermediaries. The FHA and VA insurance and assistance programs have facilitated intermediary participation, as have standardized mortgage

Table 6-2
Percentage Distribution of Nonfarm Residential Mortgage Debt
Outstanding, by Type of Holder

	Noninstitutional[a]	Savings and Loan Assns.	Mutual Savings Banks	Commercial Banks	Life Insurance Companies	Sponsored Credit Agencies[b]	Other[c]
1905	45.5	12.7	23.4	8.3	7.2	–	2.9
1915	37.0	18.3	23.5	9.4	8.7	–	3.1
1925	37.5	23.2	17.6	10.8	8.2	–	2.7
1935	31.4	14.9	17.9	10.0	9.9	–	15.9
1945	32.0	20.9	13.7	13.8	14.7	–	4.9
1955	10.0	34.0	12.6	17.1	20.0	–	6.3
1965	5.5	44.2	14.1	14.3	13.9	1.2	6.8
1970	4.6	44.6	13.3	15.1	9.5	5.7	7.2
1974	7.5	41.0	11.3	15.0	7.8	6.3	6 9
1975	7.3	42.1	10.8	14.0	7.0	6.3	8.2
1976	7.3	43.7	11.4	15.9	6.0	6.4	9.3

Source: 1905-1945 data from Leo Grebler, David Blank, and Louis Winnick, *Capital Formation in Residential Real Estate* (Princeton, N.J.: Princeton University Press, 1956), pp. 472-474. 1955-1977 data from Federal Reserve System, *Flow of Funds Accounts,* various issues, 1955-1977, Federal Reserve Board.
[a]Individual households account for the bulk of noninstitutional mortgage holdings.
[b]Includes Government National Mortgage Associations.
[c]Includes holdings of the U.S. government (especially the Home Owner's Loan Corporation during and after the depression), state and local governments, credit unions, private pension funds, finance companies, and real estate investment trusts.

lending criteria, mortgage insurance, and improved marketability of the mortgage. Greater participation by institutions has been facilitated by the gradual liberalization of legal and institutional restrictions on the portfolios of intermediaries, and this has had an especially large impact on the role of commercial banks and life insurance companies in the mortgage market.

The savings and loan associations dominate the residential finance market. Since the early 1900s, they have experienced an astounding growth. They have quadrupled their share of the mortgage market so that by 1974 they held nearly half of all outstanding residential mortgages This rapid growth in the savings and loan share of the mortgage market is primarily the result of their ability to attract a major portion of personal savings. Their total assets grew from $8.7 billion in 1945 to over $295 billion in 1974. During the postwar period until 1965, these associations were clearly the most rapidly expanding financial intermediary, undergoing nearly uninterrupted double digit growth rates. Since 1965, the savings and loan associations have experienced slower growth rates, with especially poor performance during the credit crunches of 1966, 1969, and 1974.

Since savings and loan associations specialize almost exclusively in residential real estate loans, most of their large increment of savings deposits was channeled in that direction. The portfolios of the savings and loan are highly regulated, with over 75 percent of their assets restricted to the provision of real estate credit. The remainder of their portfolio is held primarily in government securities and demand deposits and currency. These instruments provide the savings and loan associations with needed liquidity.

The mortgage holdings of these banks are primarily nongovernment insured conventional loans, with an average life of about twelve years, reflecting prepayment and the refinancing of mortgage loans.

On the liability side, the savings and loan associations hold primarily personal savings deposits, with the remainder of their liabilities representing advances (loans) from the Federal Home Loan Bank Board. Until about 1969, the majority of these savings were in passbook accounts, but since then savings and loan associations have tried to lengthen the maturity of their liabilities They have attempted to lock in longer maturity deposits, thereby reducing cash management problems by offering higher yielding certificates of deposit. In 1975, over half of all deposits were in certificate accounts. Nine percent of savings and loan association deposits were in accounts with maturities of four years or more, nearly 20 percent were in two-year to four-year maturity accounts, and only 43 percent were in regular passbook accounts.

This attempt to lengthen the liability maturity structure is of major importance to the viability of savings and loan associations and to their role as the prime mortgage lending institution. The major problem they have faced over the past ten years has been a result of portfolio imbalance; that is, borrowing "short" and lending "long." When the normal yield relationships (with short-term rates lower than long-term rates) invert, the savings and loan associations face substantial cash flow and liquidity difficulties. This process, known as disintermediation, presents a major problem for savings and loan associations during periods of tight money. By attempting to lengthen the maturity of their liabilities, these institutions hope to achieve a better matching of their assets and liabilities and so reduce the difficulties that the frequent yield curve inversions of the past ten years have caused.

In addition to the regulation of their asset and liability structures, the ceiling interest rates that associations can pay on passbook accounts and on certificates of deposits are set under the provisions of Regulation Q. Actual interest rates paid are set by the market except when they reach Regulation Q ceilings. The Regulation Q ceiling interest rate provisions were initially applied to savings and loan associations during the liquidity crisis of 1966. It was hoped that by forcing a uniform rate differential between their services and those of commercial banks, the outflow of funds from savings and loan associations would be stemmed, and mortgage lending would be encouraged. These controls were meant to be a temporary emergency measure, but have now become a seemingly permanent feature of the market. These controls have achieved a major portion of their initial purpose of preventing interest rate competition from other banks. They have, however, failed to solve the problem of fund outflows because of their inability to control all competitive interest rates. During the past two periods of tight credit, open capital market rates rose substantially above the Regulation Q ceilings, and this led to the disintermediation or outflow of funds from savings and loan associations. This, in turn, led to a scarcity of mortgage funds and a sharp curtailment of mortgage lending.

Mutual savings banks make up the second set of institutions traditionally specializing in mortgage lending. In the early 1900s, mutual savings banks were the largest institutional holder of residential mortgages. Since that time, however, their share of the mortgage market has declined dramatically. At present they hold about 11 percent of outstanding residential mortgages. This reduction in market share has not been a result of decreased specialization in the residential mortgage market; to the contrary, as table 6-3 indicates mutual savings banks have become increasingly specialized in the residential mortgage market. The share of mutual savings bank assets invested in mortgages has risen continually except for the depression and World War II periods. At present nearly 60 percent of their assets are invested in residential mortgages, up sharply from the one quarter to one third of their portfolios allocated to residential mortgages in the early portions of this century.

Savings banks have declined in importance in the mortgage market because of the regional shift in population growth away from geographic areas in which mutual savings banks have traditionally been concentrated. Mutual savings banks cluster in New England and the Middle Atlantic States, but since much of the population growth and housing stock growth in the past fifty years has been concentrated in the South and the West, the ability of these banks to attract savings and to find opportunities for mortgage investment has diminished in relation to more geographically dispersed financial intermediaries.

Mutual savings banks are less constrained by regulation than are savings and loan associations. In most cases, their portfolio allocations are determined by management decisions rather than government regulation. This increased portfolio flexibility allows them to take advantage of market opportunities and to achieve a more balanced matching of assets and liabilities. On the liability side, mutual savings banks face Regulation Q provisions on ceiling interest rates by type of account similar to those faced by savings and loan associations. For this reason, mutual savings banks face similar period disintermediation crises.

The commercial banking system provides the third major source of mortgage funds. The historic share of commercial bank participation in the mortgage market has doubled since the early 1900s. By 1974, the commercial banking system held the second largest portfolio of mortgages, with their $81.9 billion of mortgage assets comprising nearly 18 percent of all outstanding residential mortgages. As shown in table 6-3, commercial banks now allocate over 10 percent of their portfolio to residential mortgages as compared with only 2 to 4 percent in the pre-World War II period. This portfolio diversification has in turn been attributed to a gradual lifting of previous federal and state restrictions on

Table 6-3
Assets of Financial Intermediaries: Total Assets and
Residential Nonfarm Mortgage Assets

	Savings and Loan Associations	Mutual Savings Banks	Life Insurance Companies	Commercial Banks
Residential Nonfarm Mortgages (dollars in billions)				
1905	.448	.882	.254	.293
1915	1.098	1.41	.522	.566
1925	3.994	3.03	1.408	1.846
1935	3.301	3.98	2.20	2.051
1945	6.076	3.387	3.706	3.395
1955	30.614	15.568	21.213	15.888
1965	102.35	40.09	38.4	32.387
1974	225.60	62.2	42.4	81.9
1975	249.50	63.8	41.2	83.1
1976	289.30	67.4	35.5	94.3
Total Assets (dollars in billions)				
1905		3.08	2.71	15.53
1915		4.41	5.19	27.39
1925	4.628	8.02	11.54	57.47
1935		11.17	23.22	52.34
1945	8.747	16.962	43.946	142.408
1955	37.656	31.346	87.856	185.025
1965	129.58	58.232	154.089	336.354
1974	295.616	109.55	255.0	796.3
1975	338.2	121.1	279.7	832.0
1976	392.0	134.8	310.9	910.0
Percentage of Assets in Residential Nonfarm Mortgages				
1905		26.6	1.1	9.4
1915		32.1	2.1	10.1
1925	86.4	37.8	3.2	12.2
1935		35.7	3.9	9.5
1945	69.5	19.9	2.1	8.1
1955	81.3	49.7	8.6	24.1
1965	79.0	68.8	9.6	24.9
1974	76.3	56.8	10.4	16.1
1975	73.8	52.7	14.7	10.0
1976	73.8	50.0	11.35	10.3

Source: 1905-1945: Leo Grebler, David Blank, and Louis Winnick, *Capital Formation in Residential Real Estate* (Princeton, N.J.: Princeton University Press, NBER, 1956), pp. 481-485.
1955-1976: Federal Reserve System, *Flow of Funds Accounts.*
1905-1935: from Raymond W. Goldsmith, *A Study of Savings in the United States* (Princeton, N.J.: Princeton University Press, 1955), I.

bank lending to the real estate market. In terms of present regulations other than reserve requirements, commercial banks are able to allocate their assets in accordance with prudent management goals. The interest rates they are allowed to pay on accounts of various maturities and size, however, are limited under the provisions of Regulation Q. Commercial banks presently are restricted to a ceiling interest rate on passbook accounts which is .25 percent below the ceiling rate on savings and loan association and mutual savings bank accounts. This differential is partially meant to compensate thrift institutions for restrictions on the liabilities they can offer (no demand deposits) and the assets they can hold. Nevertheless, despite this interest rate differential, commercial banks appear to have the most viable long-run potential as a financial intermediary and as a mortgage lender, because of the lack of restrictions on their asset and liability structure.

The life insurance companies make up the fourth major source of residential mortgage loans. Over the long run, life insurance companies have a role that has varied in importance. Their share of outstanding residential mortgage loans has risen from 7 percent at the beginning of the century to over 20 percent at the peak in the mid-1950s. Since then, their share of the residential mortgage market has dropped dramatically, so that they now hold only 5 percent of the outstanding loans. This represents their lowest relative share in the residential mortgage market in this century. The long-term variation in their market share has been the result of variations in the rate of asset growth and dramatic shifts in the allocation of their asset portfolio. After World War II, life insurance companies moved their assets into the mortgage market, and residential mortgage-holding expanded from 10 percent to nearly 25 percent of their assets—largely because of the acquisition of a large portion of the VA and FHA mortgages that originated during the postwar housing boom. Since the mid-1960s, however, the interest rate on mortgages has fallen in relation to other assets, and the life insurance companies have virtually ended home mortgage loans Instead, they have confined their lending to the multifamily residential sector and to investment in commercial mortgage loans. These changes are reflected in the sharp decline in their overall residential mortgage market share and in the proportion of their portfolios allocated to residential mortgages. This portfolio shift has been accentuated by the decline in their asset expansion relative to other financial intermediaries. This is primarily the result of the explosion in the asset growth of private pension funds, which provide a partial substitute for savings held in life insurance policies. The net effect of these changes is that life insurance companies are no longer one of the major forces in the residential mortgage market. In fact, while their assets increased $110 billion in the past ten years, their residential mortgage holdings only increased by $4 billion.

The final set of institutions that play a substantial role in the residential mortgage market are the government or quasi-government sponsored agencies. The Federal National Mortgage Association, the Government National Mortgage Association, and the Federal Home Loan Mortgage Corporation have rapidly expanded their share of mortgage holding since the mid-1960s. In 1974, they held nearly 10 percent of home mortgages outstanding. The role of these agencies in the housing finance system will be dealt with in greater detail in a later section of this chapter.

What are the implications of this institutionalization of the mortgage market? The expanded role of financial intermediaries in the provision of mortgage credit means that the mortgage markets are now closely tied to the general capital market, with increased sensitivity to general capital market conditions and to variations in monetary policy. By replacing a primarily noninstitutional personalized lending system with a highly institutionalized profit-sensitive system, the mortgage markets have gained better access to the nation's capital markets, but have sacrificed some of their previous isolation from the impacts of general financial restraints.

The Mortgage Credit-Housing Cycle Nexus

Most of the literature on short-run fluctuations in residential construction suggests that variations in monetary policy, aimed at restoring economy-wide stability, tend to destabilize the housing sector. These variations in aggregate financial restraint are translated through the housing finance system into instability in the availability of mortgage credit and into changes in the price and other parameters of the mortgage instrument. The influence of these supply and demand effects of changes in the supply of mortgage credit are then indirectly transmitted to the housing market.

Restrictive financial policies also affect the housing market through their impact on the actions of the home builder. Changing financial conditions influence the builder not only through fluctuations in demand but also through variation in the cost (and availability) of construction loans. These loans are the equivalent of working capital for nonbuilding firms. The cost of construction loans is usually tied directly to the prime lending rate and consequently reflects variations in monetary policy.

Supply of Funds

The cyclical instability of mortgage fund flows results from two portfolio choices. The first concerns the way individuals allocate their personal savings among various financial intermediaries and other assets; the second concerns the portfolio composition of the financial intermediaries themselves.

Individuals and households place their savings where they perceive the greatest benefits. They weigh the relative yield, risk, liquidity, and expected capital gains of various assets. Changes in any of these characteristics or in household preference can lead to a change in portfolio allocation. Over the course of a typical financial cycle of credit restraint and credit ease, these characteristics shift in their relationship to each other. While all of these parameters change over the normal cycle, variations in relative yields are of foremost importance. During periods of credit restraint, the yields offered by financial intermediaries—because of their portfolio composition (with a fairly large concentration of long-term assets induced in some cases by legal portfolio restrictions) or because of Regulation Q interest rate ceilings—fall in relation to open market (especially short-term) credit instruments. This is particularly true of savings and loan associations' passbook accounts. Savings and loan associations, as an outcome of historical precedent and government regulation, borrow short and lend long, attracting funds through deposits made by households and acquiring long-term assets in the form of mortgages. When the monetary authority pursues a restrictive policy, the savings and loan associations are left in a less competitive position in the general capital market, and household savings move to other intermediaries.

Figure 6-2 clearly illustrates that this disintermediation is primarily induced by changes in relative yields among asset types. It shows the relationship between savings flows to savings and loan associations and the differential between the interest rate paid on savings and loan passbook deposits and ninety-one-day U.S. government treasury bills. The inverse relationship can be further quantified using econometric techniques. A regression equation developed by the author and presented below shows the strong relationship between the interest rate differential and savings flows to savings and loan associations. Every increase of 1 percent (100 basis points) in this spread reduces savings flows to the savings and loan associations by $4.76 billion on an annual basis. The equation also shows that the differential ceiling rates between savings and loan banks and commercial banks has a positive impact on savings flows to the former, and that the flow of personal savings and of household financial wealth affects the flows of funds to the associations. Finally, the civilian unemployment rate is also directly related to the level of savings flows, reflecting the impact of consumer uncertainty which increases savings rates during periods of high unemployment.

$$
\begin{aligned}
\text{Savings Flows} = \ & -5909.6 + 1965.67 \, (\text{SLRATE} - \text{Commercial rate}) \\
& \quad (8.53.4)^* \quad (790.52) \\[6pt]
& -1163.33 \, (\text{Treasury bill rate} - \text{SLRATE}) \\
& \quad (152.33) \\[6pt]
& +465.63 \, (\text{Unemployment rate}) \\
& \quad (154.8) \\[6pt]
& +25.42 \, (\text{Personal savings}) \\
& \quad (13.35) \\[6pt]
& +1512.93 \, (\text{Financial wealth of households}) \\
& \quad (371.10)
\end{aligned}
$$

1962:3 to 1973:4   Standard error of the regression = 564 million

$R^2 = .95$ Durbin Watson Statistic (a measure of autocorrelation)
                   = 1.83

*(standard error)

Cyclical instability in the flow of funds is not unique to savings and loan associations. Flows to nearly all financial intermediaries that compete for household personal savings on a noncontractual basis have instability of a similar magnitude. Table 6-4A shows the standard deviation (as a percent of mean) of flows of funds to six intermediaries. While this measure is somewhat deficient as an indicator of instability because of probable time trends in the value of the mean, it does show that savings and loan associations, mutual savings banks, and commercial banks experience large instability in fund flows in relation to other intermediaries that have a contractual source of funds, such as life insurance companies and pension funds. Thus the intermediaries that compete with open market instruments are subject to fairly large fluctuations in fund flows. This is caused by an "inability to compete" resulting from legal restrictions and legally induced portfolio imbalances.

The cyclical instability of the flow of personal savings is the main cause of instability in mortgage lending. Institutions like savings and loan associations have little choice in terms of portfolio composition. Since they are restricted primarily to the residential real estate markets, a decline in fund flows leads quickly to a decline in mortgage lending. Such declines are somewhat mitigated by the ability to draw on liquid reserves, Federal Home Loan Bank Board advances (loans), and on the flow of repayments from outstanding mortgages. This mitigating effect is clear from the data presented in table 6-4B. Savings and loan mortgage lending is less cyclically unstable than the flow of funds to these institutions.

Other institutions have considerably more options. Mutual savings banks, life insurance companies, and commercial banks have a fair amount of portfolio flexibility over the course of a cycle, although flexibility does not necessarily work to the advantage of the housing and mortgage markets. It is generally recognized that, during periods of rising interest rates, mortgage interest rates rise less than rates on comparable assets. This is usually attributed to state usury laws, FHA-VA restrictions on interest rates, and rising business competition for funds. As a result, mortgages become less attractive investments. Financial institutions applying profit-maximizing criteria will shift from mortgages to other assets. This second portfolio shift, by intermediaries away from mortgages, compounds the problem of households directing personal savings flows away from the mortgage-creating intermediaries.

Characteristics of the Mortgage Instrument

In addition to the influence of the supply of mortgage credit on housing activity, changes in the terms of the mortgage instrument have substantial indirect effects

Savings (billions $) Spread (%)

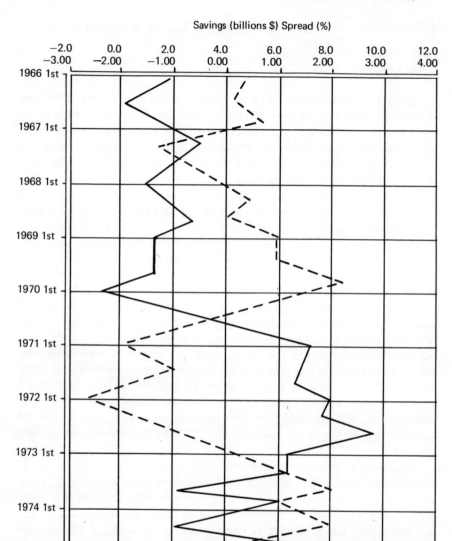

Figure 6-2. Relationship between Savings Flows to Savings and Loan Associations and Interest Rate Differential

Table 6-4a
Cyclical Instability of Flows to Financial Intermediaries

	Standard Deviation as Percent of Mean[a]
Savings and loans	80.30
Mutual savings banks	72.98
Life insurance companies	38.32
Commercial banks–time deposits	104.59
Private pension funds	37.93
State and local retirement funds	62.12

Table 6-4b
Cyclical Instability of Mortgage Lending by Financial Intermediaries

	Standard Deviation as Percent of Mean[a]
Savings and loans	55.98
Mutual savings banks	30.49
Life insurance companies	24.10
Private pension funds	76.8
State and local pension funds	68.0

Source: Kenneth T. Rosen, "The Role of Pension Funds in Housing Finance," Harvard-MIT Joint Center for Urban Studies, Paper no. 35 (Cambridge, Mass.: June 1975).

[a]Standard Deviation is the usual measure of dispersion used in the literature. For series with a substantial time trend it is a somewhat distorted measure of volatility.

on residential construction. These aspects of the mortgage instrument are important: the contract interest rate, the amount of the loan (which, in combination with the price of the house, determines the downpayment requirement), and the amortization period of the loan. These simultaneously determine and are determined by the supply of and the demand for mortgage funds and houses.

1. Variations in the mortgage interest rate have traditionally been considered one of the prime short-term determinants of new housing activity. Short-run increases in mortgage interest rates reduce the demand for mortgages and the number of housing starts.[6] There are several channels, however, through which mortgage interest might affect the demand for and the supply of housing starts. One effect occurs through a change in the real mortgage interest rate (after adjusting for expected inflation), which would be expected to have a negative impact on activity. A second works through the impact on monthly payments. Even if the real mortgage rate remains unchanged, a higher nominal rate raises mortgage payments immediately and would be expected to reduce the demand for starts. A third effect could be the result of an expectations phenomenon: when mortgage interest rates rise, households might postpone a housing purchase in the expectation of lower mortgage rates in the future. A

final effect would be on supply; higher rates might increase the availability of mortgage credit and thus increase housing starts. The supply effect, however, depends on the relative interest rate on mortgages. As a result of all the institutional factors mentioned earlier, the relative mortgage interest rate (the difference between the mortgage rate and the bond rate) declines when interest rates rise. Thus the supply effect associated with rising mortgage interest rates is also likely to be negative. The net impact of these supply and demand effects as estimated in econometric models is substantial. The estimate of the short-run elasticity of housing starts to changes in the mortgage interest rate averages −1.5. This implies that a 10 percent increase in mortgage rates will cause a 15 percent decline in housing starts.

In the long run, however, changes in mortgage interest rates do not appear to be inevitably associated with particular levels of housing activity. Mortgage interest rates have shown wide fluctuations, falling during the first half of the twentieth century, and then rising dramatically to their present peak levels. Table 6-5 illustrates these long-run variations. There appear to be no long-run correlations between these long-term fluctuations in mortgage interest rates and housing starts.

2. The downpayment requirement is the second mortgage parameter that strongly influences short-run fluctuations in housing activity. Changes in the requirements may affect the demand for housing starts in several ways. One can distinguish between an initial downpayment effect and a monthly payments effect on the demand side of the market. These two partial effects would be expected to work in opposite directions. The total demand impact of a change in downpayment requirements would thus be the sum of the two partial effects.

The initial downpayment effect depresses housing activity. Higher downpayments may eliminate families with little wealth from purchasing a house or might force them to purchase a lower-priced home. This, of course, assumes that we have an imperfect capital market in which the individual often cannot borrow more than a certain amount of funds against his future income to increase his initial equity. The monthly payment effect works the opposite way. A higher downpayment, would reduce the size of the monthly payments, and would tend to increase the number of housing starts.

A change in downpayment requirements alters the supply of mortgage credit because of the impact on the risk of default. Everything else being equal, lower downpayment requirements increase the risks of the lender, reduce his supply of mortgage loans, and thus decrease housing starts.

Together these effects result in a fairly strong inverse relationship between changes in downpayment requirements and housing starts. The short-run elasticity of housing starts with respect to the downpayment is estimated at around −2.3. This means that a 10 percent decrease in downpayment requirements will stimulate a 23 percent increase in housing starts. This elasticity results from lenders using the downpayment requirement as the mechanism with which they ration credit during periods of financial restraint.

Table 6-5
Mortgage Terms

	Downpayment (% of Purchase Price)	Contract Interest Rates (Savings & Loans)	Savings & Loan Assn.	Commercial Bank
1915	53	–	–	–
1925	35	6.9	10.9	3.1
1935	42	6.2	11.9	9.8
1945	19	5.1	14.3	9.3
1965	23	5.8	25.3	20.5
1974	21	8.7	27.5	26.3
1975		8.89	27.8	
1976		8.83	28.1	
1977		8.77	28.4	
1978		9.093p	28.7p	

Source: 1915-1945 from Leo Grebler, David Blank, and Louis Winnick, *Capital Formation in Residential Real Estate* (Princeton, N.J.: Princeton University Press, 1965), pp. 228, 234, 455.
     1965, 1974 from Federal Home Loan Bank Board, *Federal Bank Board Journal.*
ppreliminary

Over the long run, the impact of variations in downpayment requirements are less clear. The data in table 6-5 indicate that a dramatic decline in downpayment requirements has occurred since the beginning of the century. This change has probably increased the ability of the average household to become a homeowner and in turn has probably had a positive impact on overall construction activity.

3. The final mortgage parameter, amortization period of the mortgage loan, would *a priori* be expected to have a direct relation to housing activity. Longer amortization periods lead to lower monthly payments, although increasing the total payments (principal and interest) over the life of the loan. There is little econometric evidence concerning the short-run impact of changing amortization periods on housing starts. Over the course of the century, there has been a dramatic increase in the average contract term of the mortgage. In 1925, the average loan contract was three to eleven years, depending on amortization provisions. In 1974, the average contract term of a fully amortized mortgage loan was twenty-five to thirty years. This lengthened amortization period has probably had a strong positive impact on housing activity.

Countercyclical Mortgage Assistance Policies

Public policy toward cyclical instability in residential construction is based on the premise that the cyclical instability in mortgage lending is the cause of fluctuating housing activity.[7] As a result, stabilizing the flow of mortgage credit to the housing market appears to have become a major goal of federal housing policy since the mid-1960s. The establishment of the Federal Home Loan Mortgage Corporation, the reorganization of the Federal National Mortgage Association, and the new aggressiveness of the Federal Home Loan Bank Board, can all be viewed as at least partial attempts to insulate the mortgage and housing markets from a general financial restraint. The activities of these agencies have also led to an increased federalization of the private housing finance system. The federal government has become an integral part of the mortgage credit and housing production system.

Federal Home Loan Bank Board

In 1932, the Congress established the Federal Home Loan Bank (FHLB) system to oversee the actions of the federal savings and loan associations. It became the first government-sponsored intermediary for residential mortgages. The FHLB system, similar to the Federal Reserve system, has twelve home loan banks and districts presided over by a board, the Federal Home Loan Bank Board (FHLBB). The FHLBB has the power to regulate capital requirements (which, in the past several years, have fluctuated between 5 and 7 percent of savings deposits) and asset structures of the savings and loan associations. More important, it has the power to advance funds to the savings and loan associations. These advances are financed by the sale of securities on the open capital market. The establishment of the FHLB system has largely eradicated regional barriers to savings flows. By means of its provision of advances it has served as a credit reservoir and as a supply of short-run cash to the savings and loan associations.

During the 1930s, 5 to 8 percent of outstanding mortgages were funded by the FHLBB, and at times, the FHLBB would provide up to 18 percent of the additions to mortgages outstanding. This activity reached a peak just after World War II, and then fell steadily until a marked resurgence in the middle and late 1960s. There is no clear indication, however, that any effort was made before 1968 to provide direction to moderate cyclical behavior in the housing market. On the contrary, an examination of the data indicates that the provision of advances was highly correlated with the availability of other savings funds. The interest rate charged on advances was tied to the cost of funds to the FHLBB, and this was consequently an expensive source of funds for the savings and loan associations. When savings flows improved, the savings and loan associations traditionally used the new funds to repay their borrowing before expanding their mortgage lending. The FHLBB actions, therefore, seem to have been essentially passive. Some simple correlation studies show a general cocyclical movement (with respect to housing starts) of advances through the early and mid 1960s- a movement inconsistent with any goal of stabilizing housing—although on several occasions there had been efforts to restrict or ease the policy on advances. In the period since 1968, the countercyclical mandate of the FHLBB has been strengthened, and the new policy tries to encourage the savings and loan associations to borrow from the FHLBB to support their mortgage lending. Under this new policy, some loans by the FHLBB to savings and loan associations carried fixed interest and penalties for prepayments.

These policy changes seemed to produce a new aggressiveness at the Federal Home Loan Bank Board. In 1969, the board extended over $4 billion in credit and supported over 40 percent of its members' increases in mortgages. This can be contrasted to the debacle of 1966, when the FHLBB appeared to have exacerbated the housing crunch by allowing outstanding advances to decrease, showing the limited ability of the system to have a stabilizing effect on the housing market.

Federal National Mortgage Association

The National Housing Act of 1934 allowed the creation of institutions that would support FHA-insured mortgages (Title III). In February 1938, the Federal National Mortgage Association (FNMA) was created. FNMA, originally a government agency included in the federal budget and now a quasi-private corporation, has the power to purchase FHA- and VA-insured mortgages and, since 1970, the power to purchase conventional mortgage loans not backed by the government. Although FNMA is an independent corporation which acquires capital in the established markets and is no longer bound by the constraints of the federal budgetary process, it is still viewed as a quasi-governmental agency with some public policy objectives. FNMA has traditionally had a general over-the-counter program, but in May 1969, it adopted a forward mortgage commitment program allowing for deliveries of mortgages up to eighteen months after purchase. It no longer purchases at posted prices but conducts a biweekly auction, similar to the Fed's weekly Treasury bill auctions. Mortgage lenders bid for these funds by offering mortgages to FNMA at yields specified by the lenders. FNMA takes the highest yields offered and agrees to purchase the mortgages at a specified future date with lenders required to pay a small commitment fee. The supply of funds is inelastic (relatively fixed), and the market demand determines the equilibrium price. The scope of its recent operations has been impressive: FNMA's portfolio grew from $6.5 billion in May 1961, to $14.1 billion in July 1970, and to $25 billion as of January 1975. In 1970, it financed one quarter of the nation's housing starts, and floated $13 billion in new issues, second only to the U.S. Treasury.

While FNMA was initially designed to play an important role only after others had left the mortgage market, the magnitude of its activity has made it an integral element of the system.

Since its severance from the government, FNMA has had several, perhaps conflicting, targets. First, it is charged with improving the liquidity of the mortgage markets through the provision of a secondary market facility. While FNMA does not provide a "true" secondary market, since it only acquires mortgages originated within the past year, it does provide mortgage lenders substantial additional liquidity. This secondary market facility is closely related to its second purpose, to improve the ability of the mortgage and housing market to cope with cyclical instability. By providing advance commitments, FNMA can provide the necessary flow of funds and the requisite planning horizon to enable mortgage lenders to originate mortgages even though their traditional source of funds may have been curtailed. This procedure would appear *a priori* to have a potential stabilizing impact on the flow of mortgages. Finally, FNMA's third goal is to make profits for those owners and lenders who purchase its securities. In times of high interest rates, a portfolio of relatively low interest mortgages may cause some tension within the organization as it attempts to meet its separate goals. Conflicts can also arise between it, the other agencies that are still part of the federal system and are concerned with housing, and the Federal Reserve System, since the goal of stabilizing mortgage lending and housing starts can also be viewed as a charge to offset the actions of the Federal Reserve System in so far as they impinge upon the housing and mortgage markets.

Government National Mortgage Association

In addition to reorganizing and changing the status of the Federal National Mortgage Association, the Housing Act of 1968 authorized the creation of another public intermediary, still included in the federal budget: the Government National Mortgage Association (GNMA). GNMA was established primarily to provide subsidized support for low-income and moderate-income housing by providing mortgages at below market interest rates. Recently the government has also used GNMA as a countercyclical device. GNMA can purchase the mortgages at face value from the lender and then resell them to FNMA at the going market price, subsidizing only the difference between the two prices, an option known as the FNMA-GNMA tandem plan. In addition, GNMA has attempted to improve the long-run attractiveness of the mortgage market by issuing mortgage-backed securities, in hopes of attracting less traditional souuces of mortgage funds to the housing market. The most popular GNMA security is the "pass-through" certificate. Under this plan, GNMA guarantees the holder of the pass-through certificate both the principal and interest due each month on the mortgage pool, (the GNMA certificate really represents a share in a pool of FHA-VA insured mortgages), whether or not it is actually received by the manager of the pool. Thus the GNMA certificate is backed by the full faith and credit of the U.S. government.

Federal Home Loan Mortgage Corporation

A fourth intermediary, the Federal Home Loan Mortgage Corporation (FHLMC) was created by the Emergency Home Finance Act of 1970 primarily to provide support in the secondary mortgage market for conventional mortgages not backed by the government. FHLMC, like FNMA, finances its acquisitions through the sale of its own securities in the capital market, rather than issuing general federal debt. In terms of acquisitions, it can either purchase the mortgages outright or it can set the yield it wishes to receive and then purchase an interest in a pool of mortgages. This latter action can be made particularly attractive to the savings and loan associations if FHLMC sets its desired return below the average return of the pool. In 1977, FHLMC purchased $4.1 billion in conventional mortgages.

Linkages with Private Markets

The establishment of the intermediaries, FHLBB, FNMA, FHLMC, and to some extent GNMA, can be viewed as attempts to direct capital from the general capital markets toward the savings and loan associations and other mortgage-creating institutions in an effort to ameliorate the capital drain when households go elsewhere with their money. (Figure 6-3 depicts these processes.) The intermediaries have been given a variety of instruments to attract capital including overt subsidization and covert subsidization in the form of federal guarantees.

What are the specific links between these intermediaries and the housing mortgage markets? The FHLBB, reacting to conditions in the housing and mortgage markets, makes advances to the savings and loan associations, which can then expand their holdings of mortgages in excess of their inflow of savings deposits. These advances can be viewed, roughly, as borrowed reserves and, consequently, they are considered as liabilities by the savings and loan associations. The advances are financed by the sale of FHLBB securities in the open market.

The savings and loan associations and other intermediaries can also acquire liquidity by selling their holdings of mortgages and using the funds to acquire new mortgages. This can be achieved in a variety of ways. FNMA can purchase FHA-VA mortgages or conventional mortgages from the savings and loan associations and other intermediaries, financing the purchase through the sale of its own securities in the open market. GNMA can purchase mortgages of federally subsidized housing, financed through the sale of its securities to the U.S. Treasury. Recently GNMA was also authorized to purchase nonsubsidized mortgages at below market interest rates. FHLMC can also purchase conventional mortgages from savings and loan associations.

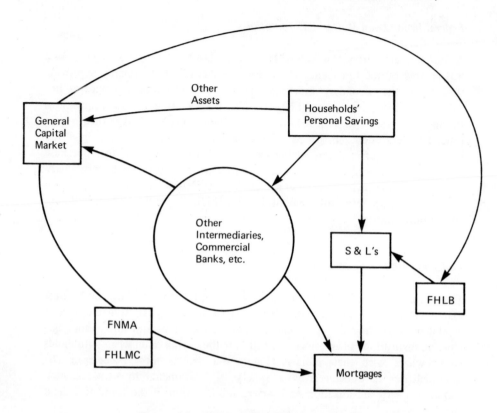

Figure 6-3. The Supply of Mortgage Funds

The intermediaries can attract a wide range of investors by issuing a variety of different securities. These can be characterized in two ways: securities of the intermediary itself and securities based on pools of mortgages. GNMA guarantees pass-through securities, and FHLMC can also issue mortgage backed securities.

Thus these organizations have two direct links to the capital markets: first through issuing their own direct obligation bonds and second through their provision of mortgage backed securities available to private and quasi-private investors. An indirect link is provided through the mechanism of selling securities to the U.S. Treasury or of borrowing directly from it, although neither mechanism has been important in the past.

Evaluating Mortgage Assistance Policies

With the link between the government intermediaries and the mortgage market delineated, it is possible to evaluate the impact of the government mortgage assistance policies on the cyclical problem. We will confine the analysis to an evaluation of the effectiveness of the countercyclical activities of the Federal National Mortgage Association and the Federal Home Loan Bank Board, since those of the Government National Mortgage Association and the Federal Home Loan Mortgage Corporation are too recent in origin to provide an adequate quantitative assessment of their efforts.

If FNMA and FHLBB do attempt to serve as a stabilizing influence in the housing and mortgage markets, two aspects of their activity must be assessed: (1) the extent to which their reactions to market events are correct in a countercyclical sense, and (2) the overall effectiveness of their activities in moderating fluctuations in mortgage lending and in residential construction activity. Several econometric models of the housing and mortgage markets, which include the actions of these two intermediaries, have been constructed by the author. The models estimate housing starts, mortgage flows, purchases of FNMA and advances of FHLBB, savings flows to thrift institutions, and open market interest rates.[8]

In their response to housing and mortgage market events, FNMA and FHLBB appear to have reacted (at least since 1968) in a strongly countercyclical fashion. With respect to savings flows to thrift institutions, the usual leading indicator of housing and mortgage market activity, both agencies again appear strongly countercyclical. When individual savers disintermediate, transferring their funds from thrift institutions to other assets and intermediaries, FNMA and FHLBB have tried to divert funds from the general capital market back to these mortgage-creating institutions. Since 1968, as shown in table 6-6, the activities of both agencies have been correct in a countercyclical sense, that is, these organizations have increased mortgage acquisitions (for FNMA) or advances made (for FHLBB) during trough periods in housing activity, and decreased them during periods of peak activity in the housing market. Prior to 1968, the activities of these agencies were not clearly countercyclical and in some cases were procyclical.

If FNMA and FHLBB have been reacting to market events in a strongly countercyclical way, it is reasonable to ask why their activities have not been strong enough to offset substantially the periodic credit crunches on the housing and mortgage markets. What limits the impact of their apparently correct reactions to market events?

The limited effectiveness of their activities stems from a number of sources. First, the nature of the institutional relationship of FNMA and FHLBB to the mortgage market limits their ability to influence the market. Both depend on lender initiative in making use of advances or the secondary mortgage market. Savings and loan associations cannot be forced to demand advances (even though quantitative and rate policies may encourage their use), and cannot be forced to use advances for mortgage purposes (as opposed to general liquidity purposes).

Table 6-6
Actions of FNMA and FHLBB Near Peak or Trough Periods

Turning Point Date in Housing	FNMA Seasonally Adjusted Change in Net[a] Acquisitions of Mortgages by Quarter					Characterization of Actions[b]
1965:4 Peak	157	171	380	773	786	Incorrect
1966:4 Trough	786	600	473	390	383	Incorrect
1968:4 Peak	732	231	271	613	723	Correct
1969:4 Trough	793	1113	1578	1699	1514	Correct
1972:1 Peak	1459	686	977	857	786	Correct
1975:1 Trough	2165	1348	578			
FHLBB						
1965:4 Peak	422	76	−18	429	717	Correct
1966:4 Trough	717	235	−417	−1089	−1178	Incorrect
1968:4 Peak	412	−119	−14	786	943	Correct
1969:4 Trough	943	878	1027	1264	356	Correct
1972:1 Peak	−249	−66	−630	−165	−144	Correct
1975:1 Trough	2178	779	−1959			

[a]Figures shown for turning point and two quarters on either side of turning point in housing starts. The turning point is underlined.

[b]For FNMA a correct stabilization policy would be to increase the rate of mortgage acquisition during trough periods, and decrease them during peak periods. For FHLBB, advances outstanding should be increased during trough periods and decreased during a peak period if a correct stabilization policy is implemented.

In the same way, FNMA cannot force lenders to sell mortgages, even though quantitative and rate policies can encourage such sales. Both FNMA and FHLBB can only react to events in the market, and to some extent, they are limited in their active ability to influence the market.

In addition to the problem of lender initiative, there is also an organizational constraint on the countercyclical activities of both FNMA and FHLBB. FNMA is a profit-making company, and it cannot be expected to sacrifice profitability completely to meet public policy objectives. During periods of cyclical tightness, FNMA faces the same problem of yield differential confronted by savings and loan associations. To some extent, FNMA has attempted to counteract this problem by lengthening the average life of its corporate debt, but this does not alter the fact that FNMA's first goal is, of necessity, profitability. The FHLBB system, while not a profit-making organization, is influenced by a somewhat similar imperative: it must remain solvent. This limits the extent to which advances below borrowing costs can be made.

The unequal regional distribution of secondary mortgage market activity points out a third difficulty of the present system. Table 6-7 shows FNMA purchases as a percentage of FHA mortgage originations, by census regions. The data clearly indicate that after standardizing for the volume of activity, the Northeast, especially the New England region, is aided very little by FNMA activities. The South, on the other hand, is clearly aided most. This regional imbalance is probably attributable to two factors—one related to market forces and the other to institutional structures. The Northeast, under usual conditions, is a capital surplus area, with mortgage interest rates 1 to 1.5 percent lower than the rest of the country. Since FNMA allocates purchases on the basis of an auction system, those mortgages offering the highest yield will be accepted first. Normally, this would be considered an equitable procedure, since interest rates should reflect the need for funds. In times of cyclical tightness, however, the price of funds does not necessarily reflect the need for mortgage funds. Credit rationing and usury limitations both make interest rates an unreliable indicator of mortgage activity.

The second probable reason for the unequal regional allocation of FNMA funds stems from the institutional structure of the mortgage market in the Northeast. In this region, savings and loan associations and mutual savings banks are the predominant mortgage lenders. Since FNMA does most of its business with mortgage bankers (individuals or firms that originate but generally do not hold mortgages) and not thrift institutions, the neglect of this region may be partially explained by this institutional structure.

The most important limitation on FNMA and FHLBB activity, however, relates to the general equilibrium (or feedback) impact of their activities. Both FNMA and FHLBB influence not only the supply and price of mortgages but also the cost of funds in the general capital market through their borrowing activities. Their issuing of debt to finance mortgage purchases would tend to increase overall market interest rates, and thus it would contribute to the marginal disintermediation problem. This, in turn, would decrease their impact on the mortgage market by reducing private mortgage availability. The net impact of any injection of funds on the availability of mortgages thus depends on the response of market interest rates to incremental borrowing and on the response to changes in free market interest rates of the flow of household savings to thrift institutions. In addition, the injections of resources into the construction sector might intensify inflationary pressures, and thus they exert further upward pressure on interest rate levels.

The sum of these general equilibrium effects can be estimated using simulation techniques with a version of the econometric model mentioned previously. This simulation shows the estimated net impact of a hypothetical attempt by the FNMA and FHLBB to stabilize the flow of funds to the mortgage market. The dollar level of response by FNMA and FHLBB is determined in the simulation by the mortgage funds required to meet the short-fall in housing activity from a target level (determined by demographic

Table 6-7
FNMA Purchases as a Percentage of FHA Mortgage Obligationsa

Census Regions, 1971		
West	19.0%	
Pacific		16.8%
Mountain		24.8%
North Central	16.7%	
West North Central		13.3%
East North Central		17.6%
South	25.7%	
South Atlantic		23.0%
East South Central		31.1%
West South Central		26.6%
Northeast	6.6%	
New England		0.2%
Middle Atlantic		8.7%
U.S. Average	19.0%	

aThis procedure thus standardizes for the volume of FHA activity in each area. As a result, comparing the figures in the various regions provides an indication of FNMA participation in those areas.

requirements). The required stabilization response of FNMA and FHLBB involves the sale of mortgages or repayment of advances during periods of excess activity (1972) as well as the acquisition of mortgages or the making of advances during periods of depressed activity (1966-67 1969-70).

The net impact of these agencies on mortgage supply in the simulation (based on actual historical parameter estimates of FNMA and FHLBB in each equation) appears to be substantially less than their gross injection of mortgage funds. Their net impact, in terms of increasing mortgage funds, appears to be less than a third of their gross mortgage fund provision. This is the result primarily of the adverse impact of their borrowings on open market interest rates and thus on the flow of private savings to thrift institutions. The impact of even this small net increment in mortgage funds on housing starts is further diluted by the adverse direct influence of interest rates on housing starts. The combination of these indirect supply and demand effects offsets a major portion of the impacts of FNMA and FHLBB. Thus while FNMA and FHLBB are clearly countercyclical in their activities, both institutional and market limitations on their effect greatly reduce their ability to moderate cyclical fluctuations in residential construction.

Alternative Ways to Stabilize Homebuilding through Mortgage Credit

The relative ineffectiveness of the present mechanisms and the increasing severity of the cyclical problem have given rise to various proposals to stabilize the mortgage and housing market. Three major suggestions-(1) adopting a variable interest rate mortgage instrument; (2) eliminating Regulation Q interest rate ceilings and diversifying thrift institution asset and liability structures; and (3) greater participation of pension funds in mortgage lending—will be briefly analyzed.

1. A variable rate mortgage, rather than the present fixed interest rate for the life of a mortgage, would allow periodic (usually every six months) adjustments in the interest rate to reflect changes in general capital market interest rates. The interest rate on such a mortgage could be set by negotiation between the borrower and the lender or could be tied to some general market interest rate. These interest rates could in turn be reflected in changes in the borrower's monthly payment or in changes in the maturity of the mortgage loan (number of mortgage payments required to pay off the loan).

Such an instrument would presumably allow mortgage rates to adjust more rapidly to changes in overall market interest rates. This, in turn, would allow the mortgage market to clear by means of price changes rather than credit rationing. Since the return on the outstanding portfolio of mortgage holdings of lenders would adjust to changing open market rates, the risk of capital gains and losses on such a portfolio would be substantially reduced. (Of course, this risk would have been transferred from the lender to the borrower.) As a result of these impacts, proponents of the variable rate mortgage allege that there would be a substantial moderation in cyclical fluctuations in the mortgage and housing markets.

There are, however, several serious flaws in the arguments of advocates of the variable rate. First, they have ignored the crucial influence of a more flexible mortgage interest rate on the demand for housing and mortgages. Since there is a fairly high demand elasticity for housing starts with respect to mortgage interest rates, the greater variance of mortgage rates in the variable rate world might increase cyclical instability. Second, since mortgage interest rates on existing as well as new homes would be flexible, the demand for *the entire* housing stock would be subject to fluctuations. The impact of this stock effect on the stability of new starts is hard to estimate, but it surely would be substantial. Third, other long-term investments would also become variable rate instruments if widespread use of a variable rate mortgage became common. Thus the initial advantage to the mortgage supply, while still positive, would be substantially reduced. Finally, the foreign experience with similar variable rate mortgages has not been successful in reducing fluctuations in housing activity.

2. The second proposal for moderating the housing cycle is the elimination of Regulation Q interest rate ceilings, thus allowing thrift institutions substantially greater freedom in their asset and portfolio choices. The essence of this strategy revolves around the belief that by removing the Regulation Q ceilings thrift institutions would diversify their liability and asset portfolios and become less susceptible to the disintermediation process (since they will be in a better position to compete for the savings from households). While such reforms would

certainly benefit thrift institutions, it is unclear that the net effect on the housing market would be positive in either the cyclical or long-run sense. The impact of these proposed changes on the cyclical nature of the market depends on the relative importance of the household portfolio shifts and intermediary portfolio shifts discussed earlier. If savings and loan associations have a better flow of funds during periods of financial restraint but use these funds for high yielding short-term nonmortgage investments, the impact on the cycle will not be positive. In the long run, the effect on housing markets will probably be negative. A shift of savings and loan assets out of mortgages will increase relative mortgage interest rates and thus may reduce the overall demand for housing. The net effect of these proposed reforms on housing and mortgage markets, both in the short and long run, is unclear.

3. A final suggestion for reducing the volatility of the housing and mortgage market involves the use of pension fund reserves. One of the key characteristics of pension plan contributions is the great stability of their net fund flows; if pension funds took a larger role in providing residential mortgage capital, they could perhaps help stabilize the flow of funds to this sector and so moderate cyclical instability in residential construction. While, *a priori*, this would seem to be a reasonable approach to the cyclical problem, the past record of pension fund investments is not encouraging. Pension funds allocate over two-thirds of their assets to common stocks and hold less than 3 percent in residential mortgages. Even this small proportion has declined rapidly since the mid-1960s. This portfolio allocation is due to very strong institutional constraints. As a result, despite their large and dynamic role in the overall capital market, pension funds will continue to play only a minor role in the residential mortgage market.[9]

Conclusion

Housing construction is very sensitive to financial restraint, and this is the ultimate cause of the industry's cyclical instability. Purchases of housing depend on credit, and deficiencies in the financing system inevitably affect the housing market through the impact on the availability and cost of loans to builders and consumers.

Government policy toward cyclical instability has accepted this institutional and credit dependency explanation and so has attempted to stabilize the flow of mortgage funds. By so doing, the government has attempted to insulate housing partly from the financial and real resource allocation impacts of general financial restraints. The Federal National Mortgage Association, the Federal Home Loan Bank Board, the Government National Mortgage Association, and the Federal Home Loan Mortgage Corporation represent efforts to divert general capital market funds to the mortgage and housing markets. Despite the efforts of these organizations, their effectiveness has been limited by institutional and market constraints.

A number of additional policies and solutions have been proposed to solve the cyclical problem. Most of these concentrate on reforms of housing finance institutions. The variable rate mortgage, the elimination of Regulation Q, and other aspects of proposed financial reforms can be viewed in this way. Other suggestions include the increased use of pension fund reserves. All these suggestions, however, suffer from the same problem—a failure to consider the general equilibrium implications of the proposals. As we have shown in the case of FNMA and FHLBB, attempts to allocate real resources indirectly by indirect financial resource allocation are not very effective. The efficiency of U.S. capital markets will invariably offset most of these attempts. In fact, some of the proposals to aid housing, by improving the efficiency of the capital markets will further decrease the effectiveness of attempts to insulate the housing and mortgage markets from general financial restraint. The foreign experience perhaps affords a good perspective on the future of these policies of indirect stabilization. Nearly every non-Communist country appears to experience short-term housing cycles that are at least as severe as those in the United States. These cycles occur despite substantial differences in the systems of housing finance, extent of government involvement in the housing market, extent of government planning, and substantial foreign efforts to moderate the cycle.

Stability in residential construction will require either increased stability in the economy as a whole (and perhaps less reliance on monetary policy as a tool of stabilization) or direct rationing of real and financial resources. Since neither is likely, the cycle in residential construction should be a characteristic of the industry for the foreseeable future.

Notes

1. Long cycles last fifteen to twenty-five years and are attributed to wars, income, immigration, and household formations. See Leo Grebler, David Blank, and Louis Winnick, *Capital Formation in Residential Real Estate* (Princeton, N.J.: Princeton University Press and National Bureau of Economic Research, 1956).

2. Leo Grebler and Sherman Maisel, "Determinants of Residential Construction: A Review of Present Knowledge," *Impacts of Monetary Policy*, Commission on Money and Credit (Englewood Cliffs, N.J.: Prentice-Hall, 1963). See also Irwin Friend, *Study of the Savings and Loan Industry*, 4 vols (Washington, D.C.: Federal Home Loan Bank Board, July 1969).

3. James B. Burnham, "Private Financial Institutions and the Residential Mortgage Cycle, with Particular Reference to the Savings and Loan Industry," in *Ways to Moderate Fluctuations in Housing Construction* (Washington, D.C.:

Federal Reserve Board, 1972), p. 81.

4. By short-term cycle we mean those variations (exclusive of seasonal factors) that occur around long-term trends.

5. Grebler, Blank, and Winnick, *Capital Formation*, p. 231.

6. For a more extended analysis see J. Kearl, K. Rosen, and C. Swan, *Relationships Between the Mortgage Instrument, the Demand for Housing, and Mortgage Credit: A Review of Empirical Studies,* Federal Reserve Bank of Boston, MIT-HUD Alternative Mortgage Study (Boston: September 1975).

7. For a more extended analysis see Kenneth Rosen and James Kearl *A Model of Housing Starts, Mortgage Flows, and the Behavior of the Federal Home Loan Bank Board and the Federal National Mortgage Association,* Harvard-MIT Joint Center for Urban Studies, Paper no. 27 (Cambridge, Mass.: June 1974).

8. For more details on the model used for the evaluation and for the results of the simulations see Rosen and Kearl, *A Model of Housing Starts;* and Kenneth Rosen, "Evaluation of Government Mortgage Assistance Programs."

9. For more information, see Kenneth Rosen, "The Role of Pension Funds in Housing Finance," Harvard-MIT Joint Center for Urban Studies, Paper no. 35 (Cambridge, Mass.: June 1975).

7

Residential Finance: Reforming the Mortgage Instrument

Arthur P. Solomon and
Lynne B. Sagalyn

Over the past decade, the residential construction industry has been plagued by several severe problems—wide swings in building activity, a diminished position in the capital market, and inflation-related fluctuations in the demand for homeownership. The cyclical sensitivity of this sector of the economy has long been recognized and has made housing production a critical instrument of federal stabilization policy. Yet with each successive period of monetary contraction, the cyclical instability has become more acute. Although the thrift institutions that specialize in mortgage lending were designed in the aftermath of the Great Depression to provide additional stability to the mortgage market and to assure a supply of capital to the housing sector, they now lack the flexibility to adjust to a more inflationary and unstable economic environment. In addition, the need for mortgage lenders to include a premium in their interest rate to protect themselves against the effect of inflation on the real value of future repayments has scaled down the total investment in housing in the United States.

The structure of the thrift institutions has been a major cause of these problems. The savings and loan associations and the mutual savings banks, which together hold roughly 60 percent of all outstanding residential mortgages,[1] are required by law, and induced by means of favorable tax incentives, to invest the bulk of their asset portfolios in long-term residential mortgages. Their liabilities, however, are primarily restricted to short-term deposit accounts. Thrift institutions are limited as well in their ability to compete for funds in periods of rising interest rates by the Stevens Act of 1966, which placed a ceiling on the rate offered by thrift institutions (Regulation Q) in an effort to protect them from complete exposure to interest rate risk and the possible financial insolvency that can come from "costly" interest rate wars.[2]

Thrift institutions have a serious imbalance in their asset-liability structure because they obtain most of their funds from short-term highly liquid deposits[3] and use these funds to provide long-term mortgage loans. When interest rates on short-term credit instruments, such as ninety day Treasury bills, increase, the Regulation Q ceiling on deposits and the low yield on older mortgages prevent thrift institutions from competing effectively for funds. Thus the "smart" money flows out of the thrift institutions in order to earn higher yields on alternative investments or loans. The flow of deposits away from thrift institutions has become even more responsive to rate differentials in recent years because financial innovations have produced short-term money market funds and other more attractive investments for individual and institutional savers. This periodic outflow, commonly called disintermediation, produces wide swings in deposit flows and results in sharp fluctuations in the supply of mortgage funds to the residential construction industry. The supply of housing thus becomes the roller coaster of the economy.

Until recently, the problem of cyclical instability within the residential construction sector had been diagnosed as a supply problem—that is, a problem caused by the institutional constraints on the availability and cost of mortgage funds. As such, reform proposals have focused on the restructuring and deregulation of the thrift institutions so that they could compete more effectively for savings deposits and thus stabilize the supply of mortgage credit. Other reform proposals, however, call for alternative mortgage instruments that reflect a growing awareness of the distortions in housing demand that are created by the standard mortgage instrument. These distortions in the demands of mortgage borrowers, a direct result of the standard mortgage instrument itself, will be the focus of this chapter.[4]

The expectation of inflation raises mortgage interest rates by an "inflation premium" which is added to the real interest rate in order to insure the mortgage lender against the erosion of his repayment stream. While the increase in the mortgage interest rate does not change the real cost—the discounted present value[5]—of owning a home, it does affect the borrower's pattern of repayment. The real burden for the average borrower is heaviest during the early years of the mortgage and decreases during the later years. Each succeeding year inflation reduces the value of the fixed monthly payments, with the consequent imbalance in the repayment stream. Since the ability of households to meet these higher payments is constrained by their current income and by the payment-to-income ratio set by the underwriter, any increase in the annual payment during the early years forces some households to forego or defer homeownership or to reduce the quantity or quality of their housing demands.

No single mortgage instrument is able to accommodate all types of borrowers under all economic conditions. The present arrangement, however, offers little flexibility to borrowers to adapt to their own changing housing needs or economic prospects. Thus, there is a distinct need to offer borrowers an opportunity to select a wider range of mortgage instruments, tailored to fit both their present individual financial and household circumstances and their future income expectations.

A number of possible adjustments can be made in the mortgage contract. Most of them involve three credit terms—the interest rate, downpayment, and maturity for amortizing the loan. Alternative mortgages have been designed to package different combinations of credit terms for individual types of borrower with different financial and household requirements. In order to illustrate the need for a more complete set of mortgage instruments, this chapter will examine the suitability of alternative mortgages for three distinct types of borrower:

Profile 1 describes an upwardly mobile young couple about to buy their first house. These borrowers, in their early thirties, earn the median household income and expect their real income to increase over time. Possessing little accumulated wealth with which to purchase a first home, they have few resources, and are highly averse to taking risks.

Profile 2 is of a homeowning household whose head is a blue-collar worker somewhere between thirty-four and fifty-five years of age. The household's real income is close to the median for all households and will keep pace with the rising costs of goods and services since the worker's wages are linked to the consumer price index (CPI). The primary asset held by these borrowers is the equity in their existing home and a small savings account. Similar to the first borrower type, these households have few resources with which to sustain the risk of default.

Profile 3 describes the family of an older worker, nearing retirement, who also owns a home. While households like this one receive an income somewhat above the median, they face a future decline in real income after retirement. Their only source of income thereafter comes from their relatively fixed social security payments or other pensions. With a significant proportion of their assets tied up in their home, households like that of Profile 3 may need to draw on their equity in order to supplement retirement income. With greater assets than either of the other borrower types, they are better able to cope with default risk, but because of the uncertainty of retirement reserves, they are equally averse to default.

In addition to offering diverse borrower groups more choice in the method used to finance their home purchase, the introduction of new mortgage instruments alters the relation between lender and borrower. These alternative mortgage contracts are risk-sharing instruments. They transfer part or all of the risk associated with fluctuating interest rates, graduated mortgage payment streams, or extensions of the amortization period. The form and degree of this risk transfer is critical to the distributional impact of such proposed changes.[6] In general, borrowers are in a less favorable position than financial institutions to bear risk due to their limited ability to assume higher monthly or annual payments, limited ability to project future interest rates, and limited access to additional credit.[7]

Changes in the terms of the mortgage contract have a different impact on the income and wealth requirements of different groups of borrowers. An assessment of who gains and who loses with each of the alternative mortgage instruments is an important policy consideration, and the subject of the sections which follow. First, to provide a basis for comparison, the distributional effects of the existing standard mortgage contract are set forth. Then, a similar analysis is undertaken for the two most important alternatives.[8] The final section summarizes and compares the results for the three borrower profiles and for the lender-borrower relationship.

The Standard Mortgage

The standard mortgage contract in the United States consists of a small number of credit terms—a nominal interest rate that remains constant over the life of the mortgage, a long-term fixed maturity for full amortization of the principal, and a low-to-modest downpayment requirement. The financial burden of homeownership, then, is expressed by the payment-to-income ratio over time (the cash flow or income requirement), the breakdown of the payment between interest and principal (the rate of equity buildup), and the original loan-to-value ratio (the downpayment or initial wealth requirement). For the institutional lender, the rate of return on mortgage loans is determined by the difference between the discounted value of the future mortgage payments and the interest paid on deposits.

It is current practice in mortgage lending to select a nominal interest rate that remains fixed for the economic life of the mortgage. The level payment schedule of the standard mortgage indicates that nominal monthly payments will be the same every month for the life of the mortgage. As table 7-1 illustrates, these payments are allocated between the interest payment and the amortization of the principal; as the mortgage is paid off, equity accumulates at an increasing rate since the outstanding balance, against which the interest has been calculated, is reduced. Institutional rules of thumb generally stipulate that the monthly payment represent no more than 20 or 25 percent of a household's gross income at the time the mortgage is granted.

The Payment-to-Income Ratio: The Cash Flow Requirement

Inflation, or the anticipation of inflation, increases mortgage interest rates by a premium to compensate the lender for the anticipated erosion, in real dollars, of the constant nominal mortgage payments. With the standard fixed-rate, level payment mortgage, the addition of the inflation premium to the real interest rate necessitates higher initial monthly payments for the same level of housing purchased in a noninflationary economy. Since the interest rate on this long-term contract is fixed, the initial monthly payments, in real dollars, are higher than they would be if the rate did not have to take into account inflationary expectations over the full economic life of the mortgage.

In an inflationary economy, these constant payments imply a stream of declining real payments; the greater the rate of inflation, the more rapid the

Table 7-1
Standard Mortgage Payment Schedule
(payment and debiting factor of 3.5%)

Year	Principal at Start of Period	Payment Per Annum	Payment Breakdown		Real Payments in Constant Dollars
			Interest	*Principal*	
1951	$30,000	$2,110	$1,050	$1,060	$2,110
1952	28,939	2,110	1,012	1,097	1,956
1953	27,841	2,110	974	1,136	1,914
1954	26,704	2,110	934	1,176	1,900
1955	25,528	2,110	893	1,217	1,890
1960	19,000	2,110	665	1,445	1,715
1965	11,247	2,110	393	1,717	1,610
1970	2,038	2,110	72	2,038	1,308

decline in the real payment stream (see figure 7-1).[9] For the same $20,000, thirty-year mortgage, assuming a 3 percent real interest rate and a 4 percent inflation rate (7 percent nominal interest rate), annual payments would be $2,300, or 125 percent higher. In these situations, borrowers are obviously unable to buy as much housing as they could in a noninflationary period, or they must do so by allocating a higher percentage of their annual income—even if their income is expected to rise at the same rate as the general price level.

Definite distributional consequences result from adjusting the standard mortgage for inflationary expectations. Higher initial interest rates and a declining real payment stream distort the burden of mortgage payments over time for the borrower. The borrower's real cash burden, measured by the ratio of payment to income, is higher in the early years of the mortgage when compared to the real cash burden in later years. Furthermore, while the borrower must cope with higher nominal payments at the time the mortgage is written, it is only in the future, after a possible lag of several years, that inflation-induced adjustments in salaries and wages yield the higher income with which to make these payments.

The standard mortgage, therefore, works particularly against the needs of the young, upwardly mobile households with little initial wealth but potentially high future income—Profile 1 borrowers. The higher initial cash burden induced by inflationary expectations affects the quantity and quality of housing they can purchase. Whether by choice or institutional underwriting tradition, households that are constrained by current income to a particular monthly payment-income ratio and wish to buy the same amount of housing as in a noninflationary period must do so by making higher downpayments. The higher downpayments must be financed either by accumulated savings, loans or gifts from relatives or by secondary financing. Unfortunately, young households typically have fewer assets and savings than older households or previous homeowners. Also, since the

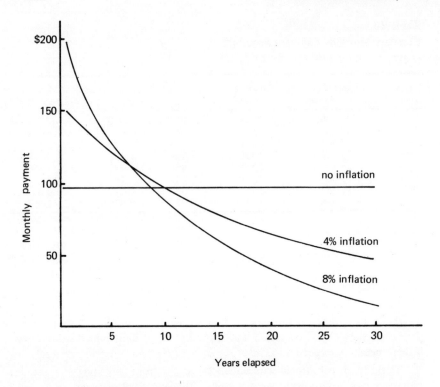

Figure 7-1. Real Value of Monthly Payments on Level-Payment Mortgage—With Different Rates of Inflation ($20,000 Loan, 30 Years)

payment-to-income ratio is set when the mortgage is issued and then frozen into level monthly payments, upwardly mobile young households must settle for less housing than they would be able to afford if their monthly mortgage payments were scheduled in a way that could reflect the upward changes in their income. In practice, institutional lenders seldom are willing to adjust the terms of the mortgage to reflect the life-cycle earnings of younger households.[10]

Even in periods of stable prices, the level payment mortgage is not ideal for young and upwardly mobile households (Profile 1), or for older households nearing retirement (Profile 3). For these the annual cash flow requirement is often at variance with either current or future expected income. This generates an uneven burden of payments over the life of the mortgage. Indeed, the schedule of payments for the fixed standard mortgage coincides only with the life-cycle earnings of Profile 2 borrowers—those households whose future real income is expected to remain constant.[11]

*The Loan-to-Value Ratio: The Initial
Wealth Requirement*

The downpayment requirement on a mortgage loan establishes the borrower's initial equity in his property and the lender's exposure to default risk. With the standard-fixed nominal-rate mortgage, two considerations determine the amount of the downpayment: first, the trade-off between the initial equity investment (the downpayment) and the rate of equity accumulation (the monthly amortization payment); and second, the trade-off between equity and debt financing. Both choices affect the probability of default. In the conventional mortgage market there is a trade-off between the risk of default or foreclosure a lender is willing to take and the rate-of-return required for assuming a given risk. The higher the risk, the greater the return or interest rate the borrower is expected to pay. Given the minimum downpayment or equity investment stipulated by the lending institution, larger downpayments imply lower interest rates.[1,2]

The risk of mortgage default is generally a function of the initial equity investment, the borrower's capacity to repay the mortgage (payment-to-income ratio), and the risk attached to the asset itself (the property value), which is determined by conditions in the local real estate market. While no clear-cut rule determines whether the amount of the downpayment will be 20 or 30 percent of the initial home value, lenders take into account the credit risk, the supply of funds, and the level of demand for mortgages in setting the loan-to-value ratio. It should be noted, moreover, that the downpayment or wealth requirement is an expedient means to ration credit during periods of tight money supply. Since wealth is less evenly distributed than income in the United States, increases in the loan-to-value ratio, the wealth requirement, limit homeownership more than increases in the payment-to-income ratio, the income requirement.

In an inflationary economy, higher initial nominal monthly payments mean higher real payments in the early years of the mortgage. In turn, the higher real payments reduce the real outstanding debt more rapidly than in a noninflationary world and thereby induce a faster accumulation of equity. This rapid equity build-up implies a reduction in default risk. Yet, in an inflationary economy, mortgage lenders do not tend to respond to the accelerated accumulation of equity by lowering the downpayment requirement, since the lender still assumes an interest rate risk from possibly underestimating the inflation premium.

The Maturity or Amortization Period

The standard mortgage establishes a fixed twenty-five-year or thirty-year period for amortizing the loan with constant monthly payments determining the pace of equity build-up. Prior to the enactment of the Federal Housing Administration's (FHA) mortage-insurance programs in the late 1930s, the average maturity on conventional mortgages was eight to nine years. With the protection of the government insurance programs, conventional lenders extended the repayment period. Thus, the existence of FHA insurance enabled cautious lenders to learn about the actual relation between the terms of the mortgage and the actual risk of default.

While the length of the maturity or amortization period is obviously a determinant of default risk, empirical studies indicate that it is not very significant. The most critical years of risk for mortgage default are the first few; thereafter, as the amortization period increases, the risk is only slightly increased, so that the difference in the probability of default between a twenty-five-year or thirty-year mortgage, all else being equal, is not really significant. Although the increased maturity and lower annual income requirements enhance the opportunity for many moderate-income families to become homeowners, it makes the real value of future repayments more difficult to anticipate. Given this uncertainty, the possibility undoubtedly increases that lenders will underestimate the future rate of inflation.

Alternative Mortgage Instruments

All alternative mortgage instruments seek to alleviate the problems of the standard fixed-rate mortgage during inflationary periods—the wide swings in the supply of mortgage funds and construction activity and the tilt in the real value of mortgage payments (higher in the early years, lower in the later years). Although the list of potential nonstandard mortgage instruments is extensive, this chapter can only suggest the potential utility of increasing the range of options available to mortgage borrowers.[13] For illustrative purposes, then, the discussion will focus on two major alternatives: the variable rate mortgage (VRM) and the price-level-adjusted mortgage (PLAM).

The Variable Rate Mortgage

The variable rate mortgage is the most commonly cited alternative mortgage because it is relatively simple and currently in use in several parts of the country.[14] The characteristic feature of the VRM is that the interest rate on the outstanding loan balance is allowed to fluctuate with some specified reference rate. Variable rate mortgages are commonly tied to a *nominal* as opposed to an inflation-adjusted *real* interest rate; for example, the current cost of funds to thrift institutions. The interest rate on the variable rate mortgage is adjusted through one of three approaches: (1) the monthly payment may vary while the loan maturity remains fixed; (2) the monthly payment may remain constant while the loan maturity varies; or (3) changes may be made in both the payment and maturity. As with most alternative mortgage forms, the frequency, magnitude, and timing of mortgage adjustments remains adaptable over the life of the mortgage.

While the VRM provides a means of adjusting to inflationary conditions, the choice of a nominal rather than a real interest rate implies that the reference rate, and therefore the mortgage interest rate, will contain a premium for anticipating inflation. In this respect, it resembles the standard mortgage and does not completely eliminate the "tilting" of the stream of mortgage payments. With a VRM, therefore, the real payment stream may still decline over time. (See figure 7-2.)

The stream of nominal and real payments for a $30,000, thirty-year variable rate mortgage for the period from 1951 to 1970 illustrates this point. The reference rate is the three-to-five-year U.S. government bond rate. In the first year, an interest rate of 3.82 percent applied against the $30,000 principal yields a monthly payment of $180 (and an annual payment of $2,159); $1,146 of this annual amount is applied to interest and $1,013 to equity, which reduces the outstanding loan to $28,987.[15] With a VRM, each change in the reference rate causes a recalculation of the payment schedule in order to amortize the payment of the loan over the fixed term of the mortgage. While the payment stream fluctuates with the nominal reference index, inflation causes real payments to decline over the life of the mortgage.

The Price-Level-Adjusted Mortgage

The essential characteristic of the price-level-adjusted mortgage (PLAM), the second major alternative, is that the principal is adjusted periodically to reflect changes in a real reference index such as the Consumer Price Index (CPI). The interest rate written into the mortgage contract, therefore, is a fixed real interest rate—free of any inflation premium. With every change in the price index, the principal of the loan is revalued and the payment stream is recalculated using the contractual real interest rate. Such adjustments obviate the need to anticipate inflation and thereby eliminate the initial high payments common to both the standard and the variable rate mortgage. In contrast to these mortgage forms, the real value of the PLAM mortgage payments remains constant over the life of the mortgage (figure 7-3).

With a PLAM, for $30,000 loan at 3 percent real interest for twenty years, the first year's payment equals $2,176—$971 for interest and $1,205 for principal or equity accumulation.[16] This equity payment is subtracted from the outstanding balance, which is then recalculated to reflect the change in purchasing power brought on by inflation. At the end of the first year (1952),

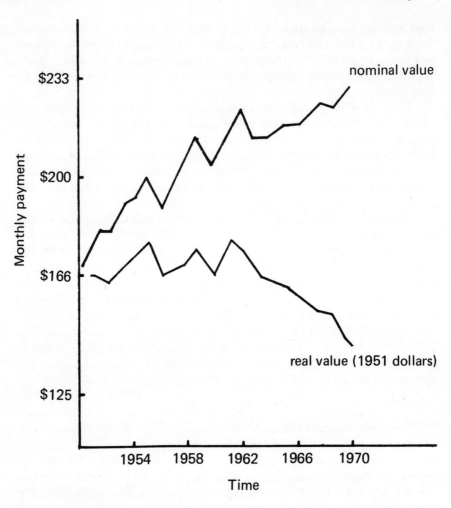

Source: Richard A. Cohn and Stanley Fischer, "Alternative Mortgage Designs" in *New Mortgage Designs for Stable Housing in an Inflationary Environment,* Conference Series no. 14 (Boston: Federal Reserve Bank of Boston, 1975), table 3.

Figure 7-2. Payment Stream For a Variable Rate Mortgage (fixed maturity, variable payments)

the borrower owes $31,168—the principal payment ($1,205) is subtracted from the original outstanding balance ($30,000) and the remaining balance is then adjusted upward ($2,373) to account for the 7.9 percent inflation rate. Because the principal is revalued by the *actual* rate of inflation, the real monthly payment remains constant while the nominal payment changes. The initial real

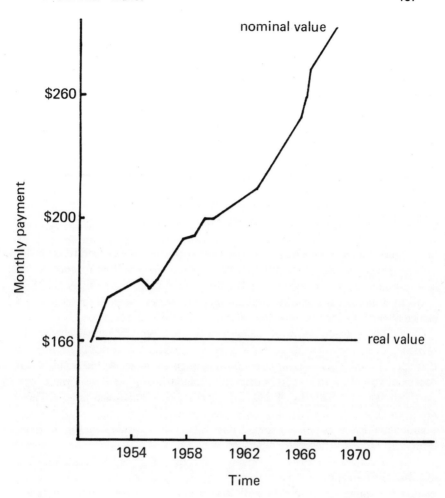

Source: Richard A. Cohn and Stanley Fischer, "Alternative Mortgage Designs" in *New Mortgage Designs for Stable Housing in an Inflationary Environment,* Conference Series no. 14 (Boston: Federal Reserve Bank of Boston, 1975), table 5.

Figure 7-3. Payment Stream for a Price-Level Adjusted Mortgage

payment is less than that of a standard or variable rate mortgage because this mortgage instrument eliminates the inflation premium. After a number of years, however, the real monthly payment on the PLAM exceeds the real payment on the standard mortgage.

The Payment-to-Income Ratio:
Selecting the Reference Index

Each alternative mortgage instrument involves adjustments in the terms of the mortgage contract during the life of the loan. By adjusting either the mortgage interest rate or the balance on the outstanding loan or both to reflect changes in purchasing power due to inflation, each eliminates the need to anticipate future inflation *at the time the mortgage is granted.* Instead, the mortgage is linked to a reference rate that corresponds to inflationary changes. Without the anticipated inflation premium, the borrower may be able to buy the same amount of housing at a lower initial cost than at present, or more housing at the present cost. The most significant benefit is that the real burden of buying a home would be more evenly spread over the economic life of the mortgage.

The timing and degree to which such index-linked mortgages reflect inflationary changes depend upon the choice of the reference rate. For the variable rate mortgage there are two obvious reference indices to consider: a cost-of-funds index, for example, what thrift institutions have to pay for their funds in a competitive market; and an index of wages for urban workers. The choice of the reference rate has important distributional consequences.

Any index based on wage changes will, for example, reflect changes in worker productivity as well as inflation. Since wages have historically risen faster than prices, linking the mortgage terms to such an index would yield a real continuous windfall to lenders. Furthermore, inflation-induced wage gains have not been shared equally by all industrial sectors or occupational groups. These problems notwithstanding, any mortgage pegged to a wage index would discriminate against those borrowers past their prime earning age or on fixed retirement incomes—the group described as Profile 3.

The cost of funds, the other major reference option, is an average measure of what thrift institutions have to pay for their funds in a competitive capital market (assuming the elimination of Regulation Q, which presently limits the competitive interest rate thrift institutions can offer on time and savings deposits). Most suggestions for variable rate mortgages favor such a reference rate. Denominated in nominal rather than real terms, a cost-of-funds index reflects an element of inflationary expectations. This means that the mortgage borrower will experience some uncertainty and risk not present with the standard mortgage, since there is a time lag between the increase in this index (and hence the mortgage payment) and increases in household earnings generated by inflation.

Many specific references would provide either a singular or composite index of the market cost of funds. For example, there are U.S. government securities (the ninety-day U.S. Treasury bill and the three-to-five-year U.S. government bonds), some corporate bonds, the thrift institution's offer rate on deposits, or the composite figures issued by the Federal Home Loan Bank Board. If mortgages are linked to the thrift institution's deposit rate or even to the FHLBB's standard mortgage rate, such reference rates are said to be internal, as opposed to external, indices and thus more beneficial to the lender since they can be subject to direct or indirect influence. In contrast, interest rates on U.S. government securities or on corporate bonds are external indices, not subject to individual or thrift industry influence and are directly determined in a competitive market.

The Payment-to-Income Ratio: Adjusting the Maturity or the Payment Level

With the standard mortgage, the payment stream is constant in nominal dollars over the life of the mortgage. The lending institution bears the entire risk associated with fluctuating rates of inflation that exceed those anticipated at the time a mortgage is granted. A VRM transfers all or some of this interest rate risk to the borrower by adjusting the mortgage repayment schedule. With a PLAM, revaluations in the loan principal resulting from inflation also lead to changes in the nominal monthly payment stream. For the lender, when market interest rates increase, so will the income from the institution's outstanding mortgages. Mortgage reform thereby overcomes the current "lock-in" risk of old loans in which the yield on long-term outstanding mortgages is lower than the interest rates paid to compete for short-term deposits, certificates, and other sources of funds. Nontheless, variable rate and price-level-adjusted mortgage proposals do not completely eliminate interest rate risk. The risk is primarily associated with the long-term nature of mortgage assets, the particular institutional structure of thrift institutions, and the existence of inflation. The question then is how to allocate the costs and the burden of risk.

Adjusting the Maturity

If the maturity of the variable rate mortgage varies while monthly payments are held constant, part of the equity component of the monthly payments must be transferred to the interest portion of the account. In periods of rising interest rates, this creates an increased risk of default because of the slower build-up of equity. Changing the maturity of the loan is a more agreeable adjustment for the consumer since it insures stability in the payment-to-income ratio and a relatively low level of uncertainty about the cost of the mortgage. From the lender's perspective there are two limitations to this form of adjustment: (1) it is an accounting change that does nothing to alleviate the cash flow problem thrift institutions experience during periods of credit restraint; and (2) there is a limit to which the lengthening of maturity can adjust for increased interest costs and this limit is quickly reached when one starts out with a twenty-five-year or thirty-year mortgage. For example, a variable rate mortgage issued for $30,000 at 6 percent for twenty five years would have monthly payments of $193.30. If the rate increases to 8 percent after three years, unchanged monthly payments would extend the mortgage life to forty-five years. If the rate increased to 8.25 percent, the loan could never be paid off at the initial monthly payment level. Depending upon the size of the payment, within a relatively short period of time, interest charges could therefore represent the total payment or even an amount which exceeds the total monthly payment.[17] By leaving monthly payments unchanged, borrowers do not risk unexpected changes in budget allocations for other household expenses. Among borrower types, Profiles 2 and 3—the prime age blue-collar worker and the older worker—are less able to absorb larger payment-income burdens. They benefit more from maturity extensions since their real income is less likely to increase over time. The slower equity accumulation, however, increases the risk of default for the lender. Underwriting standards would inevitably have to be revised substantially in order to account for the slower build-up of equity. In addition, should interest charges exceed constant nominal monthly payments, it would be necessary to deduct the additional interest from the accumulated equity. Clearly this technique has limitations. Furthermore, without changes in bank charters, maturity extensions would quickly reach the legal maximum.

Adjusting the Monthly Payment

If the nominal monthly mortgage payments are adjusted to reflect changes in either the real value of the loan principal (PLAM) or the changes in interest rates (VRM) while the maturity of the loan is held constant, borrowing households will be uncertain how to budget for housing. Thus, for the borrowers, there would be considerable insecurity about their ability to meet increasing monthly payments. For example, the annual payments on a twenty-year variable rate mortgage of $30,000, taken out in 1971 with an initial interest rate of 8 percent, would have been $3,450, approximately $285 per month. Nominal payments would have declined 11 percent between 1971 and 1974; the 1974 escalation in interest rates, however, would have increased nominal annual payments 14.5 percent between 1974 and 1975.[18] With a PLAM, changes in monthly payments would not be as severe because the interest rate that is used to calculate the nominal monthly payments is a "real" interest rate and consequently, during inflationary periods, is lower than a nominal interest rate (figure 7-4 and figure 7-5).

The long-term ability to finance such increases obviously depends on the borrower's income potential and access to credit. For those borrowers cor-

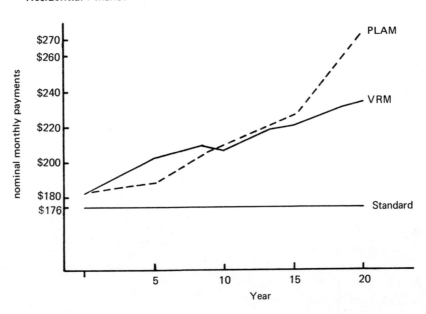

Figure 7-4. Monthly Payments on $30,000 20-Year Mortgages

responding to the profile of a young upwardly mobile household, homeowner-ship represents a decreasing financial burden as their income increases more rapidly than inflation. The costs of homeownership are likely to increase for low-income households and older borrowers who experience real income declines. To keep up with changes in monthly payments, these households will be forced to allocate fewer of their funds to nonhousing goods and services or to finance the increased housing cost, often at rates higher than the mortgage rate (see shift in, for example, Master Charge) through second mortgages or additional consumer borrowing. Although Profiles 1 and 2 are able to absorb increases in nominal mortgage payments over the long run, a major shortcoming of the variable rate mortgage is its short-term uncertainty and the instability of its payment-to-income ratio. Nor does the variable rate mortgage have the low initial monthly payment features of the price-level-adjusted mortgage or the graduated payment mortgages,[19] which act as a compensatory feature, particu-larly for young borrowers. With few savings or other assets, young borrowers are least able to handle sudden variations in the payment-to-income ratio and in the short run are exposed to greater risk of default. In the absence of a diversity of mortgage alternatives more suitable to the needs of both Profile 1 and 3 borrowers, regulatory conditions on the timing of payment adjustments and the maximum rate increase of VRM's take on added significance.

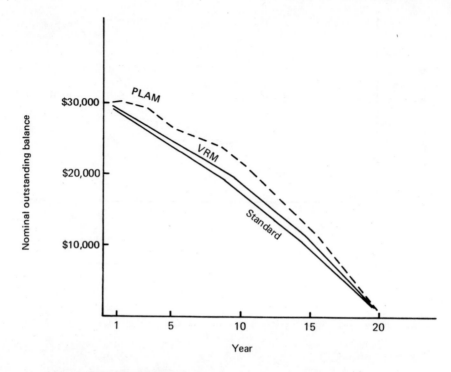

Figure 7-5. Outstanding Balance on $30,000 20-Year Mortgages

*The Loan-to-Value Ratio: Determining
the Downpayment Requirement*

The introduction of index-linked mortgages would alter the lender's calculation
of default risk because the rate of equity accumulation and the payment-to-
income ratio over the life of the mortgage differs from that of the standard
mortgage. Changes in underwriting standards, particularly downpayment requirements, would have clear distributional effects.

In the case of VRMs, the nature of the increased risk of default varies with
the option for adjusting the interest rate. A variable rate mortgage with fixed
nominal payments and a variable maturity would obviously increase the risk of
default, since equity accumulates at a slower rate as a larger share of the
monthly payment is applied to interest. Lenders might require higher downpayments to compensate for this increased risk. Since the downpayment requirement is a wealth requirement and wealth is more concentrated than income,
many young households and lower income groups may have to defer or forsake
homeownership until they accumulate additional savings.

With changes in the monthly payments, the calculation of the risk of default becomes more complex. Lenders can no longer rely upon the constant or decreasing payment-to-income ratio characteristic of standard fixed interest rate mortgages. The relative constancy of this relationship has been a natural controlling factor that has placed greater weight on the loan-to-value ratio as a guide to assessing default risk.[20] Index-linked mortgages alter this relationship. Since VRMs with adjustable nominal monthly payments imply both short-term and long-term variability in the payment-to-income ratio, the risk of default would increase. Lenders will likely assure themselves that the borrower has adequate income or reserves to cover the burden of a varying monthly payment.

The same default risk exists with the PLAMs; although the real value of the mortgage payment remains constant, borrowers accept additional risk because the nominal payment increases in step with the rate of inflation. The PLAM causes less volatility in the payment-to-income ratio, however, because it adjusts to *actual* inflation rather than the anticipation of inflation. In addition, during inflationary periods, the initial monthly payments for a PLAM would be considerably lower than under a standard mortgage or a VRM, and this would provide borrowers with a small financial cushion.

Compared to either the standard mortgage or the variable rate mortgage, the borrower can purchase the same amount of housing at a lower initial income with a PLAM. Also, during inflationary periods, the real payments remain constant with a PLAM but decline with a standard or variable rate mortgage.

For those households whose income is expected to increase faster or at the same rate as inflation—the young upwardly mobile professional and the prime age blue-collar worker—the real burden of the mortgage payment will remain constant or decline over time thereby eliminating the default risk attributable to the new mortgage payback arrangements. Equity accumulates more slowly, however, with a variable rate mortgage than with the standard fixed-rate mortgage. Thus, lenders may require a higher downpayment for the VRM than for the standard mortgage.[21]

The older home buyer, who fits the Profile 3 borrower, presents different problems. Faced with a declining real income stream, these households cannot absorb increasing payment-to-income ratios. They are more likely, however, to be able to afford a higher downpayment because of their previous homeownership or accumulated savings. Yet both PLAMs and VRMs are equally unsuitable mortgage instruments for these borrowers. They need a mortgage with a declining payment-to-income ratio or one that allows them to draw on existing accumulated equity in their home.

For low-income families whose income does not keep pace with inflation, the effects of index-linked mortgages can take one of three forms: (1) these households may be rationed out of the mortgage market; (2) they may be offered a standard fixed nominal mortgage at a higher initial interest rate than with the index-linked mortgage; or (3) they may be offered an index-linked mortgage with a high downpayment requirement to offset the increased risk of default.[22]

Conclusion

Until recently, analysis of housing finance problems concentrated upon the supply and cost of funds. Recognizing the effect on borrowers is more recent. The interaction of inflation with the long-term upward trend in housing costs has done much to expose the defects of the traditional mortgage instrument. The two alternative mortgage instruments examined in this chapter do not solve all the problems; they are only two of the many nonstandard mortgage proposals under discussion. Since no single mortgage instrument fits the life-cycle requirements and income potential of all borrowers, or the profitability criteria and aversion to risk of all lenders, neither of the above alternatives can be viewed as an ideal type. Instead, they represent two examples of the type of mortgage options that may supplement the existing standard mortgage.

With the standard mortgage, households presently engage in a trading-up process, selling their present house and buying another, in order to adjust housing needs to changes in family composition and income. While neither of the two alternative mortgage instruments, in the form presented here, completely adjusts the schedule of payments to correspond with the path of a household's potential income, alternative mortgages do offer payment requirements more suited to the conditions of different borrower types. The young, upwardly mobile homebuyer, for example, would benefit most from a specified prepayment schedule that gradually increased over time as the household's real income increased. The older worker nearing retirement would similarly benefit from a declining schedule of payments or a contract that permitted a withdrawal of the accumulated equity in their home as a supplement to retirement income. Both payment patterns seek to reduce both the involuntary household mobility and the distortions in the payment burden associated with the traditional standard mortgage.

The variable rate mortgage does not provide complete financial flexibility; nor does it provide a total solution to the inflationary tilt in the borrower's real mortgage repayment stream. Because the VRM is tied to a nominal, as opposed to a real, interest rate which incorporates expectations of inflation, it offers little relief to the young first-time homebuyer. Thus many households may still have to forego or defer homeownership until they either accumulate enough savings for a larger downpayment or decide to reduce their demand for housing quality and quantity. The VRM has been promoted primarily for its favorable impact upon the problem of the flow of funds faced by thrift institutions. The VRM, that is, provides lenders with a better match between the maturities of their assets and their liabilities.

The price-level-adjusted mortgage provides a potential solution for the uneven burden of payments experienced by some borrowers. The real value of the payment stream remains constant over the life of the mortgage since payments are pegged to a real rather than a nominal reference rate. Young households with little initial wealth but with future expectations of higher real income benefit from lower initial monthly payments; they are able to buy more housing and need not rely on the trading-up process to improve their housing consumption as family needs change. For the prime age blue-collar worker, PLAMs provide less variability in the payment-to-income ratio than the variable rate mortgage.

The ability of PLAMs to meet part of the borrower problem is clear; its acceptance is not. The lack of familiarity with contracting in real rather than nominal terms and the uncertainty with regard to nominal payments will cause some difficulties in marketing such instruments. Tables 7-2 and 7-3 summarize the major impact of the various mortgage features that have been discussed here. The choice of a reference index directly affects households at different stages in their life cycle. All households would be adversely affected by a mortgage pegged to a wage index but young and elderly households would be most hurt. In the former case real income may be steadily rising while for the retired elderly family on a fixed income the defects of a wage index reference rate are obvious. For similar reasons, elderly households would be most adversely affected by adjustments to the monthly payment schedule as opposed to a maturity extension.

The stratification of borrower types does not directly address the problem of low-income households whose real income declines during inflationary periods. Alternative mortgage instruments are not intended to provide a solution to this problem. Yet if these households do not already own homes, they are net losers regardless of the choice of mortgage instruments. If such households already own homes, they may benefit from the inflation-induced appreciation of their home and from the reduced real value of their outstanding mortgage loan. Most households have few other equity investments. Therefore, residential property is commonly the sole means for low-income as well as moderate-income households to share in the inflation-generated capital gains enjoyed by owners of other types of assets.

There is little question that the standard mortgage worked in periods of relatively stable interest rates and that it facilitated a broad expansion of homeownership in the United States. Yet the standard mortgage is a mixed blessing for many borrowers. On the one hand, there is a serious distortion in the real payment time stream as borrowers are forced to amortize their mortgage at an extremely rapid rate. On the other hand, there is certainty regarding the total value of the mortgage payment commitment. For many households, particularly the elderly or those with low incomes, alternative mortgage instruments may not be appropriate. The certainty of the payment-to-income burden of the standard

Table 7-2
Comparative Effects of Mortgage Parameters on Different Borrower Types

| Borrower Type | Standard Mortgage | | | Variable Rate Mortgage | | | | Price-Level-Adjusted Mortgage | |
| | | | | Reference Rate | | Adjustments to Payment Stream | | Reference Rate | Adjustment to Payment Stream |
	Fixed Interest Rate	Level Monthly Payments	Fixed Maturity	Wages	Cost of Funds	Monthly Payment	Maturity	CPI	Monthly Payment
Profile 1: young, upwardly mobile professional household	−	−	0	−	0	0	+	0	0
Profile 2: prime age blue-collar/ clerical worker	0	0	0	−	0	0	+	0	0
Profile 3: older worker nearing retirement (or already on fixed income)	0	−	0	−	0	−	+	−	−

Note: 0 = neutral effect.
        + = positive effect.
        − = negative effect.

Table 7-3

A Comparison of Mortgage Types with Respect to Payments, Equity Buildup and Capital Gains

	Standard Mortgage	Variable Rate Mortgage	Price-Level-Adjusted Mortgage
Purchase			
Original price	$34,500	$34,500	$34,500
Downpayment	4,500	4,500	4,500
Loan amount	30,000	30,000	30,000
Interest rate	9%	8.5%[a]	3%[b]
Maturity	30 years	30 years	30 years
Initial monthly payment (nominal)	242	232	135[c]
Year Five	242	213	159
Initial annual income required[d]	$16,400	$15,900	$11,280
Initial percentage of income	17.7%	17.5%	14.3%
Sale After Five Years			
Appreciated value[e]	$44,000	$44,000	$44,000
Net capital gain	9,500	9,500	9,500
Amortization	1,010	1,120[f]	−2,830[f]
Net equity (capital gain and amortization)	10,510	10,620	6,670

[a]The interest rate is adjustable and varies with the average cost of funds to the thrift institutions. The initial rate of the VRM, however, is assumed to be 50 basis points below the rate on the standard mortgage.

[b]The interest rate is set to approximate the real rate of interest.

[c]The payment increases each year at the same rate as the rate of inflation.

[d]Assumes that total housing expenses, including principal, interest, property taxes, and insurance, equal 25 percent of gross family income. In this case, property taxes and insurance are assumed to be $100 per month.

[e]Appreciation of property value is equal to 5 percent per year.

[f]The amount of amortization differs depending upon economic conditions over the time period.

mortgage provides the most suitable mortgage option. But for young, upwardly mobile or middle-aged blue-collar households, the nonstandard mortgages are more consistent with their real income patterns and are beneficial to the extent that they require lower initial monthly payments. The introduction of alternative mortgage instruments is not meant to preclude the continued availability of the standard mortgage, but will provide a wider choice. Individual households can then tailor their mortgage burdens more closely to their real payment capabilities, changes in life cycle, willingness to assume risks, and nonhousing debt requirements.

Notes

1. *Savings and Loan Fact Book, 1976* (Chicago: United States League of Savings Associates, 1976), p. 29.

2. As compensation for such restrictions, public policy has protected savings and loan associations by creating a secondary market for mortgage purchases and making advances available from the Federal Home Loan Bank Board (FHLBB) during periods of rising interest rates. Also, federal policy has sought to reduce competition in the capital markets by establishing large minimum denominations for Treasury bills and notes and by maintaining a differentially higher interest rate on the deposits of thrift institutions over those of commercial banks. Most significant, however, has been the federal income tax provision that provides thrift institutions with deductions for bad debts in excess of actual loss. See, for example, Leonard Lapidus, Suzanne Cutler, Patrick Page Kildroyle, and Arthur Castro, *Public Policy Toward Mutual Savings Banks in New York State: Proposals for Change* (New York: Federal Reserve Bank of New York, New York State Banking Department, 1974).

3. Since 1966, the time deposits have been supplemented by certificates of deposit, which have a longer maturity. Although these deposits have mitigated the portfolio imbalance somewhat, the essential problem caused by the mismatch in maturities still remains.

4. For a discussion of the supply problem see, for example, Lyle E. Gramley, "Short-Term Cycles in Housing Production" in *Ways to Moderate Fluctuations in Housing Construction,* Federal Reserve Staff Study, 1972, and George Von Furstenberg, 'The Economics of Mortgages with Variable Interest Rates," FHLMC monograph no. 2, February 1975.

5. With the mortgage contract, the borrower secures cash by selling, and the lender by buying, a future stream of payments. The discounted present value represents the value at the time the loan originated of the sum of mortgage repayments to be received by the lender over the life of the mortgage. The higher initial payments resulting from inflation compensate the lender for the reduction in the real value of succeeding mortgage repayments. The real interest rate represents the difference between the nominal or current interest rate and the anticipated rate of inflation over the life of the contract.

6. Obviously the nature of the regulatory policies designed to accompany these instruments will affect the timing and exposure that the financial burden imposes upon borrowers from changes in the interest rate.

7. Richard Marcis, "Variable Rate Mortgages: Their Use and Impact in the Mortgage Capital Markets," *American Real Estate and Urban Economics Association Journal* 2 (Spring 1974).

8. There are many possible mortgage instruments with various combinations of maturity loan-to-value ratio, and graduation in payment-to-income ratio including graduated payment mortgages, three-to-five year rollover mortgages, reverse annuity mortgages, and deferred interest mortgages. For a discussion of some of these various mortgage instruments see David L. Smith, "Reforming the Mortgage Instrument," *U.S. Federal Home Loan Bank Board Journal* 9 (May 1976).

9. Donald Tucker, "The Variable-Rate Graduated Payment Mortgage" working paper, U.S. Federal Reserve System, Board of Governors, January 1974.

10. The standard mortgage similarly contributes to the high rate of residential turnover in the United States as families respond to higher earnings by upgrading their housing through the process of "trading-up"—selling their home and moving into a bigger and better one as income increases.

11. See Josephine M. McElhone and Henry J. Cassidy, "Mortgage Lending; Its Changing Economic and Demographic Environment; A Call for Innovation," *U.S. Federal Home Loan Bank Board Journal* 7 (July 1974).

12. In contrast, with FHA and VA mortgage loans, a trade-off is not operative Government mortgage insurance and guarantee programs reduce the lender's exposure to default and facilitate homeownership for low-income and moderate-income households. FHA and VA mortgage loans, for example, typically cover 97 percent of the appraised value of the home or 100 percent of the selling price. See George Von Furstenberg, "Risk Structures and the Distribution of Benefits Within the FHA Home Mortgage Insurance Program," *Journal of Money, Credit and Banking* 2 (August 1970).

13. For a more complete range of alternatives see Richard Cohn and Stanley Fischer, "An Analysis of Alternative Non-standard Mortgages," in Franco Modigliani and Donald Lessard, eds., *New Mortgage Designs for Stable Housing in an Inflationary Environment,* Federal Reserve Bank of Boston Series no. 14 (January 1975); and Smith, "Reforming the Mortgage Instrument."

14. Variable rate mortgages have been adopted by several state-chartered savings and loan associations in California, Wisconsin, and Massachusetts. At present, federally chartered savings and loan associations are prohibited from issuing mortgages in which successive monthly payments exceed the initial payment; they can, however, issue mortgages in which there is a *declining* nominal payment stream. See Henry J. Cassidy and Josephine M. McElhone, "A Call for New Mortgage Instruments," Working Paper no. 46, Federal Home Loan Bank Board, 1974.

15. Richard A. Cohn and Stanley Fischer, "Alternative Mortgage Designs" in *New Mortgage Designs for Stable Housing in an Inflationary Environment,* Conference Series no. 14 (Boston: Federal Reserve Bank of Boston, 1975), table 3, p. 56.

16. Cohn and Fischer, "Alternative Mortgage Designs," table 5, p. 58. There are several options in designing the timing and number of adjustments to the loan principal. The principal can be adjusted prior to the time payment is due or at the time payment is due; obviously the former case is more workable since there must be sufficient time in which to notify the borrower of a change in the payment schedule. The length of this notification lag can vary. In this example, there is a one-year lag although three or six months would be more likely.

17. See Paul S. Anderson and J. Philip Hinson, "Variable Rates on Mortgages: Their Impact and Use," Federal Reserve Bank of Boston, *New England Economic Review* (March-April 1970), p. 12.

18. Cohn and Fischer, "Alternative Mortgage Designs," table 7, p. 60.

19. See Smith, "Reforming the Mortgage Instrument"; and Tucker, "The Variable-Rate Graduated Payment Mortgage."

20. The downpayment effects are less certain because default risk is primarily a function of both the loan-to-value ratio and the payment-to-income ratio. Since alternative mortgage forms substantially change the payment stream, previous empirical relationships implying the dominance of one variable cannot be used to predict specifically the changes introduced by a new set of mortgage terms.

21. Cohn and Fischer, "An Analysis of Alternative Non-standard Mortgages," pp. 48-49, argue that this set of relationships will mean a lower downpayment requirement for the standard mortgage than at present. This argument makes two important assumptions: (1) lenders have a matched liability with regard to maturity and (2) borrowers and lenders have equal bargaining positions. Without the first condition, the interest rate risk facing the lender would not be eliminated and without the second condition, the benefits to the borrower may not be transferred.

22. This latter option seems unlikely since higher downpayments may not be able to compensate for the household's inability to meet higher monthly payments.

8 Construction in the Electric Power Industry

Kenneth F. Reinschmidt

The electric power industry is the most capital intensive of all major American industries, and by virtue of that fact, it is the largest single industrial customer of the construction industry. From 1920 until the end of 1973, the consumption of electricity in the United States grew continuously at a rate of more than 7 percent a year. This was significantly greater than the average growth rate for all energy consumption of about 5 percent per year, or the rate of growth of the Gross National Product. Most of this increase in demand was supplied by the construction of fossil-fueled steam-electric power plants, which between 1950 and 1973 increased in total capacity at a rate of 8.4 percent a year. Hydro-electric capacity also grew exponentially during the same period, but its rate of increase was less (5.9 percent a year), and its share of total capacity declined. In recent years, nuclear power has grown with particular rapidity; prior to 1960, only one small commercial nuclear power plant existed, but since then nuclear capacity has increased at an average rate of 16 percent yearly. These growth rates mean that the electric industry built enough new plants to double its size every nine years.

Table 8-1 summarizes electrical energy production and fuel consumption for 1973. The dominant fuel was coal; it will continue to be for some time.

This growth in generation capacity requires substantial financial resources. In 1976, capital investment by the electric utilities is estimated to exceed $19 billion,[1] the largest capital investment of any single industry, and almost 16 percent of the total capital spending for all U.S. business and industry. The amount may be compared to estimated capital requirements in 1976 of $12 billion for petroleum, $3 billion for iron and steel, and $2 billion for the automotive industry. In 1977, capital investment by electric utilities is expected to rise to $22.5 billion, or $100 for every person in the United States.[2]

These expenditures are primarily for construction of new generating plants, modifications to existing plants (for example, fuel conversion and environmental controls), transmission lines, substations, and distribution facilities. While investments in transmission and distribution are substantial, generation of new power is the most critical and rapidly expanding area, and will be the primary focus of concern here.

There are over a thousand public and private electric utilities in the United States, ranging from giant systems covering several states to small municipal distribution companies and rural cooperatives. Table 8-2 shows the proportion of total electric energy generated by each major group. The investor-owned

Table 8-1
Electric Energy Capacity and Generation, 1973

Plant Type	Capacity, Millions of Kilowatts	Generation Billions of Kilowatt-hours	Percent of Electric Generation	Amount of Fuel Consumed
Coal	167	846	46	388 million tons
Gas	61	336	18	3.61 trillion cubic feet
Oil	78	311	17	567 million barrels
Hydro	65	271	15	
Nuclear	20	83	4	
Total	391	1847	100%	

Source: Reprinted from July 15, 1974 issue of *Electrical World* © Copyright 1974, McGraw-Hill, Inc. All rights reserved.

systems plus the two large federal systems comprise the backbone of the industry, and of the investor-owned companies, fewer than a hundred and fifty own and construct substantial amounts of generating capacity. In fact, almost a third of committed new capacity will be constructed by the ten largest utilities (both federal and investor-owned). Substantial economies of scale favor large utilities, but the size of a utility company has no effect on the unit cost of construction of new generating plants, on the delays in obtaining construction permits, or on any other construction factor. Larger utilities do, of course, tend to build larger power plants, and are much more likely to build nuclear power plants than smaller utilities. The Tennessee Valley Authority, for example, which is the country's largest utility, has commitments to construct almost 22,000 megawatts of new capacity, all of it hydroelectric or nuclear, in units exceeding 1,200 megawatts each.[3] A few investor-owned utilities are also committed to all-nuclear new construction, but most will build a mix of nuclear and fossil-fueled plants, or fossil-fueled plants only.

Some large utilities design and construct their own plants, but most do not do enough construction to justify maintaining a large, specialized engineering and construction management staff. Instead, they use the services of architect/engineering firms to design new plants. Some architect/engineers have the capability to construct facilities also; in other cases, separate contractors do the

Table 8-2
Distribution of Electric Generation by Utility Group

Group	Number in Group	Percent of Electric Generation
Investor-owned systems	250	78
Federal systems	2	12
Public (nonfederal) systems	700	9
Cooperatives	65	1
Total		100

construction work. These independent engineering and construction firms will design and construct 85 percent of all new fossil-fired plants and 76 percent of new nuclear plants. This aspect of the industry is also highly concentrated; fully two-thirds of committed new power plant construction will be designed or built by the fifteen leading firms. Total expenditures for the construction of a typical 1,100 megawatt nuclear station begun in 1975 might exceed $1 billion over a ten-year period; and with a typical 800 megawatt coal-fired plant exceeding $500 million over an eight-year period, it is clear that only the largest and most experienced design and construction firms are likely to be selected for such projects.

Types of Power Generation Facilities

Electric power plants generate electricity by means of turbine generators. The generator is basically a winding of copper wire on a shaft, inside a magnetic field. When the winding is rotated, electric current is generated. The generator shaft is, in turn, driven by a turbine, an arrangement of curved blades on a shaft inside a housing.[4] In hydroelectric plants, the turbine is driven by water pressure, in other plants by the pressure of steam or hot gas. All turbines in general commercial use, exclusive of hydroelectric machines, are heat engines, which produce work by means of a differential in temperature. For a reversible heat engine, the thermal efficiency, or fraction of input heat energy converted to useful work, is given by the equation

$$e = 1 - T_{out}/T_{in} \qquad (8.1)$$

in which e is the thermal efficiency, T_{in} is the temperature at which heat is received, and T_{out} is the temperature at which heat is rejected, both in degrees absolute (Kelvin or Rankine).[5] A real power plant is not actually reversible, so this equation is inexact, but useful nonetheless in defining the maximum theoretical thermal efficiency.

The equation points out that in order to increase thermal efficiency it is necessary to increase T_{in} or reduce T_{out}. Thus power plant engineers are constantly striving to increase the temperature of the inlet steam or gas through improvements in materials and systems. The temperature at which heat is rejected, however, is more or less limited by the ambient environment. Thus, if steam at 1,000° F enters a turbine and is rejected at 212° F, the maximum thermal efficiency is $1.0 - (212 + 460)/(1,000 + 460) = 0.54$. The overall plant efficiency will be much less because the actual process is not reversible, because some of the heat of fuel combustion goes up the stack, and because some power must be drawn off to run plant equipment. In practice, the efficiency of real power plants is usually described by the heat rate, which is the amount of heat, in Btu, required to produce a kilowatt hour of electrical output.[6] Heat rates range from about 12,000 Btu/kwh for older fossil-fueled plants to about 9,000 for more efficient modern plants. The heat rate will vary, for any given plant, depending on the amount of power actually being produced. At 100 percent efficiency, one Btu is equivalent to 3,413 kilowatt hours, so that a typical plant with a heat rate of 10,000 Btu/kwh would have an overall efficiency of 3,413/10,000 = 0.34. In other words, 66 percent of the heat energy input to the plant produces no electrical energy, and must be rejected as heat load to the environment. Nuclear power plants have lower thermal efficiencies than fossil-fueled plants, primarily because the operating temperatures are lower. If the inlet steam temperature for a nuclear plant is 600° F instead of 1,000° F, the theoretical efficiency falls from 0.54 to 0.37. Consequently, the overall efficiency for a nuclear plant is closer to 30 percent, and relatively more of the heat input must be wasted to the environment.

Power Plant Selection

Because electricity cannot be stored, it must be generated as demand arises, and electric demand is far from constant. The variation in demand can be imagined as a composition of three cyclical patterns. The *annual* cycle is the first pattern: Electrical consumption varies as demand shifts from winter heating and lighting to summer air conditioning. Superimposed upon this is a *weekly* cycle, with demand being lower on weekends than on weekdays. Finally, superimposed on the weekly cycle is a *daily* cycle which rises from a minimum in the early hours of the morning to a maximum around noon. These cycles are by no means firm; the time of the daily maximum, for example, may vary with the season of the year. Different utilities will have different cyclical patterns, depending upon the mix of residential and industrial customers in their systems, the type of industry present, and many other factors. In some cases, neighboring utilities are able to send power back and forth to meet differing peak requirements. For example, in former years New York City had a summer peak while upstate New York utilities had winter peaks, so that there was a net flow of power south in summer and north in winter. More recently, increased use of air conditioning has caused upstate New York demand to peak in the summer as well, so that this annual interchange is no longer significant. As the daily peak moves from east to west with the sun, some degree of power transfer is also possible, but the time change is not sufficient to solve the problem. System interconnections are, however, valuable contributors to improved reliability of service.

The ratio between the actual energy consumed in a year and the energy that would have been consumed if demand had been constant, at the maximum yearly value, is called the system load factor. It is a measure of how effectively the capacity of the system is used. The lower the load factor, the more peaked the demand curve and the less efficiently the system operates. Low load factors present an economic problem to the utilities because the generating capacity must be built to meet the peak demand (plus a reserve of 20 to 25 percent in order that there very rarely be a power shortage). This capacity is relatively expensive. As a simple example, a 1,000 watt hair drier can be purchased for about $10.00. The total cost of electrical energy to the user would be perhaps $.05 per hour of operation, depending on location, but if this appliance were operated at the peak of electric demand, an additional kilowatt of generating capacity would be required to supply it, and the cost of this capacity to the utility at today's prices would be at least $400. Obviously this poses a disastrous set of circumstances for a utility. In order to recover the utility's investment costs on this kilowatt of capacity, plus fuel, taxes, and operating expenses, this appliance should be in operation four hours a day. This amount of use would cost the consumer, in annual electric bills, seven times what he paid for the appliance originally. Luckily, all appliances are never turned on simultaneously, but the provision of electrical capacity to meet peak loads is a serious problem for utilities.

Systems load factors from 60 to 65 percent are not uncommon, and utilities take various steps to try to increase their load factors. Encouragement of electric heating, for example, makes economic sense to a utility with a summer peak, as it generates more revenue without requiring any additional plant capacity. Conversely, some utilities are experimenting with different pricing structures to discourage peak hour demand. Even so, peak hour consumption is not necessarily priced at its true marginal cost, since this would be more than any consumer would care to pay, and whether the possible increase in load factors will justify the increased cost of electric meters has not yet been determined. Experiments aside, almost all existing price structures average out costs without regard to peaks, so that utility revenue is roughly proportional to total energy consumed. A great proportion of utility costs are, however, proportional to total installed capacity. In 1973, roughly half of the cost of electricity to the consumer was due to fixed costs, for example, taxes and capital costs of facilities, and only a quarter went for fuel.[7]

The load factor is thus the key to understanding utility economics, and since utilities can do little to improve their load factors, they must try hard to reduce those costs under their control—by means of proper selection of generating equipment. Suppose that the annual cost of operating a generating plant is composed of two terms: A, the fixed cost per kilowatt of plant capacity, comprising capital costs, taxes, and so on; and BX, a variable cost, where B is the fuel and operating cost per kilowatt hour of energy generated, and X is the number of hours operated per year. Therefore the total cost per year is $A + BX$ per kilowatt of plant capacity. For a given mix of plants in a system, the utility will tend to operate the plants with the least marginal cost when possible. As revenues are based on kilowatt hours consumed, when constructing new facilities, the utility will select units with the least average cost per kilowatt hour, $A/X + B$, for the anticipated number of hours of operation, X. Because electrical demand never falls to zero, there is some load, called the base load, which must be generated continuously. For this load, X is very large (approaching 8.760 hours per year) and a low variable cost, B, is necessary, while a large value of A, the fixed cost, is tolerable. Thus base-loaded plants usually have low fuel costs and high capital costs. Conversely, plants built to operate only during peaks must have low capital cost, A, as the number of hours of operation per year is low, while the variable cost may be higher than for base-loaded plants. In between base-loaded plants and peaking plants are cycling plants.

In practice, the fixed and variable cost factors, A and B, vary inversely for real plant types. It is possible, for example, to reduce fuel consumption by increasing thermal efficiency, but to do so requires expensive additional equipment. If one tries to increase thermal efficiency by increasing the inlet temperature, T_{in}, one must use exotic high-temperature materials and solve numerous technical problems in high-temperature engineering. If one uses a cheaper fuel, additional plant equipment for safety (nuclear plants) or pollution control (high-sulfur coal plants) will be required. It thus requires more capital to save fuel. Nuclear power plants appeared to be the exception to this rule, because they were originally thought to have low construction costs (as low as $81 per kilowatt in 1965) as well as very low fuel costs. The estimates of low construction costs, however, proved to be seriously in error, and while nuclear plants now have the lowest fuel costs of all steam-electric types, they are the most expensive to construct. Fusion and solar power plants will have even greater capital costs.

As of 1975, some trends in fuel selection may be discerned. International oil prices are set monopolistically, and could therefore go up or down at the whim of OPEC, although obviously one expects them to go up. Domestic gas prices are artificially low and will rise dramatically when decontrolled. Gas has been a major fuel in electric generation (see table 8-1) because it was cheap and clean, requiring the least pollution control expense of any fossil fuel. The penetration of gas into the electricity generation sector was limited mainly by its availability, and it appears that in the future it will be scarce. While oil was widely used, particularly on the East Coast where imported petroleum was cheap, these areas paid the price for this economy in 1974 and construction of new oil-fired plants is now discouraged. Coal is the least environmentally acceptable of all fossil fuels, requiring expensive pollution control equipment. Surface coal mining despoils the countryside and deep mining is hazardous; coal is by far the most dangerous of all energy sources. It is also the most abundant in the United States and both its consumption and price will surely rise. Table 8-3 briefly summarizes the changes in fuel costs, on a cents-per-million-Btu basis, at three points. Prior to 1970, costs had been virtually constant for ten years or more. The cost advantage of gas is obvious. The future projection assumes that oil will be the price-setter, with the prices of all other fuels, even uranium, following oil upward. Coal will remain slightly cheaper to allow for the greater capital costs required to use it. Assuming that few new oil- and gas-fired steam-electric plants will be built, the major comparison lies between coal and nuclear plants.

When the approximate prices for uranium and coal in 1975 are compared, and values for the heat rates of both types of plants are assumed, the difference amounts to about 0.8 cents per kilowatt hour in fuel cost, in favor of nuclear power. By further assuming equal annual availability rates (hours of operation per year) and capitalization factors, it appears that the nuclear plant could cost $400 to $450 per kilowatt more than the coal plant to construct, for the same total electricity cost. The construction cost differential for units currently coming online is less than this amount, but the differential is increasing. Moreover, the estimates given in table 8-3 for 1980 show the decreasing advantage of nuclear fuel. The availability of nuclear fuel, because of a possible shortage of processing plants and a scarcity of uranium ore is also a question of concern.

In the light of these facts, the following plant types can be placed in perspective. Fossil-fueled steam-electric plants are by far the most prevalent form of electric generation and are generally used as base-loaded facilities. In these plants, fuel is burned in a furnace to generate steam in a boiler; the steam, at high temperature and pressure, then drives the turbine. The steam exiting from the turbine is condensed to water, forming a vacuum and lowering the temperature at the outlet, T_{out}, to well below 212° F, thereby improving the thermal efficiency of the plant. The condenser is cooled by water drawn from a river, lake, or ocean and returned directly after being heated, by cooling ponds, or by cooling towers.

Nuclear power plants differ from fossil-fueled steam-electric units mainly in the way they generate steam. In a nuclear reactor, heat is generated by the fission of the uranium atom; this heat is transferred to the reactor coolant water which surrounds the nuclear core. In a boiling water reactor (BWR), steam is generated immediately within the reactor and piped to the turbine. In a

Table 8-3
Costs of Fuels Compared

Fuel	Cost, Cents per Million Btu (¢/MBtu)		
	1970	1975	1980 (estimated)
Oil	35	165	210
Coal	30	125	150
Gas	25	50	80
Nuclear	20	35	75

Source: M.J. Whitman, "An Analysis of Current Trends in Nuclear and Fossil Powered Generation Costs," U.S. Energy Research and Development Administration, 1975.

pressurized water reactor (PWR), the reactor coolant is kept under high pressure so that it does not boil; this pressurized water is conducted outside the nuclear reactor to heat exchangers where water is boiled in a separate system to generate steam. The pressurized water reactor thus requires additional steam generators as compared to the boiling water reactor, but the steam flowing through the turbine does not pass through the nuclear reactor and therefore does not become radioactively contaminated. The safety aspects of all nuclear reactors are under the control of the U.S. Nuclear Regulatory Commission (NRC), formerly the Atomic Energy Commission, and no nuclear power plant can start construction or operation without licenses from the NRC.

Nuclear power plants, as mentioned above, have the highest capital costs and the lowest fuel costs of all steam-electric systems; therefore, they are always operated as base-loaded facilities. If demand momentarily falls below the maximum capacity of the unit, it may be throttled back to less than full capacity. The excess capacity available is termed spinning reserve, that is, reserve capacity available in the spinning turbine to meet increases in demand instantaneously. Alternately, a nuclear power plant may be coupled with a pumped storage facility in order to store this excess generating capacity for use at peak periods. Nuclear power plants are rarely shut down except for refueling or for equipment failures (forced outages).

Older fossil-fueled steam-electric power plants are generally placed in cycling service as newer units become available. Newer units are more efficient for base-load service because of their higher thermal efficiency and lower operating costs. Maintenance costs also generally increase as plant equipment ages, so that the variable cost factor, B, increases while the fixed cost factor, A (because of increases in construction costs and interest rates), may be smaller than that for newer plants. Such cost factors are more appropriate to cycling units. The economic life of power plants is considered to be about thirty years, but pollution control considerations may play as important a role as equipment obsolescence in forcing plant retirements. Because most nuclear plants have been constructed relatively recently, they have not been reduced to cycling service.

Some fossil-fired steam-electric plants have recently been designed expressly for cycling service. Such plants must start up and shut down rapidly. Nuclear plants are inherently less suited for such service because of the more complex startup procedures that are required for safety. Fossil-fueled plants designed for base-load service also generally require lengthy startup times because it takes time to build up steam pressure in the boilers and to bring a cold turbine up to operating temperature without inducing destructive thermal stresses. Plants designed for cycling service incorporate provisions for keeping equipment hot, as well as other features to reduce startup time. Even so, it takes many hours to bring a steam plant up from shutdown to full power.

Hydroelectric plants have large capital costs (which, however, vary widely with topology and other site conditions) and no fuel costs. They might, therefore, be assumed to be exclusively base load facilities, and they will, in fact, operate in this way if base-load steam-electric units are unavailable. Hydro-electric plants are unique, however, in that the reservoirs constitute storage facilities for potential electric energy, and therefore they are highly suited for peaking or cycling service. Run-of-river plants generally have relatively small reservoir capacities and may be used to satisfy base load. Multiple-use hydro-electric plant operation is also complicated by other factors, such as past and predicted rainfall and snowfall, use of the reservoir for flood protection, and requirements for water for irrigation, navigation, and other uses.

A pumped-storage plant is a hydroelectric plant in which the turbines are reversible and can function as pumps. Thus, instead of reducing power output in a nuclear or coal-fired base loaded plant when the system demand drops below the unit's capacity, full output is maintained, and the excess electric energy is used to pump water up to the storage reservoir. This water is then allowed to flow through the hydroelectric turbines to generate electricity during peak periods. Energy is lost during this cycle, and therefore pumped-storage facilities are used only for peaking power. Other methods for energy storage, such as compressed air storage, underground pumped storage, and rotating flywheels are being studied to meet the great need for energy storage.

The combustion turbine or gas turbine plant is very much like the jet engine of an aircraft (in fact, aircraft engines have been used). Combustion of the fuel with the air creates expanding gas, which directly turns a turbine. Instead of being connected to a propeller, as in an aircraft turboprop engine, the turbine shaft is connected to an electric generator. The hot exhaust gases are discharged to the atmosphere. Combustion turbines are used almost exclusively for peaking power or spinning reserve in electric utility systems; their installation costs are relatively low while their fuel costs, because of low thermal efficiency, are high. Combustion turbines also generally require natural gas or refined oil as fuel. Because of their low capital costs, however, they are widely used as standby power units in a wide variety of industrial applications.

A combined-cycle plant begins with a combustion turbine driving a gener-ator. After the combustion gases have expanded to drive the turbine, they are passed through a heat exchanger to generate steam, which drives a second turbine and generator. By scavenging the waste heat from the combustion turbine, the combined-cycle system becomes much more efficient, at the price however of substantial additional equipment. The greater efficiency makes these units suitable for cycling or even base-loaded service, in addition to peaking service, when rapid installation time is a major consideration.

Another factor that must be considered in plant selection is the length of time required to plan and construct new facilities (see table 8-4). Planning for nuclear power plants must begin at least ten years before the power is needed. Under the relatively stable conditions that prevailed until 1973, utilities were able to plan on such a long term basis. As the span of time becomes shorter before additional power is required, options must be sacrificed. In general, both fuel costs and total costs increase. Finally, if time becomes too short, there is no possibility of construction and the only recourse is the bulk purchase of electricity if any is available.

While the plant descriptions given here apply in general terms, they are not absolutely precise (the distinction between cycling and peaking service, for example, is sometimes obscure). Only the largest electric utilities enjoy the flexibility of owning all types of facilities. Most are constrained by practical considerations (plant outages, maintenance downtime, plant decisions made many years previously, long lead times on new units) to make the best use of what they have.

Construction Factors

One of the most significant trends in power plant construction has been the continual increase in unit size. In 1930, the largest steam-electric plant in operation had about a 200 megawatt (MW) capacity. Maximum unit sizes remained fairly constant through the 1950s, and then began to rise. Maximum sizes rose to 1,100 MW in 1970, and 1,300 MW in 1973. In 1969, the average size of a new fossil-fueled unit was 350 MW and the average for new units coming online in 1979 will be 575 MW, but the increase in the size of the largest plants has stopped, at least temporarily. In part, this is a result of operational problems arising from the rapid increase of turbine sizes.

Nuclear units grew in size even more rapidly. In the early 1960s, the few commercial nuclear plants built were in the 200 MW range. By 1969, the average size of new units had increased to 600 MW, and units now under construction average over 1,600 MW. This rapid escalation must be understood in the context of the lead time necessary to produce power plants: the first unit over 1,000 MW was being designed before the first 500 MW unit had been operated, at a time when there were only six nuclear reactors producing power commercially. This rapid growth, a reflection of the confidence and optimism of power plant

Table 8-4
Number of Years Prior to Need for Additional Power That Plant Decision Must Be Made

Plant Type	Lead Time in Years
Nuclear	10
Coal steam electric	8
Oil or gas steam electric	6½
Combined cycle	5
Combustion turbine	2
Purchase power (if available)	0

Source: *An Appraisal of the Reliability and Adequacy of the North American Bulk Power Systems for the Five-Year Period, 1973-1977* (Princeton, N.J.: National Electric Reliability Council, 1973), p. III-4.

designers in the 1960s meant, in fact, that little actual operating experience could be used in the design of these large units.

Several factors may have influenced this rapid increase in plant size. Certainly there are economies of scale. Thermal efficiency, for example, increases with plant size, but the major reason is that additional equipment is necessary to use the heat energy input more efficiently, and the cost of this equipment does not rise proportionally with its size. A statistical analysis of the reported thermal efficiencies of one hundred modern power plants, fossil and nuclear, showed that thermal efficiency is correlated strongly with unit size.[8] The absolute magnitude of the improvement was not extremely large, however; at pre-1973 fuel prices, increasing the size of a unit by 100 MW would decrease the fuel cost by less than 0.04 mills per kilowatt hour, on the average. The same survey showed that unit construction factors, such as engineering and construction man-hours per kilowatt of plant capacity, and construction cost per kilowatt capacity, did not vary significantly with plant size.

Economy of scale operates in other areas as well. Larger units require less land and fewer operators per kilowatt capacity than smaller units. Recently, regulatory factors have come into play; it is generally just as difficult to license a small unit as a large unit, and total time to produce an operating plant does not vary significantly with plant size.[9] Thus, under the conditions in which electric demand grew rapidly, a small unit could be inadequate by the time it was licensed and built. More recently, as demand growth has slowed, construction costs have risen, and capital has become less available; the trend toward ever larger units has declined. It would seem, then, that although some economies of scale apply in power plant design, the major factor in the growth of units has been the growth in consumer demand coupled with the ability of the industry to construct ever larger units without proportional increases in construction time. This trend may have been more attributable to the efficiency of the construction industry in constructing large projects than to the inherent efficiency of large power plants.

Some unanticipated penalties may have been paid for this trend toward larger units. A Federal Energy Administration (FEA) study reports that the average availability rate for fossil-fired plants falls from 92 percent for plants in the sixty to ninety megawatt range to 73 percent for plants over 600 megawatts. The availability rate is defined as the percentage of time for which a unit is functional and available for power production, whether it is actually called upon to operate or not, during some time period. For nuclear plants, the availability rate similarly declined from 80 percent for one unit less than 200 megawatts to an average of 64 percent for units above 600 megawatts.[10] These data indicate a significant size effect as well as a significant difference between fossil and nuclear plants. However, the FEA recognized but did not explicitly correct for the fact that larger units tend to be newer units, and newer units may not have shaken down to their long-term level of performance.[11] A multivariate regression analysis of the data, as was done elsewhere, might have clarified this point.[12] Even with lower availability, nuclear units may still be more economical than fossil units. Nevertheless, it is obviously true that low availability is a serious reliability problem and a drain on capital resources, as the real cost per kilowatt is much higher than the apparent cost.

Although the advantages of unit size are debatable, it is clear that unit sizes have increased, and this has placed greater demands on the capabilities of the construction industry to staff, organize, and manage such construction projects. Some of the problems arising from these, as well as other factors, will be discussed below.

Materials of Construction

Engineered components (machinery, electrical equipment, instruments, and the like) account for about 55 percent of the cost of a power plant. On-site construction, however, is substantial. A 1,100 MW nuclear power plant may require 16 million cubic feet of total building volume, and much of this volume is filled with pipes, cables, trays, instrument lines, and other essential equipment. Table 8-5 gives some idea of the amount of materials used in the construction of a single 1,100 MW nuclear power plant.[13] Fossil-fueled plants require significantly less material not only because they are generally smaller but also because they are not subject to the same safety regulations. Nevertheless, the quantities are considerable.

In the inflationary period 1973-1974, many items of material and equipment were in short supply. Structural steel, reinforcing steel, steel castings, railroad ties, and numerous other items were difficult to obtain or could be procured only with very long waiting periods. Nuclear units were particularly affected, because of the higher quality required. In a survey taken in January 1974, 30 percent of fossil-fueled plants and 37 percent of nuclear plants reported late delivery of major items of equipment or materials as a cause of significant delays in completion of construction.[14] By July 1975, 57 percent of

Table 8-5
Approximate Material Quantites for a Typical 1,100 MW Nuclear Unit

Material	*Quantity*
Concrete	150,000 cubic yards
Formwork	1,500,000 square feet
Reinforcing steel	15,000 tons
Structured steel	7,000 tons
Piping	3,000 tons
Cable	750 miles
Conduit	100 miles
Cable trays	15 miles

nuclear units that were at least 30 percent complete indicated that difficulties in procuring materials or equipment had resulted in delays in completion.[15] The situation eased in the recessionary period of 1974-1975, partly due to a decline in power plant as well as other types of construction, but the problem has not been solved and will appear again as economic activity recovers.

Construction Manpower

Manpower is also a serious factor in power plant construction. A survey shows a requirement of about 0.5 engineering man-hours per kilowatt to design a fossil-fueled power plant and about 5 man-hours per kilowatt to construct it.[16] Corresponding figures for nuclear power plants are 1.5 man-hours per kilowatt for engineering and 12 man-hours per kilowatt for construction. It appears that both design and construction man-hours per kilowatt are increasing with time. A 1,100 MW nuclear power plant just entering design in 1975 may require more than 2 million man-hours to design and 15 million man-hours to construct, if present trends continue.

A power plant construction job uses a wide variety of construction crafts, with pipefitters expending the greatest number of man-hours (about 25 percent of the total), followed by laborers, electricians, carpenters, ironworkers, operating engineers, boilermakers, millwrights, and miscellaneous other trades. For a single 1,100 MW unit, pipefitters would peak at about 450 men on the job and electricians at about 300; the peak total number of men on the job would be about 1,300 exclusive of nonmanual supervisory personnel. When there are two or more units on a single site, construction is usually scheduled with about one year between units, to provide a smooth transition of manpower between units. With good scheduling, the manpower peak on a two-unit project should be only about 60 percent more than that for a single unit.

The lack of skilled workmen is the most frequently encountered labor problem, cited by utilities as a cause of major construction delays for 38 percent of power plant projects. Pipefitters, electricians, boilermakers, and welders of all trades are most frequently in short supply. Lack of skilled labor substantially increases the total construction man-hours expended, partly due to high quality control standards, and lengthens the time of construction. Nuclear plants are hit harder; nuclear units reporting serious labor shortages average eleven months longer to construct than units not reporting shortages. The remoteness of many sites, particularly for nuclear and fossil-fired plants, increases the problem, as labor turnover can reach 100 percent a year.

Strikes are also serious factors in delaying construction for a third of all jobs, and add more than four months to the construction time for nuclear plants. Strikes would probably be even more common but for the growing amount of nonunion construction and the prevalent use of project agreements.

Project agreements between the owner and the locals specify work rules and generally prohibit strikes; many utilities would not use union labor to build power plants without such agreements.

Low labor productivity is of great concern to utilities and constructors, and many have developed elaborate computerized reporting systems to monitor productivity. Objective standards of productivity are difficult to establish, and some of the increase in man-hours for nuclear plants may be attributed to more complex designs and increasing quantities of materials.

Construction Time

The construction time for fossil-fueled power plants of all types and sizes takes about 36 months from construction start to commercial operation, on average. There is some variability; an 800 MW coal-fired unit might take 44 months, but schedule reliability is good. The average delay in completion is less than 2 months, and most of this is attributable to labor problems.

Nuclear plants are different. They take much longer and the reliability of their scheduling is not good. As a result, the American Electric Power Company, one of the largest utility systems in the United States, has reportedly decided not to design any more nuclear plants because the delays are so numerous and the completion dates so uncertain.[17] According to the Nuclear Regulatory Commission, the time between the award of a construction permit and the issuing of an operating license increased from 47 months for units completed in 1970 to 82 months for those completed in 1975, a 75 percent increase in 5 years. However, this is not the whole of it: the total period from public announcement to commercial operation amounts to 136 months, or 11 1/3 years.[18] At a cost of upwards of $150,000 per day in construction interest and escalation, such delays are costing the utilities astronomical sums.

Construction Costs

All the factors affecting power plant construction ultimately come together to affect total cost; indeed, the effects are compounded by the high cost of construction time. Fossil-fueled plants have had more predictable costs than nuclear plants. In a 1974 survey, fossil unit costs were increasing $18 per kilowatt per year, on the average. The average plant ran 12 percent over budget, but actual costs had a correlation of 93 percent with budgeted costs, indicating that estimates predict actual expenditures reasonably well, considering inflation.

It is otherwise with nuclear plant costs. Budgets for plants ordered in 1965 averaged $119 per kilowatt while those ordered in 1974 averaged $558 per kilowatt, an average increase of $44 per kilowatt per year.[19] However, completed plants averaged a 55 percent cost overrun, and the correlation between the estimate and the actual cost was only 43 percent. Thus not only are costs increasing, they are apparently increasing in an inconsistent manner, which makes budget estimates poor predictors of final costs. This situation contrasts with the efforts expended by many architect/engineers to develop budget estimates in great detail. This uncertainty in the cost increases for nuclear power plants may be as important as the cost increases themselves. Certainly it makes planning much more difficult and increases the risk to the utilities, and utilities are generally conservative risk-takers. Until 1974, utilities were generally able to cover cost overruns by external financing, and demand growth was sufficient to absorb the rising costs of capital facilities. By 1975, under different conditions, an increased cost consciousness had begun to penetrate the power plant construction field.

Table 8-6, from a U.S. Nuclear Regulatory Commission report, illustrates some of the reasons for the cost escalation for both fossil and nuclear plants by comparing estimates made in 1967 and 1974 for plants starting in those years. In view of the arguments above, it might reasonably be inferred that the 1974 estimates, particularly for nuclear plants, will still be lower than the final actual costs, but the point of this table lies in the relative magnitudes of the cost terms. In the period 1967-1974, the direct costs more than doubled while indirect construction costs increased fivefold; safety and environmental protection requirements added approximately equal amounts to both types. The obvious major contributors to the cost increases were escalation and interest during construction; the coal-fired plant has less interest cost because it is built faster. This breakdown shows that rapid inflation in construction costs and increased interest rates are prime factors in plant cost increases.

Because of the high time-related costs, the total cost of regulatory actions is not merely the direct cost of any required plant modifications and additional equipment, but should include the increased cost of the entire plant due to regulatory delays and increased construction time. By considering this compound effect, one analyst has concluded that regulatory actions have nearly doubled nuclear plant costs.[20] It may also be estimated that the additional cost for improved electrostatic precipitators, cooling towers, and SO_2 scrubbers, not to mention miscellaneous other environmental items, will far exceed the $50 per kilowatt listed for coal plants in table 8-6.

In short, escalation and interest costs are so great that, once a plant is under construction, it seems inconceivable that its owner would deliberately stop it or slow it down. Yet that is exactly what utilities were forced to do in the remarkable year of 1974.

Financing Power Plant Construction

The electric utility industry is highly capital intensive. It holds nearly $4.00 in assets for each $1.00 in annual revenue; the average for all manufacturing corporations is only $0.75 in capital investment for each $1.00 in annual

Table 8-6
Nuclear and Coal-Fired Plant Cost Estimates, 1967 and 1974
($ per kilowatt)

	Nuclear		Coal-Fired	
	1967	*1974*	*1967*	*1974*
Direct construction costs	105	225	85	210
Adders for safety and environmental protection	0	60	0	50
Indirect construction costs	15	75	10	55
Contingency	5	25	7	25
Escalation during construction	0	215	0	205
Interest during construction	10	125	8	80
Total	$135/kw	$725/kw	$110/kw	$625/kw

Source: *Power Plant Capital Costs, Current Trends and Sensitivity to Economic Parameters,* WASH 1345, October 1974.

revenue. Clearly, the problems of the electric industry in raising capital are different from those of other industries, and the sources from which it obtains capital are very differently distributed. Table 8-7 shows a breakdown of these sources for investment capital for the investor-owned electric utilities in 1973, as compared to the average of all corporations other than financial institutions. The differences are notable. Whereas all private industry generates 40 percent of its capital requirements from retained earnings, the electric industry generates only 10 percent. Conversely, the utilities rely upon sales of stocks and bonds for two-thirds of their capital requirements, compared to one-quarter for all corporations. Short-term loans, a source of one-fifth of all capital for corporations in general, is negligible for utilities. Not only, then, does the electric industry require more new capital than any other single industry, it also relies more heavily on external sources for this capital.

In addition, 95 percent of all utilities have indenture agreements on their bonds requiring that the interest coverage, the ratio of earnings (before interest and income taxes) to interest payment, be at least 2.0. Such agreements protect the bondholders against the risks of excessive indebtedness on the part of the utilities. Between 1965 and 1973, the interest coverage ratio had already fallen from 3.6 to 2.1, so that by 1974 many utilities were close to their maximum borrowing limits. This is one reason why utilities were shifting their new debt from bonds to stocks; from 1968 to 1973 the proportion of new capital from common and preferred stock increased from 18 percent to 33 percent. Of course, borrowing limits can be increased by increasing earnings, and earnings did increase in dollars, due to increased revenues, but they did not increase proportionally to the increased need for construction capital. For example, retained earnings as a percentage of annual construction expenditures fell from 11.8 percent in 1968 to 9.5 percent in 1973.[21]

In the same period, 1968-1973, the average of utility stock market prices was steadily declining, even in periods when the average of all industrial stocks was rising. Similarly, bond interest rates were rising. In 1974, the electric utility industry had to refinance over $1.2 billion in long-term debt; in 1975 the amount was $2.4 billion. One-half of this old debt carried interest rates of less than 4 percent, but by 1974, average interest rates were over 8.5 percent, with some utilities paying much more.

A detailed analysis of the economics of the electric utility industry is beyond the scope of this chapter. From the above description, however, it is clear that by the end of 1973 the investor-owned utility industry was not in a good position to face a severe economic downturn. It may help to understand the financial problems of the electric utilities if we consider briefly what happened when this downturn came, and how it affected power plant construction. The critical period may be dated from October 1973.

What Happened After October 1973

The Arab oil embargo of October 1973 was regarded as the salvation of the electric utility industry in general, and of the nuclear power sector in particular. The argument runs as follows: the oil embargo caused a shortage of imported oil; to combat this shortage the United States must shift to use of domestic fuels, namely coal and uranium; coal and uranium are effectively utilized in electric generating stations; therefore, more power plants, particularly nuclear plants, are being built. Unfortunately for the electric utilities, this simplified argument is fallacious. It is false because it ignores the practical realities of power plant financing. What, then, did happen after October 1973?

Immediately following the Yom Kippur War, the OPEC countries instituted an oil embargo against the United States and drastically increased the worldwide price of oil. The embargo was not particularly effective, but the price increase was. At the time, however, the threat of a serious oil shortage seemed real, and conservation was urged on electric consumers by all levels of government as well as by the electric utilities. Electric consumption did fall, but largely as a result of conservation by industrial and commercial users and not because of conservation by residential users.[22] However, as consumption fell, utilities' revenues fell. Fuel costs increased rapidly for those utilities burning imported oil, but in most cases these costs could be passed directly on to the consumers by fuel adjustment charges. These increases in electric costs added further inducement to utility customers to reduce consumption. Utilities, however, could not reduce their fixed costs, which amounted to 60 percent of revenues in 1973, and as revenues

Table 8-7
Sources of New Capital, 1973

| | Electric Utilities | | All Corporations (Other Than Financial Institutions) |
	Amount ($billions)	Percent	Percent
Internal Sources:			
Depreciation and amortization	$3.2	20%	15%
Retained earnings	1.6	10	40
Subtotal, internal sources	$4.8	30%	55%
External sources:			
Common stock	$ 3.4	21%	
Preferred stock	1.9	12	
Bonds	5.8	35	
Subtotal, stocks and bonds	$11.1	68%	25%
Loans and short-term debt	0.4	2	20
Subtotal, external sources	$11.5	70%	45%
Total	$16.3	100%	100%

Source: M.L. Weidbaum, *Financing the Electric Utility Industry* (New York: Edison Electric Institute, September 1974).

fell, earnings had to fall also, unless electric rates could be raised. After a long period of rate decreases (in 1965 eighty-three utilities had received rate decreases amounting to $113 million; no companies received rate increases that year), requests for rate increases had increased considerably; by 1972, $827 million in rate increases had been granted to ninety-four companies. This trend was largely a result of inflation and the financial problems that had already begun to creep up on the electric industry. By 1973, consumer resistance to this trend was rising, and when consumers found they were paying more money for less electricity, they were even less inclined to support rate increases. Even without this resistance, the natural lag in regulatory action, which in some states was more than a year, would have prevented rapid relief from reaching the utilities.

The increase in oil prices added significantly to the inflation rate in the United States, and the federal government tightened the flow of money in response. Interest rates rose and the stock market declined. In the midst of this, on April 23, 1974, the Consolidated Edison Company of New York announced that for the first time in its history, the company would not pay its quarterly dividend. Utility stocks have always been blue chip stocks, the widows' and orphans' stocks; they are not expected to bring riches, but they are expected to pay regular dividends. This single lapse triggered a series of far-reaching events.[23] Consolidated Edison's stock fell from $18 per share to $6 per share in July 1974, and virtually every other utility stock followed. By August 1974 the average market price of utility stocks was only 68 percent of book value; only four major utilities had stock selling for more than the book value, and Consolidated Edison was at the bottom, selling for 23 percent. In such a market, utilities cannot successfully issue stock, and so this source of capital was closed off.

The bond market fared no better. As utility earnings fell, their bond ratings also fell; in the period February-June 1974, Moody's Investors Services derated the bonds of fourteen major utilities. Derating further increased the cost of borrowing, which had already risen from an average of 4.5 percent in 1964 to 8.2 percent in 1973, and reduced the utilities' interest coverage, already eroded by falling earnings.[24] To cover its own deficits, the U.S. Treasury was also increasingly active in the bond markets, selling Treasury bills at high interest rates and competing with utilities, as well as other would-be borrowers, for the available capital. Utilities offered bonds at 11.5 percent, and many could not sell them; even the Tennessee Valley Authority had to pay over 10 percent interest on new bonds, an interesting commentary on the belief that government-owned utilities can raise money cheaply. At this time, the yield to private investors on utility stocks was less than the rate paid by the government on bonds backed by the full credit of the United States. Under such circumstances, the investor-owned utilities were generally forced, after the Consolidated Edison experience, to maintain their dividends to avoid further deterioration in their stock prices and their bond ratings.[25] Even so, by the second quarter of 1974, at least twelve major utilities did not have enough earnings to cover their dividends. Balance sheet losses were covered by the increases in asset value of new plants under construction, but negative cash flows could not be tolerated for long. As a result, utilities began to cut cash outflows in the only area that could be cut without affecting current power production: construction expenditures for new facilities.

In 1974, utilities cut back $2 billion worth of construction for power generation. Of the planned new construction extending through the early 1980s, some 65,000 megawatts were postponed or cancelled, of which 35,000 megawatts were nuclear units. Twenty nuclear plants were cancelled and 120 more deferred. Even plants under construction were stopped temporarily, in spite of the high costs associated with construction delays. Of 76 nuclear units with construction permits in 1975, one-third had been delayed for financial reasons; many of these plants were in advanced stages of construction. The additional costs incurred by the utilities for these units alone, because of escalation and interest costs during the delays, will surely exceed $1 billion. Costs from the shutting down and starting up of construction sites, dispersal of the original engineering and construction project teams, and other related expenses cannot even be estimated. Many plants that were postponed indefinitely had already incurred substantial costs for engineering and environmental studies. It is clear that while deferral of construction reduced short-term cash flows, in the long run the result will be greater cost.

As noted above, the brunt of construction deferrals fell upon nuclear plants, with more than half of all planned nuclear units being affected in some way.

There are several reasons for this. First, nuclear plants cost far more per kilowatt than fossil-fueled plants to construct, so that a given dollar volume of cutbacks would have less effect on total electric generation capacity if concentrated on nuclear units. Similarly, nuclear plants require more engineering and design effort that fossil plants, so that the cash flow reduction from postponing nuclear plants is proportionally greater. Nuclear plants also take much longer to complete, so that cutbacks would have a smaller effect on short-run generation capacity than deferrals of fossil-fueled plants. Finally, immediate financial considerations were intermingled with increased uncertainty about the future rate of growth of electrical demand; with this uncertainty, the units with the longest lead times were the most obvious candidates for reconsideration.

Thus, the increase in oil prices after October 1973, reinforced by the subsequent inflation and recession, led to an apparently paradoxical result: high capital costs tended to favor the construction of the least expensive types of power plants, namely those with the greatest fuel costs, and discouraged the replacement of oil-fired plants by more expensive nuclear or coal-fired units. The existence of fuel adjustment charges saved many utilities from financial disaster during the period of rapid fuel price increases, but these automatic adjustments do not generally cover increases in construction costs as well. If utilities are permitted to pass fuel price increases directly on to their customers but must absorb all construction cost increases themselves, at least until the next rate increase, there is a built-in bias in favor of construction of low capital cost, high fuel cost facilities. Finally, demand growth dropped during the winter of 1973-1974, but if the growth rate reverts to its historic value, or near it, as some observers believe it will, there will be a shortage of electric generation capacity in the early 1980s, as a result of plant deferrals and cancellations. A shortage of capacity in this time period could not be met by additional nuclear or coal-fired plants because there would not be time to construct them. If this situation appears to be developing, only plants with short lead times can be constructed (see table 8-4). All these factors favor the construction of combustion turbines, that is, those units that are least energy efficient and that require natural gas or petroleum-based fuels. Thus, as an indirect effect of the oil price increases, the electric utilities could conceivably find themselves consuming more oil rather than less, and becoming more dependent upon imported petroleum products. This paradoxical result may not occur, but the possibility exists as a result of economic forces not well understood by consumers of electricity. It probably will occur if definite economic measures are not taken to prevent it.

Management of Power Plant Construction

Several unique factors make the management of power plant construction particularly challenging. Power plants are always built by what is sometimes called, in other areas of construction, the fast-track method. That is, construction starts before engineering and design are complete. The obvious advantage of this is the shortening of project time by conducting some design and construction activities at the same time. There is no estimating how long it would take to complete a nuclear power plant if this were not the case. There are, however, some disadvantages. It is practically impossible, for example, to obtain fixed-price bids from subcontractors without completed engineering drawings. This may be satisfactory to the contractors, but not to the utility, which runs a much greater risk of cost overruns exceeding its budget. In fact, one of the reasons for the better cost performance of fossil plant construction may be their greater ability to fit within the confines of fixed-price contracts. The solution to this problem, of course, is to assure that engineering drawings are complete for the portions of the job being bid, even though other portions may be incomplete. This may be difficult to accomplish because the high cost of borrowing money places a great premium on the reduction of total project time. By the time the utility obtains the financing, insufficient time may remain before the desired commercial operation date to permit adequate engineering preparation before construction contracts are let. This is particularly true for nuclear plants because the time costs are higher and the complexity of the engineering required to meet safety and environmental regulations continually increases.

Changing regulatory requirements also lead to backfit of new or modified equipment. This is common with nuclear plants, but is also true of coal-fired plants, which may be required to have SO_2 scrubbers, cooling towers, and other features not originally intended by the utility. The magnitude of this problem is compounded by the fact that construction may have already begun before the new requirements are determined, requiring changes in structures and equipment already installed. Whatever the cause, design changes are a particular problem in power plant construction, where they are considered a cause of major delays for half of all projects.

The relatively high level of uncertainty is an important general condition in power plant construction. The lack of reliability of cost and time projections for nuclear plants has already been mentioned. There is also great uncertainty in the requirements to be imposed by federal and state regulatory and environmental agencies. This factor has increased in importance with the growing influence of intervenors and the use of public hearings by governmental agencies, which frequently make decisions based upon nonengineering criteria. Recently, the cancellation of many power plants for financial reasons has added a new source of uncertainty. Power plant engineers and managers have not yet learned how to handle all these problems, but time and experience will no doubt improve their situation.

Several management approaches are commonly used for power plant construction. Larger utilities may design and construct their own plants. They may use their own personnel to oversee construction, hiring the necessary craftsmen directly, or may contract out all or some of the job. Alternately, a utility may retain an engineer/constructor both to design and construct a power plant. The engineer/constructor will use his own forces on some construction tasks and contract others. Some constructors will use their own personnel only for general housekeeping and supervision, while others will contract out only those tasks requiring very specialized skills. Almost all contracts between utility and constructor are on a cost-reimbursable basis. Formerly, many plants were built under turnkey contracts in which the constructor builds a complete plant for a fixed price, but so much money was lost by turnkey contractors on nuclear jobs that the practice has been discontinued. Inflation would eventually have put an end to it in any event, but utilities are still searching for some comparable practice to reduce the uncertainty in their construction costs.

In other cases, a utility may use an architect/engineer to design a plant and assign the construction to another firm. The utility may contract the entire job to a major prime contractor, retain a construction management firm to let contracts for all work, or act as its own construction manager. Contracts may be fixed price, cost reimbursable, or cost reimbursable with target man-hours. In the last type, an estimate of man-hours required to perform the work is established and if fewer man-hours are actually required, the utility shares the saving with the contractor; conversely, if more man-hours are required, the contractor pays a penalty. The type of contract depends upon the state of the engineering drawings, the state of the economy in construction, and other factors; for nuclear plant construction it is difficult even to obtain a target man-hours contract because of the continual changes to nuclear plant designs.

Although these various management methods are available, selection among them depends primarily upon the capabilities of the utility. In general, the utility is advised to take on as much responsibility for the job as it can possibly handle, primarily because no one is more interested in controlling costs than the utility itself. Otherwise, there is some evidence that prime contractors performing construction only, under a single contract with the utility, have the best record for controlling cost overruns, delays, and labor problems on fossil units. For nuclear plants such contractual arrangements are relatively rare, and engineer/constructors seem to perform slightly better than construction managers on such jobs.

Computerized network scheduling techniques to plan engineering and construction are now used on virtually all power plant construction jobs. Cost monitoring has recently increased in importance, and cash flow projections have become of critical importance to utilities. While power plant construction networks are undoubtedly very large and complex, it cannot be said that the technology of cost and time control yet matches that used on many smaller construction projects, such as commercial office buildings. The continually escalating costs and lengthening construction times have eroded the confidence of power plant managers in their ability to control these factors. In a complex project involving many disciplines and organizations, the budget is the project manager's most powerful tool. If the budget is not taken seriously, the manager loses his control and the project organization may disintegrate, with each separate faction doing more or less as it pleases. The ability to bring power plant projects back into effective managerial control is a prerequisite to the successful accomplishment of these and other large, complex projects.

The picture is not inevitably gloomy. Power plant construction has many problems, to be sure, but so has any other construction project of similar magnitude and duration. None of these problems are insoluble except the declining supply of fossil fuels. The future of energy construction is bright, if anything is bright, simply because there is no alternative to increased construction for energy generation other than the collapse of the modern industrial state. Some changes may be necessary: the light water nuclear reactor may disappear under concentrated opposition, but no one ever conceived of it as the ultimate source of energy. On the other hand, opposition may abate in the face of increasing prices of fossil fuel and the public's desire for cheap electric energy, and the nuclear power industry may, in spite of itself, solve the cost escalation problem by means of the long-awaited plant standardization.

There are other alternatives as well, and a rational energy policy requires a shift away from reliance on diminishing petroleum reserves and unstable foreign suppliers. Ultimately, our planet will have to control nuclear fusion or learn to live with the energy it receives from the sun. While no practical fusion generator is anywhere near realization, current designs would require enormous construction resources. Similarly, the exploitation of solar power, wind power, geothermal power, tidal power, ocean thermal power, and other renewable energy sources with the common characteristic of zero fuel cost will also require substantial capital investments. In fact, high capital cost was the major reason why these resources were not exploited as long as fossil fuel costs were low. Research and development may bring the capital costs down to realizable levels, but they will still be substantial, and it is likely that total costs of energy will be much greater than at present. Moreover, major national dependence upon dispersed energy sources such as sunlight and wind would ultimately lead to a population shift away from the current concentrated urban centers to a more decentralized pattern. Such a shift would require not only new energy construction but also the rebuilding of virtually the entire physical plant of the nation.

Notes

1. *Editors' note:* This chapter was accepted for publication in mid-1976.

2. Estimates by McGraw-Hill Department of Economics, as reported in *Engineering News-Record*, November 13, 1975, p. 21.

3. R.C. Rittenhouse, "Power Generation Growth Patterns," *Power Engineering,* (April 1975):43. A megawatt (MW), the common unit of power plant capacity, equals one million watts or one thousand kilowatts of electrical power.

4. Except in diesel generators, a small fraction of total electric capacity. It is not possible here to give even a superficial description of the design and operation of power plants, so the reader is referred to the elementary presentations of power plant basics in the literature. See A.W. Kramer, *Power Plant Primer* (Barrington, Ill.: Technical Publishing Co., 1972); and A.W. Kramer, *Nuclear Energy* (Barrington, Ill.: Technical Publishing Co., 1972).

5. Absolute temperature is the temperature, in some suitable scale, above absolute zero, at which molecular motion ceases. Temperature in degrees Kelvin is equal to temperature in degrees Centigrade (Celsius) plus 273; Rankine equals Fahrenheit temperature plus 460.

6. A Btu, or British thermal unit, is the amount of heat energy required to raise the temperature of a pound of water one degree Fahrenheit.

7. The proportion of electricity revenues used to pay for fuel rose from 15 percent in 1964 to 24 percent in 1973, in spite of increased use of nuclear power; it was rising even more rapidly after that date.

8. R.G. Kilcup, "Construction Problems in the Power Industry," Research Report R74-34 (Cambridge, Mass.: MIT Department of Civil Engineering, June 1974).

9. U.S., Federal Energy Administration, Interagency Task Group on Power Plant Reliability, "A Report on Improving the Productivity of Electric Power Plants" (Washington, D.C.: Government Printing Office, March 1975).

10. Ibid.

11. See "Appraisal of Nuclear Power Plant Reliability, *Power Engineering* (May 1975):45-7.

12. K.F. Reinschmidt and R.G. Kilcup, "Survey of Power Plant Construction Problems," ASME-IEEE Joint Power Generation Conference, Meeting Preprint JPG-74-5, Miami Beach, September 1974.

13. See R.N. Budwani, "Nuclear Plant Lead Time, Costs, Labor, and Material Takeoffs," *Power Engineering* (April 1974):60-3; and R.N. Budwani, "Nuclear Power Plants: What It Takes to Get Them Built," *Power Engineering*, (June 1975):38-45.

14. Reinschmidt and Kilcup, "Survey of Power Plant Construction."

15. U.S., Nuclear Regulatory Commission, *Construction Status Report: Nuclear Power Plants,* NUREG 75/030-7 (Washington, D.C.: Government Printing Office, July 1975).

16. Kilcup, "Construction Problems in the Power Industry."

17. "Cutbacks, Cancellations Plague the Industry," *Electrical World,* September 1, 1974, p. 25.

18. U.S., Nuclear Regulatory Commission, *Construction Status Report: Nuclear Power Plants,* NUREG 75/030-11 (Washington, D.C.: Government Printing Office, November 1975).

19. F.C. Olds, "Power Plant Capital Costs Going Out of Sight," *Power Engineering* (August 1974):36-43.

20. M.J. Whitman, "An Analysis of Current Trends in Nuclear and Fossil Powered Construction Costs," U.S. Energy Research and Development Administration, 1975.

21. M.L. Weidbaum, *Financing the Electric Utility Industry* (New York: Edison Electric Institute, September 1974).

22. J. Papamarcos, "System Planning Amidst Roadblocks and Confusion," *Power Engineering* (May 1975):26-35.

23. R. Metz, "When Con Ed Set Off Ripples," *New York Times,* October 21, 1975, p. 50.

24. Weidbaum, *Financing the Electric Utility Industry.*

25. Too much emphasis should not be attached to the role of Consolidated Edison in this story. This utility was in particularly serious economic difficulties; so much so that it had to sell some of its uncompleted plants to the State of New York in order to stay solvent. Its importance, however, was greatly exaggerated by the publicity it received.

Index

List of Contributors

John T. Dunlop
Lamont University Professor
Harvard University

Julian E. Lange
Assistant Professor of Business Administration
Harvard University

Daniel Quinn Mills
Albert J. Weatherhead, Jr. Professor of Business Administration
Harvard University

Kenneth F. Reinschmidt
Consulting Engineer
Stone and Webster Engineering Corporation

Steven Rosefielde
Associate Professor of Economics
University of North Carolina, Chapel Hill

Kenneth T. Rosen
Associate Professor and Director, Real Estate Research Program
University of California, Berkeley
School of Business Administration

Lynne B. Sagalyn
Charles Abrams Fellow
Joint Center for Urban Studies of the Massachusetts Institute of Technology and
    Harvard University

Arthur P. Solomon
Associate Professor and Director
Joint Center for Urban Studies of the Massachusetts Institute of Technology and
    Harvard University

About the Editors

Julian E. Lange is assistant professor of business administration at the Harvard University Graduate School of Business Administration, where he currently teaches corporate finance. He serves as a consultant on finance and economics to industry and government, and has been senior economist for a leading consulting firm. He was appointed by the governor of Massachusetts to serve as a public member of the Special Commission on Construction in 1971-1972. A Phi Beta Kappa, magna cum laude graduate of Princeton University, he received his M.B.A., A.M., and Ph.D. degrees from Harvard.

Daniel Quinn Mills is professor of business administration at the Harvard University Graduate School of Business Administration. He was chairman of the Construction Industry Stabilization Committee in Washington, D.C. in 1973-1974. He has been an arbitrator in construction and is impartial umpire for the Impartial Jurisdictional Disputes Board which is located in Washington, D.C.

222631
22/7/60

£11.50

Students and External Readers | Staff Research Students

DATE | DA | E

TELEPEN

60 0078718 X

WITHDRAWN